BEYOND THE BANKS

CREATIVE FINANCING FOR CANADIAN ENTREPRENEURS

Also available in the series from
PROFIT: The Magazine for Canadian Entrepreneurs

BEYOND THE BANKS

CREATIVE FINANCING FOR CANADIAN ENTREPRENEURS

Allan L. Riding
and
Barbara J. Orser

WILEY

John Wiley & Sons Canada, Ltd
Toronto • New York • Chichester • Weinheim • Brisbane • Singapore

John Wiley & Sons Canada, Ltd
22 Worcester Road
Etobicoke, Ontario
M9W 1L1

Canadian Cataloguing in Publication Data

Riding Allan Lance, 1947-
  Beyond the banks: creative financing for Canadian entreprenuers

Includes bibliographical references and index.
ISBN: 0-471-64208-8

1. New business enterprises—Canada—Finance. 2. Small business—Canada—Finance. I. Orser, Barbara. II. Title.
HG4027.6.R52 1997   658.15'22'0971   C97-931691-X

Production Credits:
Cover & text design: Christine Rae
Cover photography: Mir Lada
Computer Assembly: Vesna Mayer
Printer: Tri-Graphic Printing Ltd.

Printed in Canada
10 9 8 7 6 5 4 3 2 1

To our dedicated parents,
Earl and Marion Orser
and
Sarah and George Riding

In the memory of
Brian Allan Farlinger,
an advocate and friend
who brought us closer together

CONTENTS

PREFACE

Sounds Enterprising Inc. is a highly successful Canadian growth company that manufactures unique, high-value-added audio components that it sells all over the world.[1] The Sounds Enterprisings of our country provide employment growth and make contributions to our prosperity that are disproportionate to their size—exactly the type of firm that we need to encourage and stimulate. Yet some firms, even businesses much like Sounds Enterprising, have trouble getting the financing they need. Concerns about banks' apparent unwillingness to lend to small firms are common in the media and have been the focus of numerous government inquiries

Frustration with the banks, however, is only one side of reality. The other reality is that growth capital is available within and beyond the banking system. The vast majority of Canadian small businesses use banks for debt financing through credit cards,

---

[1] Sounds Enterprising Inc. is a pseudonym. The principals of this firm preferred that their name not be identified as they are actively renegotiating their bank financing. We'll return to Sounds Enterprising Inc. in Chapter 9.

term loans, and lines of credit: banks approve more than 80% of small business loan applications. In our years of research and consulting in small business finance, we have witnessed a fundamental paradox. Business owners need money but often have trouble getting it. Financiers have money, but complain that there are too few opportunities in which to invest!

This book has been written to help you tap into the huge pool of investment capital that is at hand. We will tell you what types of financing are available, how and where to find them, how small business investors think, and how best to deal with them.

Having picked up this book, you have probably identified banks as a primary source of financing. Most small business owners do. Research shows that Canadian small businesses depend more on banks for capital than do small firms in the US, the UK, Sweden, Australia, and other countries.[2] With so many small business start-ups and established firms struggling to secure capital, this raises the question of why Canadian businesses are so dependent on banks.

Many entrepreneurs cannot believe that huge pools of capital stand ready to invest in the right business opportunity. This book is not just for those owners who cannot secure traditional debt financing. Even entrepreneurs who can obtain debt financing can benefit from non-bank sources of capital. Understanding and using less traditional means of financing allows business owners to diversify their dependence on one supplier of capital, to take advantage of the contacts and networks that accompany additional financing sources, and to benefit from the expertise and experience of the individuals who represent such financing. Unfortunately, alternative sources of capital are often not visible, can be difficult to locate, and seldom advertise. In addition, dealing with the unknown, even an unknown source of finance, can inhibit some owners from exploring non-traditional financing alternatives.

We have written this book to help remove some of these obstacles. There is no mystery to small firm finance. However, business owners require a minimum level of financial knowledge

---

[2] R. Petersen and J. Shulman. "Capital Structure of Growing Small Firms: A 12-Country Study on Becoming Bankable," *International Small Business Journal,* Vol. 5, No. 4, Summer 1987.

WHY DO WE DEPEND SO MUCH ON BANK FINANCING?

As Canadians, we expect much from our banking system. When we don't get what we expect, we get frustrated. We suggest three explanations for why Canadian business owners so often see banks as the primary source of financing:

- **Banks are highly visible.** Our large multi-branch banks sometimes seem to be everywhere. We can usually spot at least one bank from most downtown street corners in Canada. The media also seems to focus on banks' profits and the salaries of their top executives.

- **Banks are where the money is.** Historically, banks were the primary intermediary between savers and borrowers. Depositors don't want banks taking big chances with their money, so banks lend preferentially to businesses that demonstrate high sales volumes and the ability to cover their debt obligations.

- **Invisible alternatives.** We suspect that part of this dependence on banks is because many business owners are simply not aware of alternatives to bank borrowing. In this book, we will identify many of them.

for their firms to grow and prosper. By promoting a better understanding of small business finance, we can help reduce the visible tensions between lenders and borrowers, investors and entrepreneurs, and business and spousal partners. We have selected topics and areas of research that present a balanced profile of the Canadian capital marketplace. Much of this information is original. Drawing on over 20 combined years of research and teaching in small business and finance, this is the first time that much of this Canadian and international information appears in popular print. Our findings survived comprehensive reviews by other researchers and are enriched by suggestions from discussants, both academics and practitioners.

The chapters that follow will enable you to design financing that suits your particular business. For example, we show how "business angels" (people who invest their own money directly in small businesses) can provide more than just financing (they bring experience, contacts, and fresh ideas). We discuss the use of leases, trade credit, charge cards, and other alternatives to bank borrowing. We advance ideas about how to get the most out of your banking relationship; identify and describe both traditional and non-traditional sources of financing; and detail new developments in the capital market for small firms. We also provide examples of how a number of Canadian businesses have benefited from the financing sources we describe.

Bank loan account managers and investors want to know that the entrepreneurs they invest in will be good stewards of the financing. Investors and lenders require business owners to understand "things financial," at least to a minimum standard. They expect forecasts of cash flow and an understanding of financial statements. If owners do not have a working knowledge of finance, they need to engage such financial professionals as accountants and lawyers. Even with financial professionals on board, business owners still need a minimum level of understanding of financial concepts if they want to manage those professionals. This book helps people involved in small firms extend their financial knowledge. Here, we try to equip you with knowledge that will help you to locate, approach, and relate to alternative sources of financing. Our material is based on sound, up-to-date Canadian and international research to minimize proliferation of popular myths and misunderstandings.

In the first three chapters we set the stage for non-bank sources of capital. Chapter 1 presents reasons to look beyond the banks for financing and briefly outlines alternative sources of capital. Chapter 2 sketches the diverse small business sector. This chapter can help to position your own business—or ideas—in the small firm landscape. This is especially important because financing needs differ and the best source of financing for one firm may be too risky for another. In addition, the suitability of different types of financing changes as the firm evolves. The financing needs of start-ups differ from those of growth and rapid expansion stages, etc. In Chapter 2 we link business types and evolutionary stages of the firm to sources of financing. Chapter 2 also provides an overview of start-up planning and other management tasks that new entrepreneurs or would-be small business owners must face. This information relates to financing because costs are associated with each task. Investors, for example, will want reassurance that you can estimate realistically the costs of all start-up activities. Chapter 3 then outlines what you are likely to experience when dealing with a bank. It describes the kinds of lending banks do provide, how bankers make their lending decisions, and the terms of bank borrowing that your firm might expect.

In Chapters 4 through 8 we present more detailed coverage of the spectrum of alternative capital sources. Chapter 4 describes sources of start-up capital, including owners' assets, love money, and "sweat equity." Here, we also explore the dynamics and financial implications of business growth. Chapter 5 moves forward from start-up financing in the evolutionary cycle of the firm. The focus here is the roles of informal investors—"business angels." We describe how angels go about making their investment decisions, what criteria they use, and what their expectations are. Chapter 6 profiles the more formal, institutional, venture capital market. We outline how venture capitalists render decisions about investment proposals, the decision criteria they use, and what they expect in return. In Chapter 7 we examine a variety of additional sources of capital, including suppliers, customers, leases, private placements, export financing, and specialist financial institutions. This section of the book concludes, in Chapter 8, with coverage of the process of "going public." We direct Chapter 8 to those businesses that intend to raise funds from the formal financial markets by issuing shares and listing on the country's various stock exchanges. We identify what to expect regarding a public offering of common shares and describe the process of an initial public offering and the attendant benefits and costs.

Our financial marketplaces are changing rapidly in fundamental ways. Chapters 1 through 8 review the spectrum of business financing sources as they are currently. But the importance of banks as intermediaries between savers and borrowers is diminishing. This process, which economists call "dis-intermediation," has been underway for several years and is accelerating. In Chapter 9 we examine the forces behind the changes in our markets. We present our insights and speculations about the future of the financial marketplaces in which small firms must operate and about how these changes may impact your personal and commercial financial interests. The book concludes with

an extensive resource guide to small business support agencies
and a glossary of many of the financial terms used in the book.

The banking system certainly has an important place in capital formation, but it is not the only source. We start our examination of alternative sources of capital by proposing 10 good
reasons to look beyond the banks for your small business
finance needs. We hope you enjoy the stories of Canadian successes and empathize with the stories of failure. Mostly, we hope
this book provides you with information and learning and that
this resource helps you, in a user-friendly way, in your quest for
capital.

ACKNOWLEDGEMENTS

The origins of this book lie in a brief conversation during a board meeting of the Canadian Council for Small Business and Entrepreneurship. Since that eventful meeting in 1992, we have been fortunate to have worked and traveled together on projects relating to small business, public policy, and entrepreneurship. We have also been privileged with support from our respective universities (Carleton University and Ryerson Polytechnic University) and from the University of Bradford in England. We would like to express our gratitude to these institutions and several important individuals for their commitment and support. Colleagues Rena Blatt, Peter Shaver, Bonnie Patterson, Mary Foster, Sandra Hogarth-Scott, Raymond Kao, Walter Good, Lois Stevenson, Dina Lavoie, Louis Jacques Filion, Yvonne Gasse, George Haines, Dean Knudsen, and others have all played important parts in the development of our research, and hence in the development of this book. We have also been fortunate to have had a number of students who have provided research assistance in the many projects noted throughout the text, researchers such as Dominique Short, Patricia DalCin, and Lola Fabowale.

Much of the original research presented in this book could not have been carried out without the financial support of the Social Sciences and Humanities Research Council of Canada, the Canadian Bankers Association, the Canadian Labour Market and Productivity Centre, the Ontario Ministry of Industry, Trade and Technology, and Industry Canada. In-kind research assistance has also been made available to us by the Canadian Council for Small Business and Entrepreneurship.

The assistance provided by the staff and management of John Wiley & Sons Canada, Ltd must also be acknowledged. In particular, Karen Milner and Elizabeth McCurdy have provided moral and editorial support throughout the development of this manuscript. Rick Spence, Editor, PROFIT: *The Magazine for Canadian Entrepreneurs* has also been helpful in providing resources from his publication. We hope that you find the PROFIT vignettes dispersed throughout the text of interest. We also wish to recognize Mr. Charles Coffee and Ms Ann Sutherland for comments they provided on an early draft of the manuscript.

Finally, we cannot forget the support of our family, in particular David, Michael, and Amanda. The preparation and writing of this book has taken valuable time and we appreciate their support, sacrifice, and love.

A.R. and B.J.O.
Ottawa, Ontario
June 1997

CHAPTER ONE

WHY LOOK BEYOND THE BANKS?

Many Canadians have traditionally equated savings, investments, and financing with the banking system. So it is natural for business owners to think of banks for financing. Our legacy of public trust and confidence in bank institutions has induced many businesses to look no farther.

For some businesses, bank financing is completely appropriate. For example, most established firms use banks for transaction processing, operating loans, and term loans. However, many firms require other means of financing. In particular, some start-up operations, firms that are looking to finance significant growth, and individuals without a credit history must look beyond the banks. In addition to these higher risk ventures, most firms can profit by using additional sources of financing effectively—sources that can include love money, trade credit, leasing, export financing, merchant bankers, and specialist financial institutions.

TEN GOOD REASONS TO LOOK BEYOND THE BANKS

The prominence and convenience of banks, together with their apparent invincibility, overshadows other sources of finance for some entrepreneurs. The conservative lending practices that characterize the Canadian banking system frustrates others. This conservatism has both positive and negative effects. On the one hand, failures of our major banks are virtually unimaginable. This is reassuring to all of us—whether we are bank depositors or successful small business owners—and it stands in prominent contrast to the situation in the US. South of the border lending practices are less conservative, but failures of banks and savings and loan associations are much more common, and with them the attendant tax payers' bailouts. On the other hand, conservative lending practices mean that Canadian banks are less likely to support risky ventures. Lenders seek reassurances such as significant collateral and a convincing track record. Management is key.

Banks are not the only source of financial capital for small firms. There are alternatives that business owners can use profitably. But in the course of our research, we have found that not all business owners are aware of the alternatives to bank borrowing. Other owners lack sufficient confidence in their own knowledge to seek alternatives. Nonetheless, significant advantages often lie with non-bank sources of capital. Here are 10 good reasons to look beyond the banking system for financing.

TEN REASONS FOR LOOKING BEYOND THE BANKS

1. To Acquire More Than Money.
2. To Overcome Banks' Conservatism.
3. To Accommodate the Diversity of the Small Business Sector.
4. To Avoid the Limitations of Money Myths and the Canadian Mentality.
5. To Nourish Success.
6. To Forestall Failure.
7. To Reduce Dependence on Leverage.
8. To Support Innovation.
9. To Improve Networking and Community Visibility.
10. To Finance Substantive Growth.

To Acquire More than Money

Many small businesses stem from good product ideas that are the result of innovation. The successful commercialization of these ideas, however, requires good business management skills. Often the original start-up team may lack these skills. The firm needs, therefore, to supplement the founders' skills with additional business skills and mentoring. Bank loan account managers, whose caseloads frequently exceed 100 small business accounts, lack sufficient time, the specific skills, and the experience necessary for close involvement. Business skills, contacts, and syndication often accompany the use of alternative sources of capital.

THE VALUE OF NETWORKING

In the burgeoning high-tech sector, many firms are founded as spin-off operations to exploit new technology. These firms must embed themselves quickly in existing innovation networks and manufacturing chains. In technology centres such as Kanata and Waterloo, Ont., technology spin-offs are being complimented by growing and closely-knit syndicates of local investors. Tapping into the local investment network increases new firms' opportunities to match spin-off technology with financial resources, to surround themselves with experienced and successful business owners, and to develop production competencies. Networks and boards of advisors comprised of respected local business people can also help the firm in its relationship with all types of financiers, including banks.

To Overcome Banks' Conservatism

Banks obtain much of their capital from deposits by individuals. Banks have a fiduciary responsibility to their clients, especially to their depositors. As a result, most business bank borrowers are:

- relatively mature firms;
- businesses with established, long-standing commercial or personal banking relationships with their bankers; and
- firms whose cash flow prospects are clearly sufficient to support bank indebtedness.

This profile does not fit the majority of small firms in Canada. Many small businesses do not need any financing at all. Banks have not traditionally been in the higher risk, venture capital market. Banks are reluctant to lend to new firms or to firms without track records and a demonstrable ability to repay. Most banks now have venture capital subsidiaries or maintain "strategic alliances" with venture capital companies. This, however, is a very recent development. The extent to which banks become involved in investing risk capital remains an open question. Therefore, for many smaller or higher risk businesses, banks are not an appropriate source of funds. For such firms, alternative methods of financing are essential.

OVERCOMING INEXPERIENCE

Alon Ozery is president of the Pita Break, a Toronto eatery that specializes in freshly-baked pitas. The articulate, soft-spoken Ozery recently returned to his alma mater, Ryerson Polytechnic University, to talk to students about small business ownership. The recent graduate was well aware that his youth and lack of management experience increase the risk of failure in his foray into the restaurant trade. But he also has a clear vision for growth. He intends to build Pita Break into a publicly traded, franchise operation. To overcome the obstacles of youth and inexperience he called upon his father. Bank financing was only secured when his father invested equity and acted as co-signer on the loan.

Was the bank wrong to wait until equity and a co-signature were secured? We don't think so. They were playing according to the long-standing rules of Canadian banking, which say that the banks must forgo most of the rewards of small business growth to shun the risks. The margins do not allow them the luxury of guessing wrong.

To Accommodate the Diversity of the Small Business Sector

Small businesses come in a variety of forms. Some businesses are growing. Others are dying. Some firms are permanent, some transient. The small business sector embraces new firms, mature firms, technology-based firms, traditional firms, and home-based firms. The diverse needs of this wide variety of small business types demand a variety of financial alternatives. The banking system provides some alternatives, but there are many more.

Additional debt makes little sense for firms with high debt loads that are experiencing cash flow crises in high growth periods. Equity capital, such as that provided by informal investors and venture capital companies, provides growth capital that does not drain further cash from the firm's precious reserve.

A CREDIT TIP

T I P "Try to max out your credit facilities when times are good, whether you need them or not. When you need the money is definitely not a good time to be approaching the banks."

—Bob Murray, president, MSM Transportation Network, Inc., Bolton, Ont., PROFIT, June 1996

TIP

To Avoid the Limitations of Money Myths and the Canadian Mentality

For many Canadians, banks are the only source of capital. At one extreme, some business owners—and even the occasional politician—believe that small firms are entitled to a bank loan. At the other extreme are business owners whose earlier banking relationships have soured them to the extent that they reject all

---

A DIVERGENCE OF FINDINGS

Headlines document that women-owned firms have less access to bank credit than firms owned by men and that firms owned by women paid higher interest rates than firms owned by men. Our own research, a 1994 Statistics Canada study, and a 1996 study conducted on behalf of the Canadian Bankers Association carefully allowed for differences in the profiles of male and female business owners and found that banks offer similar terms of lending to similar male and female business owners. Size of firm and industry appear to determine the interest rate paid and the amount of financing received—not gender!

forms of external financing, especially banks. While banks have an important and appropriate place in the spectrum of financing methods, they remain low risk lenders.

Many people believe that banks are unwilling to lend to firms owned by women. Research about this topic has produced mixed findings and the truth is far from clear. If banks discriminate, remedial action is essential. However, if people incorrectly believe that banks discriminate, two unfortunate outcomes result. First, women who believe the myth may not seek bank loans that they might otherwise receive, thinking that they would be better off seeking alternative sources of financing. Second, politicians, policy makers, lenders, lobby groups, and the media might expend resources tackling a fable that could otherwise be directed at solving real problems. Perhaps the real question is why proportionately fewer female business owners elect to expand or grow their businesses.[1]

PUTTING FINANCIAL EGGS IN SEVERAL BASKETS

"Ask Canadian small business owners where they go for a loan and they'll say, 'the bank.' Period," says Roger Bennett. It is amazing that so few small business owners would want to be at the mercy of any other sole supplier. "Small business owners should put their financing eggs in several baskets." But then, as the President of Corporate Operations at Toronto-based Newcourt Credit Group, one of Canada's biggest non-bank lenders, Bennett is selling baskets. Newcourt's particular specialty is asset-based financing, a product that's just beginning to attract interest after being overlooked for years by small business owners."

"Banking on Your Assets," by Richard Wright,
PROFIT, October-November 1996.

To Nourish Success

Often sales volumes or revenues express success. When sales increase, inventories, receivables, and payables also expand—

---

[1] B. Orser, S. Hogarth-Scott, and D. Wright, "The Will to Grow: Gender Differences in Enterprise Expansion." *Administrative Science Association of Canada Conference Proceedings.* (St. John's, 1977).

sometimes quickly. This requires an investment in working capital that often results in cash shortages. To support the incremental investment, the firm needs additional capital. If the business relies only on bank debt, the debt-equity balance (a balance employed by bankers to evaluate a firm's solvency) can easily shift beyond a level that is acceptable. Lenders can quickly become uncomfortable if long-term debt is used to finance short-term assets.

EVERYBODY WINS...

Skyjack Ltd. of Guelph, Ont. has enjoyed spectacular growth as a manufacturer of specialized equipment such as scissors lifts. By the late 1980s, their rapid growth had outstripped their banker's ability to support them with debt financing. To finance an expansion, their Royal Bank loan account manager referred Skyjack's owner, Wolf Haessler, to the bank's venture capital subsidiary. Initially reluctant, Haessler followed the bank's suggestion. The result was a substantial injection of capital in the form of a combination of debt and equity that allowed the firm to make a quantum leap in capacity and to more spectacular growth. Everybody won.

To Forestall Failure

Businesses in distress are not attractive opportunities to bankers. Banks profit from the interest on successful loans; they lose both interest and capital on bad loans. The demands of a sound financial system require that banks respect their fiduciary obligations to depositors. This makes it problematic for banks to lend, or to continue lending, to firms they perceive to be in difficulty.

Complicating these fiduciary requirements is the fact that small firm lending is a low-margin, high-volume business. This creates an additional challenge because loan account managers must administer a high volume of loan accounts. One way that bankers manage potential problems is by designating the limit on operating loans to specified levels of the firm's receivables and inventories. The consequences of this practice can be problematic: when business conditions worsen, sales decrease and cash flow falls below the break-even point.

LOW RISK LENDERS

"Banks describe themselves as low risk lenders.... The banks have set targets for bad debt losses and these go from half of one percent to one percent. To achieve this low loan-loss ratio, the banks have to be correct in their lending decisions 99 times out of 100."

"Taking Care of Small Business."
Report of the Standing Committee on Industry, Ottawa, October 1994

In other words, fluctuations of the business cycle can lead to decreases in the levels of the very inventories and receivables that determine loan ceilings. Well-informed bankers will sometimes finance a temporary cyclically-induced expansion of a firm's credit needs; however, they must be assured that the management of the firm is competent. Otherwise, a business downturn can result in a firm squeezed for capital. Declines in sales lead to reduced access to capital—at the time firms need capital most! This situation does little to improve the state of the bank-business owner relationship.

On the other hand, there are participants in the capital markets who are willing to invest in the possibility of a business or market turnaround. Certain merchant bankers and a few venture capital funds focus on turnaround situations. In such cases, management has the added benefit of working with private and institutional investors on terms that are mutually beneficial.

To Reduce Dependence on Leverage

Businesses face two types of costs: variable and fixed. Variable costs are those that vary with the level of production (for example, direct labour and direct materials). Fixed costs are those that do not change over wide ranges in the level of production (for example, rent, overheads, interest on debt, and administration). A leveraged firm has high levels of fixed costs relative to variable costs.

Leverage can be both a problem and a benefit because it increases the sensitivity of the firm's net earnings to cyclical and seasonal business cycles. In times of prosperity, firms that have

LEVERAGE: WHEN IT'S GOOD, IT'S VERY, VERY GOOD. WHEN IT'S BAD...DISASTER!

To illustrate how leverage works, suppose that your firm had assets of $1,000,000 and makes an operating* return of 10% on assets during booms but only 3% during downturns. To keep things simple, suppose at first that you financed the firm only from shareholders who collectively hold 1,000,000 shares. The following table computes earnings per share for both booms and busts.

Scenario 1—A Firm with No Debt Obligations:

	Boom	Bust
Operating Earnings	$100,000	$30,000
Less Interest Payments	None	None
Equals Taxable Income	100,000	30,000
Less Taxes (@30%)	30,000	9,000
Equals Net Income	70,000	21,000
Earnings per share**	$0.070	$0.021

Now, suppose your firm had instead financed assets by (a) borrowing $500,000 at 8% interest, and (b) from the sale of 500,000 shares. Earnings per share would now look like this:

Scenario 2—The Firm with Debt Obligations:

	Boom	Bust
Operating Earnings	$100,000	$30,000
Less: Interest Payments	40,000	40,000
Equals Taxable Income	60,000	(10,000)
Less Taxes (@30%)***	18,000	(3,000)
Equals Net Income	42,000	(7,000)
Earnings per share	$0.084	$(0.014)

In this second case, the firm is more highly levered because it faces fixed interest costs. Earnings per share are better during prosperous times than for the original unlevered firm. However, downturns particularly threaten the earnings and cash flows of levered firms.

* Operating income is revenue less direct operating expense (for example, cost of goods sold, direct labour, direct materials, etc.).
** Earnings per share = Net Income / Shares Outstanding.
*** In the interests of keeping the example tractable, taxation and accounting treatments have been simplified.

high levels of leverage outperform firms with less leverage (other things being equal). However, in recessionary periods the earnings of highly leveraged (or levered) firms are particularly vulnerable. Firms with higher levels of leverage have cash flows and profits that are more variable than do firms with low levels of leverage. Thus, businesses with volatile cash flows are typically less able to meet their debt obligations during downturns. Leveraged firms' ability to meet fixed financial obligations, such as payments of interest and capital on debt, is compromised during seasonal or cyclical downturns. Lenders and investors therefore perceive such firms as more risky.

Given that interest payments on bank debt are fixed relative to variable production levels, reliance on bank debt can potentially increase your risk exposure. Use of alternative financing sources, sources that do not give rise to fixed obligations, reduces the leverage risk of the firm. As a result the business is more attractive to future lenders and investors.

To Support Innovation

INNOVATIVE FINANCING, TOO

Bernard Kotelko, is president of Highland Feeders Ltd., a rapidly-growing Alberta-based feedlot firm that raises 18,000 head of cattle per year. To ensure a continuing supply of cattle, Kotelko gets investors to purchase a portion of a cattle pen and share in the proceeds when the animals are sold. This provides Kotelko with the financing needed to support the operation, while sharing the risk.

PROFIT, June 1995

Innovative firms are more successful. A recent research study published by Statistics Canada concluded that successful firms were *innovative*, particularly in terms of management.[2] By employing innovative methods of financing, a firm's management demonstrates the willingness to accept external resources in the interests of success. Innovation in financing says much to lenders and investors about the quality of the firm's management and its ability to innovate across a broad range of its tasks.

---

[2] John Baldwin, et al. *Strategies for Success* (Ottawa: Statistics Canada 1994).

To Improve Networking and Community Visibility

Most Canadians are not aware of the many alternative sources of small firm financing that may be close at hand. Even the media and business school curricula commonly reflect perspectives of "big business" and deal mostly with traditional methods of financing. As a result, the supply of informal capital is less obvious and business owners seeking capital do not always know how or where to look. The informal marketplaces are usually local to your firm. In many instances, they operate on a hit-or-miss basis by means of referrals through lawyers, accountants, and consultants. As a result, supply and demand do not always meet. Finding alternative sources of capital therefore involves local networking.

Moreover, access to non-traditional sources of finance provides a widening of business horizons, often through the networking and mentoring of local, indigenous firms and individuals. This in turn increases the firm's visibility and furthers the owner's networking opportunities even more.

BUILDING A COMMUNITY NETWORK

The Ottawa-Carleton Economic Development Corporation sponsors a facility called the Special Investment Opportunities (SIO) project. SIO staff advise small firms where to go for help to develop their plans and to articulate their financial needs. Once the firms are investor-ready, the SIO presents the firm to groups of investors. Several municipalities feature similar facilities.

To Finance Substantive Growth

Exclusive reliance on bank lending and internal cash flows does not usually suffice to finance substantive growth, unless margins are very high. Material expansions of production capacity, forays into export markets, and expansions by means of takeovers usually require large infusions of additional capital. Most businesses are unable to command sufficient access to debt capital to finance substantive growth. Significant expansion usually demands additional equity (that is, ownership) investment. To the extent that the existing owners are unable to provide such capital, it is essential to involve external sources of equity capital.

Additional equity can come from several sources. Firms can raise relatively small amounts of equity ($25,000 to $200,000) from the active involvement of new business partners or by means of capital infusions from passive informal investors. More can be obtained from syndicates of informal investors, often amounts that are in excess of $500,000. Equity capital of more than $1,000,000 usually requires resorting to capital from the formal, institutional, venture capital investment firms. For even larger quantities, the sale of ownership shares on the stock market is an important method of supporting growth. In short, significant expansions of businesses require funds from beyond the banking system.

FINANCIAL NEEDS EVOLVE WITH THE FIRM

Inspection of the financing records of Canada's 1995 fastest-growing small firms indicates a clear evolution. While bank financing stayed steady at about 20% of total capital, owners' equity fell from 50% to just over 20%. Augmenting that capital was a gamut of alternative sources such as public funds, government assistance, vendor financing, lease financing, and private equity.

"We Are the World," PROFIT, June 1995

A SURPRISING DIVERSITY OF SOURCES

The good news is that there is capital available...and much of it is outside the banking system. RRSP contributions and growing pension and mutual funds have created pools of capital that must be invested somewhere. This is one of the reasons for the diminution of banks' role as brokers of capital between savers and borrowers. Routed through such institutions as venture capital investment firms and asset-based financing companies, some of the capital from these pools are making their way into small business financing. In the chapters that follow, we will review some of these developments and the various sources of funds in detail. First, however, we present an overview.

Financial professionals distinguish between two broad classes of financing: debt and equity. Debt financing involves a legal, usually contractual, requirement to make fixed interest payments and to repay the capital advanced.

AN ILLUSTRATION OF DEBT OBLIGATIONS

Institutions such as banks or asset-based lenders make term loans so that businesses can purchase a specific new piece of equipment. Often the equipment acts as collateral, or security, that the lender would repossess in the event that the borrower defaults. The loan usually requires, come what may, periodic payments of interest and capital.

Equity usually is the investment of ownership capital. With equity there is usually no requirement for the repayment of the capital, and payments to equity investors from the firm's earnings are usually at the discretion of the board of directors. However, the investors become owners, along with the original founder(s) of the firm, and often acquire a certain degree of control over the business. Loss of control can be bad news to some business owners.

AN EXAMPLE OF EQUITY CAPITAL

To finance an expansion of production capacity, businesses often raise capital by approaching individual investors. In return for the capital necessary to finance the expansion, the new partner typically becomes a member of the board of directors. Often, new partners also contribute management skills, an expanded network of contacts, and other forms of expertise. The additional equity also broadens the ownership base of the firm, thereby making it easier for the firm to obtain further financing, either debt or equity.

Beyond The Banks...Financing Your Small Business

You probably have your own reasons to consider financing beyond the banks. However, it may not be clear what sources of alternative financing are best. The list that follows provides a sense of the breadth of the supply of capital, a taxonomy of sources, and an overview of the market for capital for the small business sector. We discuss each of these sources in more detail in Chapters 3 to 8.

PARTICIPANTS IN THE MARKETPLACE FOR SME FINANCING

1. Personal Assets
2. Love Money
3. Credit Cards and Personal Lines of Credit
4. Partners and Business Angels
5. Suppliers and Customers
6. Lending Institutions
7. Venture Capitalists
8. Leasing and Asset-Based Financing
9. Merchant Banks
10. Initial Public Offerings
11. Specialized Financial Institutions

Personal Assets

Business owners' first source of capital is often their own asset base. These assets comprise personal savings (including pension funds, RRSPs, mortgages, life insurance) and so-called "sweat equity." Often, lenders and investors will regard the business founders' investment of time and labour, priced at a reasonable rate, as ownership capital (sweat equity). Lenders and investors invariably expect the owners to have made a material investment in their own firms.

Love Money

Friends and relatives often invest in businesses owned by family members, associates, and friends. Love money is one of the most frequent sources of capital from beyond the banks. This can sometimes be an accessible source of funds, but must be managed appropriately. Using friends' and relatives' money also carries implications for the owner(s)' personal relationships as well as their professional relationships. It often involves emotion and can create vulnerable relationships.

Credit Cards and Personal Lines of Credit

For very small firms and home-based businesses, credit cards often provide a ready means of obtaining small scale debt capital. While convenient, they bear relatively high rates of interest and limit the amount of capital available. Recently, lending institutions have expanded personal lines of credit for certain classes of professionals. The costs, management, and benefits of personal lines of credit vary widely.

FINANCING VERY SMALL BUSINESSES

Many lenders have introduced fast, one page applications, and user-friendly monthly reporting, sometimes on the internet. For example, the Royal Bank recently inaugurated a new line-of-credit facility for small firms. Sole proprietors and partnerships can apply for a loan facility of up to $35,000 using a one-page application. The evaluation is based on the principal's personal creditworthiness. The loan acts as a self-managed line of credit from which the proprietor can transfer funds to a business account using cheques or through the Interac system. When introduced in October of 1996, the facility bore an introductory interest rate of almost 4% above prime. Further, fees included a $75 set-up fee and monthly administration fees of $15. The arrangement also includes purchase discount packages and, optionally, a variety of insurance features.

Partners and Business Angels

Angels are simply wealthy individuals who invest directly in small firms owned by others. In 1992, the pool of capital represented by business angels ranged from two to four times that of institutional venture capitalists: between $250 to $500 million invested annually by angels. In Canada, angels have financed approximately twice as many firms as have institutional venture capitalists. Informal investments, however, tend to be small in scale relative to financing provided by institutional venture capitalists. The two sources act in complimentary ways. Angels tend to finance the early stages of the business with investments in the order of $100,000. Institutional venture capitalists prefer larger investments, in the order of $1,000,000.

Suppliers and Customers

Suppliers and customers can provide a permanent infusion of capital. This results from close management of the balance between current assets (account receivable, inventories, etc.) and current liabilities (accounts payable, etc.). There are two aspects to this: the use of a float or delay in payments, which can make suppliers unwitting financiers, or the alternative—to work closely with suppliers especially in the early stages of a project or during tough times, so that they are actively and knowingly helping out.

In addition, **factors**, or financial intermediaries who specialize in purchasing accounts receivable, allow firms to convert their investments in receivables into capital.

LE MOUVEMENT DES CAISSES DESJARDINS

Caisses populaires originated as parish-based cooperative banking institutions in Quebec, New Brunswick, and Manitoba. Today, most caisses are part of le mouvement des caisses Desjardins. Le mouvement controlled $74.7 billion in assets as of the end of fiscal 1993. Most ($53 billion) of this resides directly with the network of caisses; the balance reflects le mouvement's holdings of the Laurentian Bank of Canada, Desjardins Securities, Desjardins Trustco, Laurentian Life, etc.

More than five million individuals are, by virtue of a purchase of a qualifying share, members of le mouvement (most are in Quebec). Approximately 3,500 branches, service counters, or automated banking machines serve the members. Each caisse is autonomous and individually capitalized. They are grouped into fourteen geographical federations. A central body coordinates the federations. A "caisse centrale" acts as the financial agent for the system and ensures liquidity and stability.

Le mouvement des caisses Desjardins caters to smaller borrowers. According to their estimates, their share of the Quebec market is 40% of SME borrowers and about 24% by volume of lending. This is approximately one-half of the chartered banks' combined share of the SME lending market in those regions served by cooperatives and caisses.

Adapted from "Alternative Sources of Debt Financing for Small and Medium-Sized Enterprises," by C. Conner, The Conference Board of Canada, March 1995

Lending Institutions

Banks and cooperative institutions remain the foundation of many small businesses' financing. And yet, the marketplace among traditional lenders is changing. For example, the share of the market held by cooperative lending institutions, such as credit unions and the caisses movement in Quebec, is increasing rapidly. So is the share of market for new entrants such as Hongkong Bank, a bank that is using a niche strategy to attract small business.

Venture Capitalists

Institutional venture capitalists are among the more important, and least understood, source of risk capital. Venture capitalists are usually private or publicly sponsored pools of capital that take an equity position in the firm. The recent growth of labour-sponsored venture capital funds is a dramatic development in this industry, resulting in the formation of large pools of investment capital. Venture capital can be an effective means of enabling the growth potential of the firm.

RISK AND RETURN

Venture capitalists, being investors rather than lenders, don't charge interest on their money, so the short-term cost of venture funds is lower than that of bank loans. In the long-term, however, venture capital usually costs more. Because of the risks they are taking, venture capitalists look for high rates of return, typically the equivalent of 30-40% compounded annually. This is a rate of return far in excess of that earned by lenders on debt financing. The greater the risk perceived by the investor, the more the venture capitalist will expect to take out of the business at the end of the day.

While not involving themselves in the day-to-day operations of the business, venture capitalists will take an active position with the firm and will expect a say in terms of significant decisions. Venture capital is a long-term investment, with investors expecting to be involved in the firm for at least three and often seven years or more.

Leasing

An alternative to debt is leasing and is among the most frequently employed and rapidly growing sources of finance. Using
leases, businesses can obtain the use of producing assets without
having to raise the cost of the asset in advance. Through the sale-
and-leaseback structure, businesses can convert existing assets
into capital, yet retain the use of the underlying asset.

The evolution of firms that specialize in asset-based financing
is a significant development in the market for capital for SMEs.
Such firms base debt or lease financing arrangements on the
specific asset being acquired. The asset typically acts as collateral because asset-based financiers tend to be expert with respect
to the particular assets.

LEASING EXAMPLE

One of the most common uses of asset-based financing is to acquire
heavy equipment. In one example, a sole operator leased a dump
truck to use in his business. The leasing company purchased the
vehicle and leased it to the operator on terms that reflected the seasonality
of the truck's earning power. At the end of the lease, the truck will remain the
property of the leasing firm (the lessee does have an option to purchase the
truck at the end of the lease). Because the lessor leases many such vehicles
nationally, it knows the after-market for used vehicles. This takes much of the
risk out of the transaction. It also provides the operator with the use of the
machine or tool of his/her trade on terms that reflect the underlying earning
power of the asset. The deal earns investors in the lessor firm a reasonable
rate of return.

Asset-based lenders obtain their capital, in part, by reselling
"bundles" of lease and loan obligations to institutional investors.
This practice of "securitization" allows asset-based financing
firms access to large pools of capital at low cost. Because of their
specialized knowledge of the assets, they have good estimates of
the resale value of the equipment on the after-market. That
knowledge, and the low cost of funds, allows them to provide
lessors with attractive repayment terms.

Merchant Bankers

Merchant banks are a relatively recent development of North American financial markets. These institutions are similar to venture capitalists in that they commonly take an equity stake in the firm. However, merchant bankers are particularly active in larger deals and assist in buyouts, mergers and acquisitions, turn-around situations, and strategic alliances. Merchant bankers are also active providers of "mezzanine financing," or high-interest-rate subordinated debt, usually for amounts of more than $2 million. For example, Roynat Inc., the largest merchant bank in Canada provides financing in the $250,000 to $25,000,000 range. Other firms, such as Sharwood and Company lean more to the lower end of the market and also assemble multiple sources of finance as syndicates of investment capital.

Initial Public Offering (IPO)

An IPO is the process whereby a private firm sells equity through investment dealers to the public by issuing shares. An IPO often provides the exit that allows venture capitalists and merchant bankers to reap their return on their early-stage investments. It is also a means whereby the firm can raise significant amounts of capital required to make possible substantive expansions of production. After a period of scarcity in the late 1980s and early 1990s, the market for IPOs has become much more active and has again become an important consideration in mobilization of capital. As venture capitalists, for example, see better opportunities for profitable exits through IPOs, they become much more amenable to investing at earlier stages.

Specialist Financial Institutions

Specialist financial institutions include firms that hold expertise in a particular aspect of financing. These include insurance companies, commercial mortgage lenders, specialty equipment financiers, and international trade finance companies. Such firms tend to focus on financing very particular assets or activities.

SUMMARY: THE CANADIAN SMALL BUSINESS
FINANCIAL MARKETPLACE

What types of financing do firms use most often? The chart on page 21 shows the proportion of small firms that report having used various sources of finance. This chart shows that most firms use internal sources, such as personal funds and profits, as primary means of financing. Particularly for growing firms, these sources are of limited use. Second most important are commercial loans: debt in the form of operating and term loans. There is no question that banks dominate the market for debt capital, particularly as sources of commercial loans.

Fortunately, other sources of financing are available. Commercial loans are available from cooperative lending institutions, particularly in the province of Quebec, and from subsidiaries of foreign banks. Cooperative lending institutions and insurance companies are at least as important as banks as sources of commercial mortgages. Leases are largely the domain of specialized financial institutions, known as "asset-based lenders," lenders that are also making commercial loans. There is a sustained movement towards deregulation of the financial services sector. As a result, the lines between various types of financial institutions will become less clear and competition will become more intense—good news for business owners!

Equity capital is also available from a variety of sources: informal investors, institutional venture capitalists, and public equity markets. But the chart shows clearly that small businesses resort to external debt financing far more frequently than to external equity. Undoubtedly, there are good reasons for this. Nonetheless, by concentrating on debt, small business owners may handicap themselves in terms of financing growth.

Clearly, not all types nor sources of capital are appropriate for all firms. Use of the various types of capital depends on the nature of the firm, the preferences of the owner(s), the types of capital available, and the intended uses of the capital. But before we examine sources of debt and equity, we review the diversity of the small business sector in the next chapter. What are typical financing needs of businesses at various stages of development and of various types of firms? In future chapters we link these needs to alternative sources of capital.

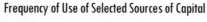

Frequency of Use of Selected Sources of Capital

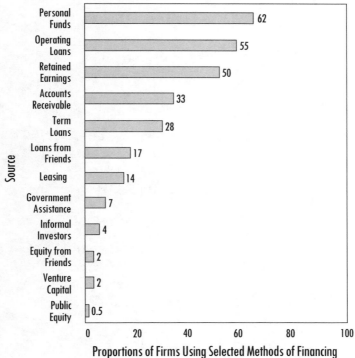

Proportions of Firms Using Selected Methods of Financing

Source: Secondary analysis of data assembled provided to the authors by The Canadian Labour Market and Productivity Centre, 1995.[3]

---

[3] This chart reports the proportion of firms that used each source, not the proportion of the value of capital they obtained. Obviously, one initial public offering can raise far more capital than multiple investments of informal capital.

THE CANADIAN SMALL BUSINESS LANDSCAPE
Implications for Financing

When preparing presentations for lenders or investors, it's crucial to understand and communicate where your own business fits on the business landscape. While many small businesses may exhibit similar operating characteristics, most small business owners can also point to aspects of their own operation that make it unique and that transcend traditional management practices. The diversity within the small business landscape is such that lenders and investors cannot deal with the entire breadth of the business landscape. Lenders and investors usually understand that small businesses are not smaller versions of big business. Administrative and fiscal concerns differ from those of traditional management. Therefore, the chances of successful financing depend on the entrepreneur's ability to identify the right source of capital for the right situation. There is no "one size fits all" in SME financing.

Diversity arises from differences in the objectives of business owners, from differences in the management styles of owners, and from differences in growth rates and growth strategies. In this chapter we present our definition of "small business," one that stresses the diversity of the sector; we outline what we believe to be several myths about small business; and we provide an overview of small business development, linking organizational activities with capital requirements. Finally, we identify some strategic financial choices that face many business owners and address several myths about small business finance. This information:

- provides a backdrop to where your own business, or idea, fits in with the changing small business landscape;

- identifies types of capital requirements that you can expect at various stages of enterprise development; and

- gives an overview of the minority of small businesses that exhibit growth and identifies factors that relate to growth.

WHAT IS "SMALL BUSINESS"?

There is no generally accepted definition of the term, "small business." Firms that we in Canada consider large are often tiny by international standards. Even our banks, arguably among the largest businesses domestically, are dwarfed by many international financial institutions. For this book, we use the term, small business, to include all businesses up to and including the point where they get listed on a stock exchange. This definition means that the information in this book is relevant to the principals of almost 2,000,000 enterprises, more than 99.5% of Canadian businesses.[1] The following chart provides a sense of the types of capital that are the most suitable according to a variety of firm sizes.

One element that is consistent amongst these types of firms are simple organizational structures, structures that provide speedy market response and product or service adaptability.[2] What distinguishes the most successful of these operations are

---

[1] *Quarterly Report on Small- and Medium-sized Enterprise,* Entrepreneurship and Small Business Office, Industry Canada, December 1995.

[2] A. Gibb, "Do We Really Teach Small Business The Way We Should?" *Journal of Small Business and Entrepreneurship,* Vol. II, No. 2 (1994).

Types of Capital By Size of Firm [3]

Start-up Operation	Very Small Firm (<$200,000)	Small Business ($200K-$5M)	Medium Business ($5M-$25M)	Large Business (>$25M)
• Personal savings • Credit cards • Household mortgages • Micro-business loans • Love money • Operating loans • Term loans • Supplier credit • Government assistance	• Personal savings • Supplier credit • Cash flow • Credit line • Operating loan • Term loan • Love money • Equity from friends • Accounts receivable • Government loans	• Personal savings • Retained earnings • Accounts receivable • Leasing • Government assistance • Informal investors • Infusion of money by partner(s) • Government loans	• Retained earnings • Venture capital • Informal investors • Leasing • Infusion of money by partners • Institutional loans without personal guarantees • Government loans	• Sale of equity (shares) • Venture capital • Institutional loans without personal guarantees • Government loans • Retained earnings

informal yet sophisticated **strategic alliances, networks,** and **operating partnerships.** In a recent study of growing small firms in Canada, research finds that "the winners," those exhibiting consistent growth, demonstrate more advanced, innovative approaches to managing their business and marketplace. Growing firms customize products and services, and tailor their deliverables to the needs of customers, quickly.[4] They also pursue innovative avenues for financing.

To nurture your small business, accurate information is needed to understand patterns of small business growth. We'll start by reviewing some of the popular misconceptions of very small business financing.

---

[3] This chart draws heavily from the work of the Canadian Chamber of Commerce, "Breaking Down the Barriers: Final Report on the Aim for a Million Project," Ottawa, 1994.

[4] John Baldwin, et al., *Strategies for Success,* (Ottawa: Statistics Canada, 1994).

SOME COMMON MYTHS
ABOUT VERY SMALL BUSINESS FINANCING

There is no consensus about how to define "very small business," a sector that includes, among others, self-employed individuals, contract employment, quasi firms, micro-enterprises, and home-based businesses.

Self-employment or very small business is often the embryonic stage for larger enterprises. From a traditional banking perspective, however, lending to self-employed individuals has not been perceived as cost-effective. Here are several reasons why:

- Doubts about legitimacy of a home-based business can be problematic when negotiating with suppliers, customers, and lenders.

- Micro-business owners must cover payroll and government taxes even when receivables remain outstanding. As a result, small employer firms are particularly vulnerable to cash flow problems.

- Contract workers may operate with little more than a telephone, computer, and software as assets, not much to pledge as collateral in support of a loan. Consequently, lenders often seek to use personal assets as security.

- Quasi businesses often operate without credit histories and a lack of guaranteed cash flow is problematic for the self-employed.

PLAYERS IN THE SMALL BUSINESS SECTOR

Self-employment refers to one-person businesses. Approximately 17% of the Canadian workforce is self-employed. Those Canadians whose primary source of income derives from self-employment enjoy freedom from corporate work distractions, independence, and the ability to determine hourly or project fees. However, the average earnings, overall, for self-employed persons are low relative to other types of very small business. This is not from lack of effort. Statistics Canada reports that self-employed Canadians work longer hours than employees, an average of 4.5 weeks more per year, and are unemployed 1.7 weeks less than paid workers![5]

Contract employment includes long-term freelance workers, long-term lease employees, and professionals on long-term retainers. These are the least autonomous and most vulnerable of very small business to suppliers' and clients' intentions. Job security is low and benefits are often minimal. Individuals are often tied to a few clients, lack entrepreneurial scope, and have little time to pursue new contracts. Contract employment often stems from large firms seeking to reduce human resource expenses and benefit premiums by outsourcing.

Quasi businesses are single ventures formed for the exploitation of temporary opportunities. They have no paid employees, are short-lived, lack conventional business organization, and may represent part-time activities by the owner who has full-time employment.[6] While difficult to monitor, these businesses often represent other types of businesses in transition, including those firms incubating ideas, struggling with maturation, or defending against decline.

Home-based businesses include business operations that operate in or from the home. They often serve as incubation centres for new businesses or can be a site for retrenchment during recessionary times. It is estimated that some 13% of Canadian households undertake some form of home work. Owners must deal with unique concerns. These include demands of managing family-work conflicts, municipal legislation, approval of the business by neighbours and friends, and working close to a fridge![7]

Unlike self-employed and contract workers, owners of **micro-businesses**, defined as firms with less than $100,000 in sales and one to three employees, have additional administrative hurdles such as employee payrolls, employment taxes, health insurance expenses, and worker's compensation payments. These activities increase the firm's administrative requirements and financial exposure.

Thus, alternative means of financing need to be identified for self-employed persons. This is why we are now beginning to see financial services being targeted to very small businesses, services such as commercial charge cards, micro-lending programs, and fast-track loan application procedures.

---

[5] B. Orser, and M. Foster, *Home Enterprise. Canadians and Home-based Work.* (Ottawa: Queen's Printer, 1992).

[6] Alvin Star, "The Proliferation of 'Quassi Businesses,' *Journal of Small Business,* (January 1981).

[7] B. Orser, and M. Foster, 1992.

Not all in small business management is at it seems. We often labour under perceptions and beliefs that are not well founded. Attracting capital requires being realistic, therefore, it makes sense to address several myths at the outset of this chapter.

SOME MYTHS ABOUT SME FINANCING

- Self-enterprise requires minimal investment
- The smaller the business, the higher the financial risk
- Self-enterprise is a great way to earn money

Self-enterprise requires minimal investment

Many business owners think so! However, there is a difference between being poorly financed and requiring little investment. In Canada it is often the former that prevails. Canadian start-ups rely heavily on debt versus equity capital. Details on debt versus equity financing are presented in Chapter 3. Many very small firms begin with too little capital, remain underfinanced, and continuously struggle. They have insufficient financial resources to sustain growth, to finance important start-up activities such as market research or product development, or to weather a difficult economy.

How much do most start-up owners invest? One Ontario study finds that the average size of start-up investment is less than $100,000.[8] On average, men invested slightly more than women—approximately $95,000 while women invested approximately $83,000. Of these amounts personal investments averaged $65,000 for men and $48,000 for women. Among the owners of these start-ups who were able to secure additional start-up funding, more than half received it from a bank or financial institution.

The smaller the business, the higher the risk

Intuitively, some readers may consider very small businesses as higher risk for lending purposes, but new research indicates otherwise.

---

[8] Rena Blatt, "Young Companies Study 1989-1992," *Small Business Advocacy, Report #46*, (Toronto: Ontario Ministry of Economic Development and Trade, 1993).

The largest published study of the lending practices of micro-businesses in North America found that very small Canadian firms are *less likely* to default or exceed their line of credit limits than larger businesses.[9] This same research also indicates that women-owned businesses are less likely to default or exceed their line of credit than small businesses owned by men! While the economies of scale that lenders enjoy with larger customers make micro-businesses less appealing, it is safe to say that we are only now beginning to understand the risk factors associated with the very small business sector. This is one reason why streamlined loan applications and simple summary audits have become popular with the bank. Very small business lending is a growth market.

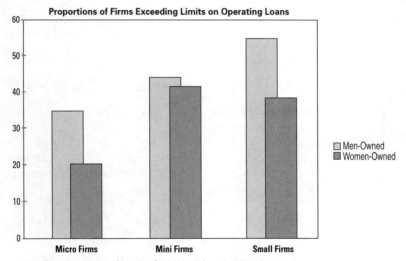

Proportions of Firms Exceeding Limits on Operating Loans

Micro Firms: Annual sales of less than $200,000 and fewer than 3 employees.
Mini Firms: Annual sales of $200,000 to $500,000 and 3 or more employees.
Small Firms: Sales in excess of $500,000 per year

Source: Fabowale, L., B. Orser, and A. Riding, "Gender, Structural Factors, and Credit Terms Between Canadian Small Businesses and Financial Institutions", *Entrepreneurship, Theory and Practice*, Vol. 19, No. 4 (1995).

[9] Fabowale, L., B. Orser, and A. Riding, "Gender, Structural Factors, and Credit Terms Between Canadian Small Businesses and Financial Institutions," *Entrepreneurship, Theory and Practice*, Vol. 19, No. 4, (Summer, 1995).

Self-enterprise is a great way to earn money

Yes, and no! In terms of job satisfaction, Canadians who work for very small firms report being more satisfied in their jobs than employees of large corporations. Greater job satisfaction appears to come from openness of management, flexibility of hours for family, workplace safety, and advancement opportunities. However, most small businesses are less generous than large public and private institutions. Less than half of small businesses have any type of medical, group life insurance, or incentive plan.[10] Even computed differences in labour quality and job quality cannot explain the wage differential between small and big business.[11] Don't underestimate the personal costs associated with business owners. You may have chosen to own a business for the benefits of employment flexibility and autonomy, but associated costs such as dental and health coverage should be factored into decision making.

BENEFITS AND COSTS OF BUSINESS OWNERSHIP

When weighing the benefits and costs of business ownership remember that the majority of the self-employed and very small business owners report earning less than their corporate counterparts; that is, paid employees involved in similar work. For example, our study of Canadian home-based workers suggests that they report (on average) 68% of on-site workers.[12]

A disproportionate number of self-employed workers fall into low earning categories, particularly in retail, agriculture, hospitality, and some service sectors. There are also significant differences between male and female business owners. Regardless of the type of business, research tells us that businesses owned by women tend to be smaller and less profitable than those owned by men.[13]

---

[10] R. Lirchfield, "Here's Lookin at You, Kid." *Small Business*, (June 1988).

[11] *Human Resource in Small Businesses*, Ekos Research Associates Inc., (Ottawa, April 1996).

[12] B. Orser, and M. Foster.

[13] B. Orser, and S. Hogarth-Scott. "Growth, Gender and Managerial Capacity: An Exploratory Study on Canadian Small and Medium Enterprises." Conference Proceedings from the 18th ISBA Annual Conference, (Scotland: University of Paisley, 1995).

While self-enterprise has advantages in terms of job satisfaction and quality of life, the financial costs must be weighed seriously. Not all businesses are alike. What is it that differentiates those businesses that grow and survive, from those that fail, and those that only provide subsistence incomes for their owners?

INGREDIENTS FOR GROWTH

Success ultimately depends on the ability of the entrepreneur or the firm's management team to commercialize successfully the product or service idea. The will or desire to grow, to assume risk, and to be innovative are paramount to ensuring that a good idea reaches the marketplace and subsequently achieves revenue growth. In the words of Jerry Goodis, a Canadian advertising icon, "Good ideas don't just float by—entrepreneurs must be willing and able to swim out to meet opportunities."[14] Business owners assume risk as soon as they enter the water!

The product or service must also embody competitive advantage. Without such, long term success is unlikely as neither investors nor lenders are willing to advance capital. Research reveals that these three elements—the business ability of the management team, their desire or attitudes towards future growth and the potential of the product—are the most important factors that prompt investors and lenders to reject or approve financing.

CRITICAL ELEMENTS FOR SUCCESS AND FINANCING

• **Capability of the Management Team**. The ability to transform a good idea for a product or service into a commercial reality and to act as good stewards of the financial resources entrusted to the firm by lenders and investors.

• **The Will or Desire to Grow**. The conscious decision to pursue a growth strategy, and intention to overcome barriers to the growth objective.

• **Potential of Product or Service**. The product or service must embody competitive advantage. Without such, long term success is unlikely and neither investors nor lenders are willing to advance capital.

---

[14] J. Goodis, Presentation to "New Ideas in Self-employment Conference," (Gravenhurst Ont.: October 23, 1996).

Given the importance of these three dimensions, a closer look at each is warranted.

The Role of Managerial Capacity

Energy, enthusiasm, and a good idea are not sufficient to ensure business success. While survivorship and growth may reflect certain factors external to the firm, the most important ingredient both to business success and to access to capital are the management competencies in the business: the firm's **managerial capacity**.

Managerial capacity refers to the general knowledge, skills, and abilities resident in the management team of a firm. Managerial capacity is demonstrated in the firm's business planning, the ability to obtain the requisite equity and debt capital, and the capacity to allocate resources efficiently and effectively. Managerial capacity takes many forms—commercial, people, technological, and financial capabilities, domestic abilities, network management skills. Management capacity reflects the total contribution of owners, managers, employees and others associated with the firm. Stakeholders include the firm's board of directors, consultants, mentors, family members, and key advisors.

Investors and lenders will often base decisions on their subjective judgements of a firm's managerial capacity. In the words of Greig Clark, president of Horatio Enterprise Fund (a venture capital firm specializing in early-stage deals), "I would rather invest in an 'A' individual with a 'B' idea, than in a 'B' individual with an 'A' idea." Since the business plan is the primary means by which investors and lenders can learn of the management abilities of the principals of a firm, it follows that these attributes should be evident from the business plan. The following chart summarizes a number of the management skills that comprise the firm's managerial capacities.

Sound financial management is one aspect of the firm's managerial capacity that is of particular importance to lenders and investors. Good financial management assures financiers that the management team of the business will be good stewards of their money: that their risk and debt capital will be treated with fiscal responsibility. Moreover, good financial management provides the staying power that will allow very small businesses to move beyond subsistence and reduce the risk of failure.

MANAGERIAL CAPACITIES FOR SME GROWTH[15]

Commercial management includes previous sector or industry experience, previous SME start-up experience, education and training and other experience gained in the paid market economy. The value of this type of capital at start-up is supported by numerous studies that demonstrate previous managerial experience to be a factor that differentiates financial performance and survival of SMEs.

People management refers to the ability of the entrepreneur to manage others, to delegate and to ensure effective human resource management practices that encourage commitment and productivity among employees. This is a big issue for entrepreneurs!

Financial management, like commercial management, is multifaceted and includes skills and knowledge requisite to the fiduciary responsibility of firm ownership. Such skills include cash flow management practices, asset management, balancing debt and equity, etc. Knowledge regarding sources of capital and lending protocols are additional factors that reflect the capacities.

Domestic management is defined as skills acquired through work in a home environment. This can include financial management, asset management, multiple task management, social skills, etc. The managerial sciences have historically provided little insight into this aspect of management. Traditionally, the study of management has negated marketable skills derived in the unpaid, volunteer, or domestic economies, skills relevant to the life experiences of many women. As such, managerial skills are acquired through household productivity and through non-paid (i.e., home care or household budgeting) work, and are therefore included within the domain of managerial capital.

Network management is defined as the ability to build upon and maintain useful commercial and social contacts that facilitate skill, information, and technology exchange for commercial purposes.

Technological management includes an ability to conceptualize, understand, and use technology in the product development or commercialization process.

---

[15] B. Orser, and S. Hogarth-Scott, "Enterprising Intentions and the Likelihood of Growth: A Predictive Model of Firm Performance." *19th Institute of Small Business Affairs*, (University of Central England, England, November 1996).

PAYING FOR THEMSELVES: ON FINANCIAL PROFESSIONALS

Canadian firms with a financial professional on board are more likely to obtain bank loans than equivalent firms without financial professionals; they also get bank loans on better terms.[16] This fact
may reflect lenders' perceptions that these firms recognize the importance
of fiscal responsibility.

T I P

Early enterprise development often reflects the technical and
creative excellence of the founder. Most of us know a craftsper-
son or artisan, an individual who excels in creating a service or
product that communicates the owner's desire of uncompromis-
ing quality. In spite of creative and technical talents, few people
can make the leap from managing a low volume, low risk operation, to one that promises growth. Early growth of any small
business venture requires the ability to marshal additional
human resources, resources such as skilled labour, technology
and an ability to delegate responsibilities for the day-to-day operations of the firm.

Important financial decisions are made very early in the life
of a business. In addition, businesses often require seed or
early-stage investment capital. Unfortunately, none of us are
born with the ability to be good financial managers. We all have,
however, the raw talent. Fiscal responsibility requires both training and experience. It makes good sense to involve financial
professionals in the business at the very early stages of business
development. Their counsel and a formal working relationship
with a financial professional could make the difference between
getting loans and risk capital; their involvement on record keeping and bookkeeping often paves the way for future infusions of
funding; and their networks and command of the financial lingo
can provide the firm with backers and partners.

---

[16] B. Orser, and S. Hogarth, 1995, *Ibid.*

MAKE ADEQUATE PROVISION FOR CAPITAL.

T
I
P

Two frequently-cited causes of small firm failure are limited access to capital and cash flow problems. The business plan should therefore also include several best- and worst-case scenarios and estimates of the anticipated revenue and capital required to start and operate the firm. Because investors don't like surprises, provide potential backers with realistic projections of the capital required to manage the business effectively. Adequate provision for your firm's capital requirements demonstrates to investors that you understand the cost of doing business.

T I P

The business plan should clearly articulate how financial management skills are demonstrated within the firm. For investors and lenders, then, the management abilities, including financial skills of the ownership team, is at least as important a factor as the potential of the product in their decision to lend or invest.

The Desire For Growth

Investors look for small firms with growth potential. Firms that are unlikely to grow are less likely to attract capital. "Growth" is most often defined in terms of a firm's financial performance and employment record. However, growth can also be considered to include personal development, domestic or family development, technological innovation, and professional recognition. Attention is warranted to the latter concepts of growth given the frequency with which business owners cite non-fiscal benefits of firm ownership.

THE WILL TO GROW

Not all business owners want their firms to grow. A recent Ontario study of new business owners finds that one-third of respondents indicated no desire to expand their business.[17] They preferred to maintain an existing lifestyle. Desire to expand a business reflects an owner's expectations of what growth will mean to the owner, his or her family, and the founder's management style.

---

[17] R. Blatt, "Young Companies Study (1982-1992)," Toronto: Ministry of Economic Development and Trade, 900 Bay Street, Toronto, Canada, M7A 2W1.

Our research on owner's growth intentions and their perceptions of personal success tells us that personal financial gain is often well down the list of motives for growth. The opportunity to make a contribution to the community, to achieve professional and industry recognition, to work autonomously, to develop their employees, and to create a work environment for their family are more important elements of the decision to grow a firm.[18]

Business owners also tell us of the personal costs associated with growth. The threat of losing control of their work environment, time away from family, the impact on employee morale, increased stress, and the prospect of additional administrative burden are significant turn-offs to growth. While we talked to both very small and medium-sized business owners, it was the smallest of business owners that were most concerned with the issue of "maintaining management control." Contrary to the concerns of owners of small firms, owners of larger businesses suggest that the opportunity to delegate allowed them to better control both the firm and their own livelihoods.

Most of the business owners we talked with worked in excess of 50 hours a week. The concept of stress associated with growth is in no way related to the number of hours worked nor the amount of income earned for the business owner's efforts!

The attitudes of the owner and management team are critical in the building of relationships with investors. A statement that clearly projects the intentions and aspirations of the owner(s), including how they view growth, helps potential investors understand where the firm and the owners are headed.

Product or Market Development

A third critical factor in the success of a new or growing venture is the product concept. As we will detail in Chapter 4, the development process involves a series of stages or steps, hurdles over which the owner must jump. For example, a firm's inception often involves little more than an idea or concept. But to move from inception to successful commercialization involves costly steps, steps that include prototype development, product testing,

---

[18] B. Orser, and S. Hogarth-Scott and P. Wright, 1996.

and prototype refinement. Early commercialization involves establishing a market identity, customer loyalty, and distribution network. Growth can then be pursued through market expansion, additions to the product line or service offerings, increased efficiency, and a host of other strategies. These activities might also include market development. Many of the most successful small firms, particularly in the high-tech marketplace, have built markets in parallel to new product introductions. These steps all require capital.

ASSESSING THE POTENTIAL FOR GROWTH AND INVESTMENT

Having considered the elements and characteristics of growing firms, we now present an overview of firm types relative to the stage of product or market maturity and the level of managerial capacity of the firm.

Of the three elements needed for growth, two of these three dimensions, **level of development of the product** and **managerial capacity of the principals**, can be considered simultaneously to map the growth process and growth potential. This grid also allows you to evaluate objectively the position of your firm as lenders and investors might. In addition, the mapping that results provides the basis for a grid that lenders and investors employ in their decision making. We will employ this grid throughout the remainder of this book to show how the various sources and forms of capital that we outlined in Chapter 1 fit a given stage and business development situation.

Most new businesses start in the bottom left corner of this chart. Many new firms are focused on product development, without regard to the firm's collective managerial ability, or managerial capacity as discussed earlier in this chapter. For them, growth involves movement, first upwards on the chart, and then (if they survived) along the managerial capacity continuum. Investors and lenders perceive these firms as highly risky, in part because they may not have the management to exercise fiscal responsibility and in part because the owners are often emotionally tied to their invention and may not be "listening to the market." Such firms may be limited to financing from family and friends. Eventually, such organizations mature and are able to develop second-stage products, traditional lenders may consider some financing, but without a demonstrated managerial capacity, public financing is difficult to secure.

Conversely, market-centered firms begin with a product or market concept and quickly add management capacity so that they can better ascertain the needs of the market before moving upwards by developing and refining the product. Usually, firms that show good management and the ability to satisfy needs of the market have an easier time getting financing from traditional sources.

Ideally product and management development must occur together. Such managerial capacity may take the form of partnerships, employment, or through the services of professional consultants. As the firm evolves, so do the requirements for capital. The financial decisions that owners make, especially those made early in the life of the business, can have far-reaching effects. Decisions you make now will speak volumes about you in the future when you might try to interest potential lenders and investors. Choices of how much money to draw from the firm and how to finance it can return to haunt you.

SME Risk and Growth Grid

Stage of Product and
Market Development

Second stage production and new competitive entries	PRODUCT-CENTRED FIRMS		ESTABLISHED FIRMS (LEAST RISKY)		
Product or service line expansion and market development					
Early commercialization stage of product or service					
Prototype stage of product or service	START-UP VENTURES (MOST RISKY)		MARKET-CENTRED FIRMS		
Concept stage of product or service					
Stage of management development →	Technically trained owner/founder	Multiple owners (Few experienced or trained managers)	Multiple owners with a financial professional involved	Multiple owners (marketing and management abilities)	A fully developed management team

We close this chapter with a look at one of your most important planning tools, the business plan, and several of the key financial decisions that must be made early in the life of a firm.

STRATEGIC FINANCIAL CHOICES:
WHAT YOUR BUSINESS PLAN SAYS ABOUT YOU

"Failing to plan is planning to fail" is an adage that carries considerable truth, and for good reason. In a recent study involving over 1,000 Canadian small business, growth or expansion appears to be a function of size, age, and planning. Planning was more closely associated with growing firms than the firm's ownership structure, level of technology, gender of the owner, degree of difficulty in securing capital, and industry or sector. Yet, the majority of Canadian businesses do not have a business plan![19] Why does planning make such a significant difference on the performance of businesses?

• Planning forces the owners and managers to articulate important strategic decisions, decisions that bear long-term implications for the very essence of the firm; and,

• The planning document, usually called a business plan, conveys to potential lenders and investors—better than any other medium—the state of the managerial capacity of the business.

Business planning tools, including computer templates for the firm's financial plan, are available in a variety of forms, many at no cost. Most of the chartered banks and several of the accounting firms provide potential customers with planning templates. Building a firm's managerial capacity and product offering requires strategic thinking and planning. So does the financial management of any firm. Without some form of planning, research and good management sense suggest that expansion is not likely to occur.

Formulating a financial plan also requires the stakeholders in a firm to make some important decisions. Some key financial questions that need to be addressed early are:

---

[19] B. Orser, and S. Hogarth-Scott, 1995.

NO SURPRISES PLEASE!

The young president of the firm was perplexed. The company had been doing well. Sales had been increasing rapidly and a profitable year-end was almost a shoo-in. Payroll was due in two days and the firm could demonstrate lots of accounts receivable. Why, then, had the bank refused yesterday's request to provide an operating line of credit? The refusal placed the president in a terrible position. The president was sure the cash shortfall was temporary.

This scenario plays out all too frequently. As mentioned in Chapter 1, growing firms can face cash flow problems due to the increased investment required in inventory and receivables. However, such cash flow shortfalls should not be surprises! They are entirely predictable. What is also predictable is that bankers and other investors will give the firm the cold shoulder if the management is taken by surprise by this type of cash flow problem. Barring major catastrophe (which can occasionally happen), the management should be able to make good predictions of cash flow deficiencies. Poor cash flow forecasts speak volumes to lenders and investors about the management's (in)ability to be good stewards of loans or capital investments.

The worst time to approach a bank for a loan is on the eve of a crisis. Far better to sort things out with the loans account manager well in advance, according to reasonable estimates based on a well-considered financial plan.

- To what extent should the firm rely on debt, as opposed to equity, capital?
- How big a dividend, if any, should the firm pay to its shareholders?
- How much cash should the owner(s) draw from the business?

These and other decisions should be made by the owner at the early planning stage, rather than through seat-of-the-pants decisions at the implementation stage. Planning forces owners to visualize how they want the firm to look in the future.

Some Important Early Choices

Even at early stages of business development, business owners make choices that can come back to haunt them years later when they may need external financing.

Balancing Debt and Equity

The balance between sources of debt and equity is important. In Chapter 1, we introduced the concept of financial leverage. Fixed financial costs associated with debt increase the sensitivity of earnings to economic changes. That is, increased use of debt increases the vulnerability of the firm to economic conditions; increased use of debt increases the financial risk of the firm and we called this risk financial leverage. The risk of the firm, however, can also be affected by any fixed expenses. In many cases, fixed expenses result from the nature of the firm's operations. For example, businesses that face high fixed production costs, are more risky than firms that might be otherwise similar. Innovative production techniques allow flexibility in response to economic decisions. Just as fixed financial expenses increase sensitivity to economic conditions, so too do fixed operating expenses. The risk that results from fixed operating expenses is called operating leverage.

To some extent, all firms are subject to both *financial* and *operating leverage*. In choosing a balance between debt and equity, owners and managers need to take into account the *degree of operating leverage*. Firms that have high operating leverage and that rely extensively on debt (that is, they employ financial leverage) are riskier than firms that have high operating leverage but use little debt. In effect, choosing the balance between debt and equity allows managers to control, to some extent, the risk of the firm.[20]

Dividend Policy

In articulating long-term financial plans, owners and managers also have to come to grips with the dividends the firm will pay out. This, too, is a decision that speaks to future investors. Investors and lenders like to see owners with a large financial stake in the firm. If owners and managers decide to pay themselves from the

---

[20] Notice that in this discussion of risk, the aspect of failure or bankruptcy is not considered. Bankruptcy or failure risk is a different type of risk than that being discussed here. The risk from leverage (both operating and financial) relates to the amount of variability in the level of cash flows during good times and bad.

earnings of the business, less equity capital, in the form of retained earnings, is plowed back into the firm for future expansion. Again, owners and mangers must make this important financial planning decision early in the life of the firm.

Owners' Draw

The third policy issue that needs to be settled early in the life of the firm is the draw that the owners take from the firm. This is frequently a contentious issue between business owners and investors. Lenders and investors want to see the business principals fully committed to the business and as much of the earnings as possible plowed back into the firm to generate growth. On the other hand, the owners need to extract some draw so they can live while developing the firm. It is not a good idea for owners seeking loans or equity capital to go to meetings wearing their Rolex! Too large a draw from the firm is a definite turn-off, particularly for venture capitalists and angels.

SUMMARY

This chapter profiled the changing character of the small business landscape and how businesses at different stages of development face different challenges. We noted that investors and lenders examine the competency of the management team and the potential product. The attitude towards growth of the founder or owners is equally important in an investment decision.

In this chapter, different kinds of risk were defined. The first is the risk of failure faced by lenders and investors when the business' product and management are not fully developed. The second is the sensitivity, due to operating and financial leverage, of a firm's cash flows to business conditions. These are risks with which lenders and investors are familiar. Most are capable of assessing both types of risk; because of the risk, suppliers of capital require competent financial management. Using the extent to which product and management development has been completed, an investment risk grid was constructed from which you could map your firm's maturation relative to various stages of firm development.

To provide a backdrop for our discussions of alternate sources of capital, we now turn our thoughts to the most frequently used type of SME finance—banks. In Chapter 3, we set the stage for our subsequent discussion of alternative sources of capital with a review of bank lending.

CHAPTER | THREE

THE ROLE OF
BANK BORROWING

"In the late 17th century, Samuel Johnson wrote that "small debts are like small shot; they are rattling on every side, and can scarcely be escaped without a wound: great debts are like cannon; of loud noise, but little danger."

Samuel Johnson (1709-84), English author, lexicographer. Letter, 1759, to Joseph Simpson. Quoted in: Boswell, *The Life of Samuel Johnson* (1791).

In this chapter we set the stage for examining alternative means of financing by first reviewing bank borrowing. We provide an overview of the debt financing market, give examples of the main forms of bank loans, describe how lenders make decisions, and we identify the profile of the "average" bank borrower. In addition, we outline the terms of bank credit and how lenders make decisions. From this, business owners will have a better understanding of what they can expect regarding the lending/borrowing process, interest rates, fees, and collateral requirements.

THE MARKET FOR DEBT CAPITAL

Although the Canadian banking market appears concentrated, banks and other lenders compete intensely within it. Six national multi-branch banks (the "Big Six") dominate the market for loans to small businesses: the Bank of Montreal, Bank of Nova Scotia, Royal Bank of Canada, Toronto Dominion Bank, CIBC, and National Bank. Other lenders include credit cooperatives (such as credit unions and caisses populaires) and subsidiaries of foreign-owned banks (such as the Hongkong Bank of Canada).

T
I
P

SHOP AROUND!

Even though many people believe that banks do not compete, the fact is that they do. Not only do lenders compete with each other, but the power of technology and communications means that institutions are getting ready to compete with "virtual" banks that are not necessarily based in Canada. For business owners this has a basic implication: if one lender is not meeting your needs, shop around.

T I P

Forms of Bank Lending 101: Term Loans

Bank loans to small enterprises generally take one or both of two forms: term loans and operating loans. Businesses use term loans to acquire specific items of plant or equipment, or to support the business' need for permanent working capital. Term loans can be for almost any principal amount. The term of a loan can range from one to five years but longer terms can be arranged for equipment, depending on the useful life of the asset.

Businesses repay term loans by means of periodic payments that, like residential mortgage payments, include both an interest and a principal component. Banks charge interest either at a rate that remains fixed for the lifetime of the loan or, more frequently, at a fixed premium above prime rate (prime rate is the interest rate banks charge their very best corporate customers). Prime rate varies in accordance with the general level of interest rates in the country. The schedule of periodic payments, broken down into its interest and principal components, is an "amortization schedule." It is useful because the interest component of the payment can be deducted from income for tax purposes.

A SIMPLIFIED EXAMPLE OF A TERM LOAN

Equinox Management Consultants Ltd. acquired a new computer system that cost $25,000. To purchase it, they negotiated a four-year term loan from their banker for the full amount, $25,000, at a fixed rate of 9%.

This arrangement entailed an annual payment of $7,717 made at the end of each anniversary of the loan. Each $7,717 annual payment is a different blend of interest and capital repayment.

For the term loan that Equinox arranged, the amortization schedule is as follows:

Year	Principal Outstanding at Start of Year	Interest Portion = 9% of Principal	Principal Repayment = $7,717 − Interest
1	$25,000	$2,250 (=9% x $25,000)	$5,467
2	$19,533	$1,758 (=9% x $19,533)	$5,959
3	$13,575	$1,222	$6,495
4	$ 7,080	$637	$7,080

Collateral requirements usually reflect the asset acquired by the firm and the risk as perceived by the lender's loan account manager. The lender and borrower can, to some extent, negotiate the form and amount of collateral. Collateral security usually comprises both fixed and floating charges on assets. For term loans, the collateral security is often the asset that the loan is financing. In addition, lenders often require that the principals of smaller businesses provide personal guarantees and even pledge personal assets as security for the loan. For sole proprietorships and new businesses, it is common for banks to require a co-signer to back the loan application.

Often, the value of the assets pledged as security exceeds the value of the loan, a fact that sometimes concerns business owners. However, lenders are in business to earn interest, not to sell used assets. Lenders would rather not face the prospect of having to realize on the collateral. For this reason, lenders rate highly the demonstrated ability of the borrower to generate cash flows that are more than sufficient to cover the debt obligations.

Forms of Bank Lending 102: Operating Loans

Operating loans, or lines of credit, provide businesses with credit on an "as-needed" basis, usually up to a predefined limit. Such loans provide working capital and bridge firms' cash flows between payment of expenses and subsequent receipt of revenues. Operating loans can be particularly useful for seasonal businesses.

With operating loans businesses access credit in a manner that is similar to that of overdraft protection on personal bank accounts. The firm owner(s) and the lender negotiate the upper limit of borrowing (the "credit limit" or "operating loan ceiling") in advance. Lenders often establish the credit limit on an operating loan as a function of the borrowers' levels of particular current asset items. For example, agreements sometimes express limits of operating loans in terms of a base amount and a proportion of accounts receivable. Once established the firm can borrow from the bank, up to the specified limit, at its discretion.

The interest rates on operating loans are usually floating rates, comprised of prime rate, which varies in accordance with the overall level of interest rates, and a risk premium above prime rate. The lender and borrower usually negotiate both the premium and any collateral security requirements. Operating loans can also involve several types of fees. These include commitment fees, standby fees, and set-up fees. A rule of thumb for debt lending is that the additional cost of these fees is approximately one percent of the loan amount. However, all fees are usually negotiable and sometimes lenders waive some fees.

Both term and operating loans are demand loans. Lenders can request repayment at any time. We hear periodically about business failures that are blamed on banks that have called in a loan. Media coverage of some of these situations and ongoing public criticism of banks' lending practices has prompted lending institutions to develop a Code of Conduct for their business lending and to establish mechanisms for resolution of disputes.

EXAMPLE OF AN OPERATING LOAN

The owner of Equinox Management Consultants Ltd. was facing a cash crisis. The firm's government client had temporarily misplaced Equinox's last invoice. The invoice was located but payment would be late. The delay in receipt of contract revenues meant that Equinox could not meet payroll on time. To survive this dilemma, Equinox negotiated an operating loan with its bank. According to the terms of the loan, Equinox could borrow as much as 75% of the face value of accounts receivable of less than 60 days outstanding and 90% of accounts receivable associated with government contracts. The interest rate on the borrowing balance was prime rate plus a premium of 1.75%. Under his arrangement, Equinox could avail itself of credit, on an ongoing basis, to provide bridge financing between invoicing its clients and subsequent receipt of revenues.

In addition, a system-wide bank ombudsoffice hears disputes that are particularly difficult to resolve. We review the Code of Conduct later in this chapter.

Other Forms of Bank Financing

Commercial Mortgages

Essentially, these are mortgage loans (secured by fixed assets such as plant and equipment) used by businesses to acquire fixed assets. While banks are active commercial mortgage lenders, life insurance firms are also a primary source of commercial mortgages in Canada (see Chapter 8).

Financing International Transactions

Banks also provide financing to firms engaged in international trade. Such financing alternatives include direct loans in US dollars and letters of guarantee in Canadian dollars. An important means by which banks finance international transactions is through letters of credit. A commercial letter of credit issued by a bank, on behalf of an importer, is an agreement by the bank to respect a draft drawn on the importer's account. Essentially, the letter of credit reduces risk for the importer's supplier by replacing the importer's creditworthiness by that of the bank. More details on letters of credit and other forms of export financing for small firms are found in Chapter 8.

Banking Terminology: Credit Authorizations and Credit Outstanding

As of June 1996, the Canadian Bankers Association reported that banks had made almost $42 billion of credit, in various forms, available to small business customers. Of the $42 billion, bank clients had used approximately $29 billion, leaving a balance of $12.5 billion of credit that had been authorized but not yet used. The following example illustrates these terms.

SMALL BUSINESS CREDIT EXAMPLE[1]

The following example clarifies the terms authorized credit and outstanding credit.

The owner of ABC company, Ms. Smith meets with her banker to discuss financing. The banker reviews ABC's financial records, cash flow, business plan, and assets. Based on this information, a $100,000 credit limit is authorized.

Of this credit limit, Ms. Smith states that she needs:
• a $20,000 loan to upgrade equipment,
• a $10,000 line of credit to purchase raw materials, and
• a bankers' acceptance of $5,000 for payment to one of her company's suppliers.

A few months later, Ms. Smith has repaid $1,500 of the outstanding loan. As a result, ABC company has the following credit position with the bank:

Authorized Credit Limit	$100,000
Credit Used (Outstanding)	
Original loan outstanding	$ 20,000
Less amount repaid	$ 1,500
Loan balance outstanding	$ 18,500
Charge on line of credit	$ 10,000
Bankers' Acceptance	$ 5,000
Total Credit Used (outstanding)	$ 33,500
Credit Still Available:	$ 66,500

---

[1] The example used here is drawn from "Small Business Credit," Canadian Bankers Association, October 24, 1995.

THE PROBLEM WITH SME LENDING

"Banks just don't understand small business" is a lament often heard from small business owners and their lobbyists. By understanding why this outcry arises, business owners may be able to improve their banking relationship and be proactive in short-circuiting potential difficulties.

The root of the problem is that most small business clients require only modest borrowing—one half of all bank loans to small firms are for less than $50,000.[2] After allowing for the lender's costs of funds, a provision for bad debts, and direct costs and overheads, the margins on lending to small business are low. Therefore, to make lending to SMEs profitable, loan account managers must administer high volumes, often 80 to 120 accounts. As a result, loan account managers' caseloads typically leave them with less than two working days per year per client! Banks are attempting to improve this situation by relying on technology, simplified application procedures, and by using account managers that specialize by sector. Nevertheless, heavy caseloads mean that account managers have little time to devote to each client, so the ground is fertile for misunderstandings. It is not surprising to learn that more than 10% of business owners are dissatisfied with their banker. And dissatisfaction is even more common among owners of smaller firms.[3]

What can be done about dissatisfaction? Again, it makes sense to shop around and negotiate for the best package of services, including personal services. Even if switching bankers is inconvenient and costly in the short term, switching lenders can bring long-term benefits. Banks realize that business clients also translate into personal banking clients. If a bank obtains the owner's personal banking, such as RRSPs, mortgages, etc., the package of personal and professional banking becomes much more attractive to the institution. Banks compete for such business.

---

[2] G. Haines, and A. Riding. *Access to Credit: Lending Priorities and SMEs*. (Ottawa: Industry Canada, 1994).

[3] The data in this section are from *Small and Medium Sized Businesses in Canada: Their Perspective of Financial Institutions and Access to Financing*. Toronto: Canadian Bankers Association (CBA), 1996, pp. 121-140.

Recently, this relationship between banks and small business borrowers has received considerable criticism and press coverage. Lobby groups and some individual small business owners cite difficulties of access to capital. Banks and investors, on the other hand, decry the lack of financial planning and management skills of some business owners. The result is a tenuous relationship between banks and some small business clients. Differing perspectives can lead to frustration.

The Tenuous Lending Relationship	
Small Business Owners' Perspective	**Lenders' Perspective**
Lenders:	Small firms:
1. Require excessive collateral	1. Do not understand lenders' requirements
2. Provide insufficient financing	2. Lack management skills
3. Provide inadequate advice and financial counsel	3. Do not realistically appraise product and market potentials
4. Do not tell individuals who have been turned down about other sources of capital	4. Communicate poorly, and in untimely manner, their financial requirements
5. Charge excessive interest rates	5. Do not understand the fiduciary responsibility the bank holds with respect to its shareholders and government
6. Do not compete with each other	6. Invest too little personal equity in their firms
7. Account managers lack sufficient skills to understand specifics of small firms	7. Assume banks are the only source of financing
8. Account managers lack local authority to make credit decisions	8. Do not understand the economics and inefficiencies of small firm lending
9. Are unwilling to lend on character	

Many of these contentions of both lenders and small businesses do not hold up to scrutiny. However, it remains that many small business owners view banks with suspicion, while bankers do not always appreciate fully the situations faced by their clients. Some banks are taking concrete and authentic steps to address this difficult situation. Such steps include placing greater emphasis on small firms in training, reducing account manager turnover, and undertaking staff exchanges with small businesses.

Also among the initiatives is a code of conduct that the "big six" banks have developed with the Canadian Bankers Association. As presented in the next chart, this code of conduct outlines the responsibilities of lending institutions to clients when a change in the relationship is contemplated.

CODE OF CONDUCT

If a change in the client-credit relationship is contemplated:

- banks must carefully review the existing arrangement before taking any action;
- banks must give clients a reasonable opportunity to provide any additional information they request;
- banks must ordinarily provide clients at least 15 days notice of any actions to be taken because of a change in the credit relationship;
- banks must inform clients when changes are made to the terms, conditions, fees, or lending margins specific to that client's relationship; and
- if a bank declines to grant a request for credit, the bank must provide a clear reason for the decline and advise the applicant of other suitable sources of capital.

The creation of bank ombudsoffice is another such development. Each of the major banks have created an ombuds function within the institution and a federal ombudsman was appointed in 1996. Thus, two levels of appeal are available and, of course, clients can always change financial institutions.

BEYOND THE "BIG SIX" BANKS

Credit Cooperatives

Credit cooperatives are membership-owned savings and loan institutions. Composed primarily of credit unions (in English Canada) and caisses populaires (in Quebec, New Brunswick, and Manitoba), credit cooperatives are community-based, non-profit organizations established within cultural, geographic, or parochial boundaries. Boards of Directors are elected by members to govern local cooperatives. Each "branch" operates independently but is part of a provincial central. The provincial centrals are part of the Credit Union Central of Canada. This three-level organization allows for autonomous local operation within provincial regulation and a national pool of liquidity.

While credit cooperatives' primary business is to support the savings and loan needs of their members, they also loan to small businesses. By 1995, almost 20% of SMEs in Canada used credit cooperatives as their primary financial institution. Most of this share reflects le Mouvement des Caisses Desjardins (with a 16% share of the Canadian market) which holds a major share of the Quebec market.

THE BUSINESS DEVELOPMENT BANK OF CANADA

Among the Business Development Bank of Canada's small firm initiatives are:

- **The Micro-Business Program** intended to provide loans of up to $25,000 to assist start-ups (or as much as $50,000 for established firms) coupled with an assessment of owner's managerial skills and training. Lending criteria under this program are similar to those employed by commercial banks. The funds are to help owners develop a business plan, and they must agree to accept continued mentoring.

- **The Patient Capital Program**, is intended to provide innovative firms in early stages of development with long-term capital.

- **The Working Capital for Growth Program**, according to which the BDC will add to, or "top-up," existing operating loans for firms in a position to exploit opportunities for growth.

- **Venture Loans**, royalty-based financing for growth firms whereby the bank shares in the profits of the firm.

- **Venture Capital** for growing firms with an emphasis on knowledge-based firms and exporters.

- **Term Loans**, that emphasize complimentary lending with special reference to knowledge-based and exporting firms.

In addition, the BDC is teaming up with banks in various parts of the country to undertake further initiatives geared more specifically to regional needs.

The Business Development Bank of Canada

Formerly the Federal Business Development Bank, the Business Development Bank of Canada (BDC) has been repositioned with new responsibilities. Once, as a "lender of last resort," the Federal Business Development Bank required businesses to show that commercial lenders had refused them. In its reincarnation, the BDC views itself as a complimentary lender. The BDC will now consider conventional financing for new technology-based firms that might lack collateral, established firms that have reached the limit of their operating loans, and for business start-ups whose owners are willing to accept BDC-sponsored training. The BDC is a Crown corporation solely dedicated to small business. During 1995 the BDC made more than 5,500 loans for a total of $900 million.

HOW BANKERS MAKE DECISIONS

It is indeed more difficult for small firms, compared to larger firms, to obtain bank capital. When they do receive credit, small businesses face higher interest rates and more stringent terms than their larger counterparts. We compared access to, and terms of, credit across firm size with the following results:[4]

Terms of Credit by Firm Size (Term Loans)		
	Firms with less than $200,000 annual sales and fewer than 3 employees	Firms with sales in excess of $500,000 per year
Loan turn-down rate	10.3%	6.9%
Average interest rate (margin above prime rate)	1.59%	1.17%
Frequency of co-signature requirement	32%	20%

[4] Haines and Riding, 1994; L. Wynant, and J. Hatch. *Banks and Small Business Borrowers.* (London, Ontario: Western Business School, University of Western Ontario, 1991).

LOAN APPROVAL RATES IN CANADA [5]

Most small and medium loan requests are approved by the bank or financial institution approached. A recent survey conducted on behalf of the Canadian Bankers Association finds that 79% of firms requesting loans from Canada's major banks reported their request was approved in full (73%), 6% were approved in part, and 6% were pending at the time of the survey. Among all requests, 15% were turned down. At least one-third of the turn-downs were given an opportunity to rework the request.

Knowing how bankers think can help improve these odds and help to ensure a good working relationship. In their 1996 survey of bank business borrowers, the Canadian Bankers Association reported that customer satisfaction depended on how bankers made certain decisions.

PRIMARY DRIVERS OF BANK BORROWERS' SATISFACTION[6]

- flexibility in meeting changing financial needs
- support in good and bad times
- timeliness of financing decisions
- speed with which main contact reacts to problems

For business borrowers, the evolution of the lending decision begins with an approach to the loan account manager. Finding the right banker means being prepared. The questions that follow provide a guide for approaching and dealing with a banking institution.

Because the loan account manager is typically pressed for time (remember, 80 to 120 accounts) maintaining a good working relationship means keeping the loan account manager fully informed. Ensuring that the lender has appropriate and reliable information at hand is important. For small business owners, knowing how lenders make their decisions helps to anticipate these needs. Typically, lenders make three types of decisions with respect to business borrowing:

---

[5] CBA, 1996.

[6] CBA, 1996, p.152

- whether or not to grant credit;
- what fees and interest rates to levy; and
- how much collateral security to require.

Our own research tells us that in making these decisions, commercial loan account managers use information such as financial statements and business plans, as well as their subjective impressions of the principals behind the firm.

The Decision to Grant Credit—or Not!

While some small business owners may not agree, our own findings tell us that the lending decision is not just based on numbers. Subjective impressions and track record are weighted heavily for start-up and very small operations. Research suggests that for very small firms, firms with annual revenues of less than $3 million, bankers accord little importance to financial statements. Instead, they stress the character of the owner. Thus, the business owner's relationship with the banker is a key element in lending decisions.

More and more, lenders are using "credit scoring" methods to make decisions. Credit scoring entails the use of selected data from the loan application and data obtained from a credit bureau to automate the business lending decision. This trend reflects lenders' attempts to reduce the high per-dollar cost of administering small lending balances. Credit scoring brings both good and bad news. The bad news is that credit scoring removes some of the human element from what, ideally, is a relationship. This can bias lending decisions against ventures that are unusual and that don't fit the mould. Therefore, some people call credit scored lending "cookie-cutter loans." The good news is that loan decisions for the majority of businesses are rendered in an objective and timely manner. In theory, borrowers get better terms of credit because they share in the lender's cost savings. But, it is not clear that this holds in practice.

For larger firms, with annual sales in excess of $3 million, lenders weight audited financial statements more heavily. Lenders, as a matter of course, also conduct ratio analyses of larger firms' financial statements while carrying out other formal credit checks.

DEALING WITH YOUR BANKER

Here is a checklist of tips that Barrie Martin, a commercial lending officer with the Canadian Imperial Bank of Commerce, suggests creates a good banking relationship.

• **What's the Chemistry?** Look for a banker with whom you feel comfortable. Recognize that you should pay attention to personal chemistry. If you don't "take" to your bankers, you are going to find it difficult to confide and to accept advice.

• **Look for a Commercial Banking Centre**. Consider the nearest commercial banking centre, even if it is some distance from your place of business. These centres offer access to a good deal of expertise and experience. Many have teams that specialize in small business.

• **Evaluate the Range of Client Services**. Most financial institutions offer a wide range of support services for small business. Consider all of your current and future needs. For example, in addition to a term or operating loan, banks offer: franchising loans, leasing, business deposit services, current and savings accounts, term deposits, retirement savings plans, cash management services, computerized payroll services, night depository services, credit card services, foreign exchange services, mail and cable payments, and so on.

• **Look Around for Financing Terms**. Check collateral requirements, service fees, loan limits and so on. Look for favourable terms but keep in mind that the cheapest might not be the best.

• **Ask about collateral**. Most bankers will require some or all of the following: personal guarantees, assignment of accounts receivable, pledges of life insurance, or a mortgage on real property, such as a house. Which mix suits your bankers and your circumstances best?

• **Remember that servicing a small business is expensive**. Recognize that while bankers want your business, servicing a small business account is expensive. Current interest rates do not generally cover the costs involved. The costs still have to be covered.

• **Discuss the Status of Your Application**. Be aware that having a loan application considered, even if it is turned down, has value. Finding out why it was accepted or rejected will provide useful information.

T I P

It is not surprising then that the most likely loan recipients are those with long-standing relationships with their banker or bank. A well-prepared business plan, one to which the owner can speak with conviction, is also critical. Incidentally, most lenders accord little weight to business plans produced by consultants or students unless the owner is able to demonstrate complete familiarity with it.

Most bank loan account managers have the discretion to approve loans up to a prescribed limit. Approval rates and ceilings vary according to the education, experience, and track record of the manager. In the event that the requested amount of the loan exceeds the account manager's authorization limit, the manager makes a recommendation to a higher level of authority. Most lenders try to limit the number of authorization levels to no more than two in the interest of timeliness.

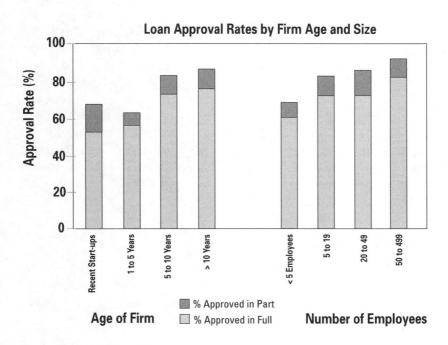

Source: CBA, 1996, p. 196.

Loan approval rates vary by age of business, size of business, and industrial sector.[7] Lenders turn down businesses in the retail and accommodation-food-beverage sectors more frequently than firms in other sectors. Lenders also turn down loan requests from very young firms (especially firms less than five years old) and very small firms (less than 5 employees or businesses with annual sales of less than $250,000) with high frequencies. These attributes reinforce each other: small, young businesses in the retail or food service sectors face an uphill battle!

Of course, charts don't tell the whole story. Turndowns happen at various stages of the application process. Informal turndowns often occur during preliminary discussions when the lender representative might imply—even unknowingly—that the client is not eligible for a loan. The number of small business owners that seek financing and do not get to the formal loan application stage is not known, although University of Western Ontario researchers estimate that "the vast majority of declines occur at the informal stage."[8]

Chances of receiving at least part of a formal loan request are high. Formal loan turndowns occur once the client has submitted a loan application. According to the Canadian Bankers Association, 78% of formal loan applicants get their loan approved in full. An additional 6% have their loan approved in part. Lenders turn down 16% of applications. Of the turndowns, about one-third get the opportunity to rework their request and resubmit. About half do so. Of those clients who do rework their request about seven out of 10 have their request granted either in full or in part. After allowing for these factors, lenders ultimately accept about 86% of loan requests.[9]

Assessing Business Risk

Several national studies have recently attempted to determine how lenders assess "risk." According to loan account managers, there are two key determinants of the loan acceptance decision.

---

[7] CBA, 1996, p. 196.

[8] Wynant and Hatch, 1991.

[9] CBA, 1996, pp. 82-92.

Firms most likely to obtain bank credit:

• have cash flows that are high relative to assets and debt; and

• have substantial levels of current assets.

These criteria are lenders' means of reducing their exposure to the possibility of default.

KEY DETERMINANTS OF LOAN ACCEPTANCE DECISIONS[10]

• Age of business

• Size of business

• Ability to service debt (that is, expected cash flows)

• Strength of guarantee or security

• Value of collateral

• Ratio of debt to equity

• Level of working capital

• Credibility of projections

• Client risk

• Strength, depth, and experience of client management team

The most important measures of risk are the client's debt-to-equity ratio and financial ratios that measure the ability of the client's cash flows to cover financial expenses. Lender's risk is lowest for those firms with low debt-to-equity ratios and high coverage ratios.

"Small and medium enterprises which are most concerned with access to credit are businesses which have cleared the start-up hurdle and which now wish to grow their businesses to the next plateau; these businesses are typically younger (one to less than five years old), and have sales volumes in the $500,000 to $1 million range."

CBA, 1996

---

[10] CBA, 1996, pp. 106, 109.

Amount of Credit Extended

Once the lender has agreed to a loan, most borrowers receive the full amount of the requested financing. The maximum size of the loan is usually guided by rules of thumb or formulas. For example, lenders do not like to see total debt exceed 75% of total assets (that is, a debt-to-equity ratio of less than 3). Lenders also link ceilings on operating loans to particular levels of specified current assets. In some instances (about 7% of cases), borrowers receive a loan, but for less funds than they had sought.[11] Account managers appear to base such decisions on judgements of what the SME actually needs.[12]

The level of owner equity is important. Too little equity makes it much more difficult to obtain bank credit. Owners must demonstrate that they hold a material stake in the firm, to spread risk between both owner(s) and lender.

THE COST OF BORROWING:
SETTING INTEREST RATES AND FEES

Interest Rates

Bank borrowing involves two primary financial costs: interest rates and fees. For lenders to make loans to small enterprises, overall revenues must obviously exceed the total costs of lending. To appreciate more fully the lenders' situation with respect to small business clients, consider the costs and benefits to the lender associated with the "average" small business loan.

It is easy to see why loan account managers must administer 80 to 120 accounts. This case load leaves the account manager with an average of about two days per year to spend on each account. It is not surprising that many small business owners complain that their banker "just does not understand our business." This situation is ripe for misunderstanding and miscommunications.[13]

---

[11] CBA, 1996, p. 82.

[12] Wynant and Hatch, 1991, pp. 153-154.

[13] Because of this caseload, banks are sometimes accused of "credit rationing" to small firms. The premise of credit rationing is that borrowers have more information about their prospects than lenders. This information asymmetry means that lenders are unable to distinguish good credit risks from bad one. If lenders cannot measure risk with confidence,

LENDING TO SMEs: THE LENDERS' PERSPECTIVE

The principal amount of the typical small business loan is $50,000 and the average rate of interest is approximately prime plus 1.25%. We shall suppose also that the lender's cost of funds is prime minus 2%, a value that is not unrealistic. Lenders try to keep bad debt expenses below 1%. The lender's "income statement" for the typical loan, therefore, looks something like this:

LENDER INCOME AND EXPENSE FOR MEDIAN LOAN

Annual Income from Loan
    Equals: Premium over cost of funds
        = (1.25% + 2%) X $50,000 $1,625
    Less: Provision for bad debts
        =(1% X $50,000)   −500

Contribution of loan to account manager, $1,125
    (Including overhead and profits)

That is, the median loan contributes just over $1,000 per year to the salary of the loan account manager, associated overheads, costs of monitoring and assessment, and profit.

Interest rates in Canada are relatively uniform.[14] Interest rates on loans to small Canadian enterprises are rarely more than three percentage points above prime.[15] Long-standing bank SME borrowers receive credit at or near prime rate and the median level of interest rates on loans to SMEs is prime plus 1.25. For loans to Canadian SMEs, the size of the borrower firm is the primary

---

they are not able to price loans according to risk. According to the credit rationing argument, they should therefore charge all borrowers the same rate of interest. However, they limit the amount of credit available, restricting lending to customers with which they have had a sufficiently long relationship, clients about whom they have greatest confidence. This theory implies that interest rates do not vary greatly across the spectrum of borrowers and that banks refuse credit to risky firms and those about which they are unsure (for example, new firms).

[14] Overall, interest rates assessed by Canadian banks appear to be lower than those assessed by lenders in the US. In the US, by comparison, 14% of all loans are at more than prime rate plus 4% (*Small Business and Banks: The United States*, 1988, The National Federation of Independent Business Foundation, p. 19).

determinant of interest rates. Data drawn from an analysis of bank lending illustrate this relationship graphically.

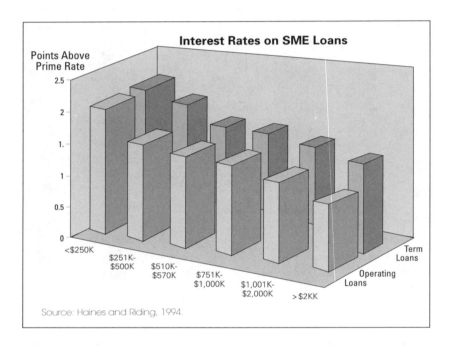

Source: Haines and Riding, 1994.

Fees

Fees on loans can take three forms:

1. Loan application fees;
2. Transactions fees;
3. Loan management fees.

---

[15] Haines and Riding (1994, pp. 28-29) report mean premiums of approximately prime plus 1.65% overall. Wynant and Hatch 1990 report a higher amount, 1.7 to 1.8%, but they failed to weight their sample to reflect the population of SMEs. According to Wynant and Hatch (1990, p. 158) 2.6% of operating loans and 4.0% of term loans are at more than prime plus 3%. Nonetheless, both estimates are significantly lower than the premium of 2.1% reported by the NFIB (*op.cit.*) for the US.

Application fees are typically 0.5 to 1% of the loan. Lenders also charge fees to recover some of the costs associated with the initial investigation of the loan request. Transaction fees recover lenders' incremental costs of transactions and client services, services such as cheque processing, deposits, transfers, etc. Finally, management fees reflect specific lender tasks that relate to the banker-client relationship, such as monitoring the performance of the loan. Fee practices vary widely across lenders: many lenders are willing to negotiate fees. As mentioned earlier, lenders often waive or partially refund application fees for successful borrowers. Fees can also be part of a banking package or can be unbundled. It still makes sense to shop around and have a clear understanding of the loan transaction fee.

Collateral Requirements

Small firm owners are concerned with the amount of personal and commercial collateral required to secure a loan.[16] The amount of collateral available does make a difference in assessing the risk of any lending situation. For example, when management researchers compared the profile of businesses that were successful in acquiring debt capital with those that were not successful, the amount of collateral available was almost 50% greater for borrowers than that for firms with loan turndowns.[17] Moreover, the strength and value of collateral are among the primary factors that govern loan acceptance.[18] Availability of collateral is a critical factor of the loan acceptance decision.

While collateral is important, lenders prefer that clients be sufficiently sound so that the need to seize collateral in case of default is minimal. It is expensive for lenders to execute on collateral and lenders do not usually realize the full value of the security. Lenders do not want the bad publicity and bitterness that attends bank seizures. At the end of the day, bankers would far rather deal with well-managed firms that have cash flows sufficient to carry the requisite loan payments.

---

[16] See, for example, Canadian Labour Market and Productivity Centre (CLMPC), *Canadian Business Speaks Out on Access to Capital*, Ottawa, 1995.

[17] Wynant and Hatch, 1991.

[18] CBA, 1996.

Nonetheless, banks do require collateral security for most lending. Term loans are usually secured by fixed and floating charges on assets. Lender and borrower usually negotiate collateral on operating loans. Borrowers and lenders often differ about the value of collateral; however, lenders often require (in the borrowers' estimation) more than $2 of collateral for each dollar of loan.[19]

PROFILES OF SUCCESSFUL BANK BORROWERS

As mentioned previously, lenders employ "credit scoring systems" to evaluate loan requests. According to these systems, firms that hope to borrow must meet a minimum "score" across a variety of lending criteria. Together, these attributes determine the "bankability" of the loan. Applicants whose score exceeds a threshold level of bankability get loans; others do not. Our own research indicates that successful bank borrowers tend to be older and larger companies than unsuccessful borrowers. A high proportion of successful borrowers are typified as incorporated businesses.

To appreciate these differences the following chart compares the financial attributes of Statistics Canada's profile of all Canadian small firms and that of successful Canadian borrowers.

	"Average" Canadian Small Firms	Successful Canadian Borrowers of:	
		Term Loans	Operating Loans
Total Assets	410	591	568
Total Equity	156	181	141
Total Current Assets	138	314	262
Total Current Liabilities	108	236	219
Total Revenues	193	992	861

Selected Financial Statement Data of SME Borrowers and Canadian Small Business Profiles

---

[19] Riding and Haines, 1994, p. 34.

Drawing on the presentation of data in this chart, successful applicants or borrowers:

- have higher levels of assets and equity than the "average" Canadian small firm;

- have higher sales volumes than those of the "average" Canadian small business;

- regardless of loan type are considerably larger than the typical Canadian small business; and

- are more efficient, and use their assets to generate extremely high levels of sales revenues, resulting in far greater turnover.

Another aspect of the approach lenders use in evaluating the solvency and operating efficiency of businesses is the analysis of financial ratios. The next table continues our comparison of small- and medium-sized bank borrowers with the larger population of Canadian small and medium firms. A summary explanation of

SME Borrowers and the Small Business Profile: Financial Ratio Data			
Ratio	Statistics of Canada Profile of Small Businesses	Borrowers with Traditional Operating Loans	Borrowers with non-Small Business Loan Act (SBLA) Term Loans
Current Ratio	1.3	1.5	1.25
Debt/Equity	1.8	1.7	1.7
Interest Coverage	2.0	9.2	6.9
Debt/Assets	0.6	0.8	0.9
Current Debt/Equity	80.4	200.0	220.0
Revenue/Equity	1.8	9.7	9.9
Gross Margin	39.9%	36.1%	34.0%
Return on Equity	7.4%	35.0%	35.0%
Return on Assets	5.1%	10.3%	10.0%
Fixed Assets/Equity	88.6	127.8	170.6

key financial rations is found in the Glossary. Further explanation is also available in most introductory finance and accounting text-books. Business owners who hope to convince prospective lenders and investors of fiscal responsibility need to have some familiarity with financial ratio analysis.

From this comparison, the total debt-to-assets position of bank borrowers is higher than that of the average of Canadian small business. The current debt portion of the debt (that is, short-term loans, accounts payable, accrued taxes, and current payments due on long-term debt) tends to be high, yet total debt-to-equity is in line with the small firm profile. Thus, borrowers must exhibit lower-than-average levels of long-term debt.

Coverage and turnover measures (ratios such as interest coverage, revenue to equity) of borrowers, as compared to the benchmark profiles of small businesses, demonstrate borrowers' ability to service debt. Overall, successful small business borrowers have high levels of revenues and particularly high levels of turnover and profitability. They also present high levels of fixed assets, assets that can be available for collateral. These data clearly indicate that "creditworthiness" relates closely to a firm's ability to cover interest expenses.

For Firms that Don't Fit the Borrower Profiles

For businesses that do not fit the profile of the bank borrowers, all is not lost. Governments have taken several measures to help viable small businesses obtain credit. One of these initiatives is the Small Business Loans Act (SBLA).

The SBLA

The SBLA has been part of the Canadian financial scene since 1961. According to the Act, small businesses that might not ordinarily get loans can obtain a term loan from an institutional lender and the federal government guarantees a high proportion of the loan to the bank. Without the guarantee, lenders may refuse to loan to new firms or to firms that the lender otherwise perceives as being too risky. Without the SBLA, lenders may require considerably more collateral security (collateral such as the family home). The guarantee specifies that even if the borrower defaults on the loan, the lender will be able to recover much of the loan from the SBLA administration. Since 1989, more than 180,000 loans have been made that provide lenders with comfort in the form of a federal guarantee.

T
I
P

SBLA LOANS

Applying for SBLA loans is relatively straightforward. To do so, a potential borrower must approach an "approved lender." All Canadian chartered banks are approved lenders, as are several other lending institutions. The SBLA program provides exclusively for guarantees of term loans (as opposed to operating loans). Proceeds of the loan must finance land, premises, equipment, and certain other items. Borrowers may not use proceeds to finance working capital, share acquisition, refinancing, or intangibles. Under current regulations, the loan must be for less than $250,000 and the firm must not have sales in excess of $5,000,000 annually. From time to time, terms of eligibility for the SBLA are amended. Approved lenders maintain up-to-date eligibility criteria and we advise interested readers to obtain the most recent information.

It is up to the lender and borrower whether or not an SBLA guarantee is advisable. If the lender and borrower agree, the lender registers the loan with the SBLA administration. However, the guarantee is not free. The borrower must pay an initial fee as well as an annual fee, fees that are paid through the lending institution which passes them on to the SBLA. These fees, even when added to the usual lending fees and bank interest, still allow Canadian small firms access to debt capital at reasonable rates by international standards. In virtually all other respects, the involvement of the government is "transparent" to the business borrower.

T I P

Business Development Centres

Another means by which the federal government tries to ease the market for credit to small firms are the Business Development Centres associated with Human Resources Canada Community Futures Program. The intent of Business Development Centres is to help provide additional employment in disadvantaged rural areas. Each centre (and there are approximately 288 in Canada) can make loans and provide loan guarantees of as much as $75,000. Terms of lending depend on collateral and risk; however, repayment provisions are flexible and can take into account the borrower's cash flow patterns. The earnings from Business Development Centre loans are retained in each centre's portfolio; accordingly, some are able to support financially several small firms.

BANK CLIENTELE

Clearly, banks prefer to deal with established firms. In terms of the product development-management development matrix introduced in Chapter 2, banks tend to lend to firms that have established management teams and a proven product. These are firms in the top right corner of the landscape.

Stage of Product and
Market Development

SME Risk and Growth Grid

Second stage production		BUSINESS DEVELOPMENT CENTRES/ SBLA		BANK LENDING	
First stage production					
Early commercialization stage of product or service		BUSINESS DEVELOPMENT CENTRES/SBLA		BUSINESS DEVELOPMENT CENTRES/SBLA	
Prototype stage of product or service					
Concept stage of product or service					
→ Stage of management development	Technically trained owner/founder	Multiple owners (Few experienced or trained managers)	Multiple owners with a financial professional involved	Multiple owners (marketing and management abilities)	Fully developed management team

COMMANDMENTS FOR A
GOOD BANKING RELATIONSHIP

Most loan account managers want to meet their clients at least annually and loan account managers like to receive, regularly, certain designated pieces of information (for example, interim cash flow forecasts, inventory levels, receivables aging). Whether seeking a first loan or facing an annual loan review, it is a good idea to prepare. We close this chapter with ten tips we hope will contribute to a sound and successful lending relationship.

T I P

COMMANDMENTS FOR GOOD BANKING RELATIONSHIPS

• **Remember that most account managers are overworked**. Prior to your meeting, provide your banker with a written, concise, yet complete summary of the previous year. Identify turning points and explain any material changes in your financial statements.

• **Pretend your account manager is new**. At each annual review, describe frankly the nature of and trends in your industry and identify clearly where your firm fits.

• **Be comprehensive**. Remember that lending to SMEs is not always profitable for banks. However, personal banking business is. Remind your lender about the other ways your firm brings additional business to the bank.

• **Review your business plan**. At your annual review your banker will expect you to be perfectly conversant with all features of your plan. The business plan should move from your vision for the firm to the strategies you are planning to use, to investments in assets, marketing plans, exports or imports, and then to the implications for cash flow and what you expect from the bank.

• **Allow no surprises**. On an ongoing basis, make sure to inform your banker about all material developments, be they good news or bad news. Your banking relationship, like a marriage, is a long-term relationship during which you must maintain trust. Keep the banker informed of all developments. This will not only help the account manager to understand the business, it will improve your credibility and sustain a long-term relationship.

• **Take the initiative**. Remember Commandment #1. The more opportunities, formal and informal, you have to keep the loan account manager familiar with your situation, the better. At the outset, shop around. Look for a banker that specializes in your sector. Make sure your banker visits the site of your firm so that he or she relates to it in a realistic manner. Get to know your account manager's boss. This helps significantly when an account manager leaves and/or you need help in a crisis.

• **Be realistic**. It is easy to be enthusiastic about your firm. Bankers can read through sales forecasts that are excessively optimistic. A record of overestimating sales will not instill confidence in your management acumen.

• **Plan for the worst**. Small firms often rely on relatively few customers. Make sure that you have plans in the event that one or more important clients do not, or cannot, pay.

• **Learn the lingo**. When your banker talks about subordinated debt, know what the manager means. Misunderstandings rooted in a lack of understanding of financial terms is still a misunderstanding.

• **Hire a pro**. Businesses that have an association with a financial professional are less likely to have loans turned down. They also receive loans at interest rates that average a quarter of a point below those of firms that do not have access to a financial professional.

T I P

CHAPTER FOUR

START-UP
AND SEED CAPITAL

There are many myths and misconceptions about small business financing. Where they create over-expectations, these misconceptions can be dangerous—to your business and to your financial health. Fortunately, there is new research that sheds light on the lending behaviour of banks and other capital suppliers. We are also learning more about why some small firms fail while others flourish. This information can help you plan your financing needs more strategically. Much of this research is original and this is the first time it appears in a book. We have balanced the theory with several very practical assessment tools to help position your own business and ideas in the research findings.

We start by identifying activities involved in small business start-up and the financial implications of these start-up activities. This leads to a review of sources of capital for start-up firms. We include a discussion of the early stages of business formation and present the Threshold for Growth Evaluation Tool. The Small Business Opportunity Continuum then provides a visual map to help position your own ideas against those of your competition.

While we focus almost exclusively on financing issues in the rest of the book, we believe that our overview of the process of the early stages of enterprise formation will help prepare business owners better for the financing steps that support the stepping stones of the growth process.

Lack of awareness of the financial and management hurdles of start-up and early commercialization increases the probability of failure. We hope this chapter will also be useful to those would-be entrepreneurs who are evaluating the merits, costs, and benefits of self-employment. This information may provide some preventative medicine against potential mistakes and misfortunes. The chapter closes with an overview of professional services that can assist in managing the firm's financial affairs.

BUSINESS FORMATION AND GROWTH

Recent surveys of Canadian households have reported some astonishing results:[1,2]

- 7% of respondents had been involved in a new business start-up within the previous 12 months.
- 1 in 10 respondents plan to start a new business within the year.
- More than 1 in 3 respondents considered the idea of a new business sufficiently to have reviewed financial requirements.
- Fully 54% of respondents had given the idea of starting a business some consideration within the past year.

Implied in these statistics is the fact that more than two-thirds of those who consider the financial aspects of a new business start-up abandon the idea. Maybe for good reason. No question about it, it is more difficult to raise capital for a business start-up than for any other stage. From the viewpoint of a potential financier, not only is the product unproven and the market uncertain, but the cash flows are usually too small to acquire the

---

[1] Angus Reid, a report prepared on behalf of The Royal Bank of Canada, *The Globe and Mail*, Tuesday, October 24, 1996, B16.

[2] *Small and Medium Sized Businesses in Canada: Their Perspective of Financial Institutions and Access to Financing*, prepared by Thompson Lightstone & Company Limited, on behalf of the Canadian Bankers Association, April 1996.

management skills so essential to success—a real "Catch-22." To unravel this Catch-22, we start with an overview of business growth.

Most firms begin with an innovative idea. The challenge is to turn a good idea into a business opportunity: to commercialize the idea by identifying and satisfying a market need. In Chapter 2 we discussed the importance of **managerial capacity**, **attitude**, and a **competitive product offering** in enterprise development. SME growth also warrants attention because a firm's financial needs change over time, and planned growth requires that owners and managers anticipate their future financial requirements.

The early phases of enterprise growth follow a pattern akin to that of many new products or services, that is, a series of steps or stages. These include:

• idea generation and gestation;

• early commercialization;

• early expansion; and

• growth and maturity.

At first, the product or service is little more than an idea or concept. In this initial stage of **idea generation**, the originator of the idea has little sense of the market for the product and at best, hazy estimates of production costs. Ideas must be refined, customer markets developed, and the firm's infrastructure built. An early task following **idea gestation** is the development of a **prototype** of the service or product concept. At the prototype stage, the technical viability of the idea can be evaluated and an early sense of the market response to the idea assessed. The capital required for prototype development, market research, and sustaining the livelihood of the firm owner is seed capital.

Early commercialization involves the initial introduction of the service or product into the marketplace. It is at this stage of the firm's evolution that costs of business design, product refinement, and market development are maximized. At this same time, revenues to offset these expenses are minimal. Cash flows are mostly outward bound and the firm is particularly vulnerable during this early commercialization step. Cash flow problems at this juncture can also jeopardize the firm's credit rating for the future and do irreparable damage to supplier relationships. Sound financial planning is therefore crucial: planning is required to balance cash demands with the availability of the firm's scarce capital resources. Perhaps the first threshold of growth in business development operation is obtaining the depth of capital to build the business, see the firm through early stages of commercialization, and then to manage early cash flows. Lack of adequate capitalization is a principle reason that many start-ups fail to survive.

The next stage, **early expansion**, is the step at which the firm attempts to market the product or service to a broad clientele. This stage entails a second critical threshold of growth, a transition when the owner looks beyond the immediate needs of the firm.[3] Only then can one begin to manage both the longer term market prospects and internal financing needs of the firm. At this point market research must establish the size and nature of the market. Potential demand needs to be understood. Ideally, the firm's management is in place with, at least, informal affiliations with marketing and financial professionals. The product by now reflects the experiences of early consumers, and financial controls are established to ensure minimal bad debts. Definition of both the product and the management structure marks the end of this first step. At the seed capital and early expansion stages that many owners attempt to secure informal equity investment.

Second stage expansions and maturity. In the second stage, the firm gears up its productive capacity to meet the demand assessed in the first stage. That is, it requires expansion of the production capacity. Additional growth thresholds occur as the firm ramps up production to meet the demands of larger markets. This often entails an expansion of the national market followed by further market expansion as the firm initiates international trade. Each expansion usually requires an investment in productive capacity, further additions to working capital, and the hiring

---

[3] This section on the theory of threshold management draws heavily on the work of Colin Aislabie, specifically "On Modeling the Small Firm Growth Process" in W.C. Dunlop and B.L. Gordon (eds.) *Small Business Research: Proceedings of the Second National Conference,* Institute of Industrial Economics, (Newcastle, England: University of Newcastle, 1984), pp. 129-142, and "The Implications For Survival in Small Firm Failure Studies," *Proceedings of the Fifth National Small Business Conference,* convened by The School of Management, University of Southern Queensland, Toowoomba, New South Wales.

of additional employees. Expansions may also involve cost and productivity modifications.

Many business owners are surprised by the time commitment required to secure the external financing so often necessary for future expansion. This quest is impeded or supported, however, by the financial track record the firm has already established! Credit worthiness of the business is a matter of record. Suppliers, early-stage investors, and others who have had financial dealings with the business can attest to the firm's record—one way or the other. Ultimate success, therefore, depends to a great extent on the firm's ability to survive the early stages of growth with integrity intact and good supplier and lender relationships. This takes professional help. The surprise for many business owners is that such help is needed earlier rather than later!

The Growth Record

The process by which firms grow is obviously not as straightforward as we depicted it above. Not all businesses have equal potential to grow. While one business is spawned, another is maturing; others are succeeding, while others falter. Many business owners begin new businesses at the same time as they operate existing firms. Only a small percentage of businesses, about 25%, will demonstrate consistent revenue growth throughout a growth cycle.[4] Market and industry differences, an owner's willingness or desire for growth, and of course firm attributes combine to produce a variety of growth scenarios. Less than one percent of all firms ever reach the point of being publicly traded.

Experienced lenders and investors understand that mortality rates are high. While rates vary depending on the definition used, a conservative estimate suggests that almost 50% of firms cease trading by their fifth year of operation and 80% cease trading by their tenth year.[5] Investors are not interested in low growth firms. The growth potential of a start-up business is a critical factor in the decision to provide equity capital. So, if you are the owner of a

---

[4] P. Reynolds, and B. Miller, *Minnesota New Firms Study: An Exploration of New Firms and Their Economic Contributions*, (Minneapolis: University of Minnesota Press, 1987).

[5] *The State of Small Business and Entrepreneurship in Atlantic Canada, 1991*, Moncton, NB: Atlantic Opportunities Agency, 1992.

very small or start-up business and you intend to stay small, if you have not yet developed a growth strategy, or if you lack management skills and financial acumen, then you cannot hope to move beyond the banks for financing. Investors will not be interested!

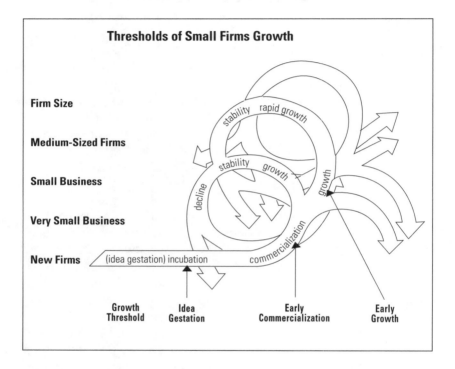

These theoretical thresholds represent significant stages of firm development. While not all the activities listed below will neccessarily be accomplished, a number of these management tasks require completion prior to subsequent growth. They represent benchmarks in firm management development.

Comparatively few firms reach the second and third thresholds of growth, growth capitalized through internal equity such as retained earnings and external equity investment. Few Canadian firms sustain consistent growth. As a consequence there is a tendency to rely on bank financing and personal savings. Moreover, too much reliance on debt can over-lever the firm, making it susceptible to economic cycles.

Growth Threshold	Idea Gestation	Early Commercialization	Early Growth
Product Development	• Prototype developed and refined • Customer credibility established • Supplier credibility established • Firm meets sales commitments to customers • Other _____	• Business plan refined • Geographical expansion • Regional customer loyalty established • Second generation product innovation underway • Other _____	• Continued sales expansion • Exporting (if not already underway) • International network established (if applicable) • Increased competition anticipated • Other _____
Management Development	• Growth ambition clear • Business plan completed • Statement of management goals and objectives • Administrative and related support systems in place • Other _____	• Management's style from entrepreneur to manager • Delegation of work • Strategic thinking • Marketing and networks established • Attempts to minimize expenses and increase efficiencies made • Other _____	• Financial officer hired • Management team in place • Strategic alliances, networks established • Sales and purchase contracts fulfilled • Employee compensation competitive • Other _____

Financial Implications	• Financial objectives stated:
	  – service debt obligations
	  – go public
	  – leveraged buyout
	  – infusion of equity
	  – acquisition of a company
	  – purchase of asset
	  – other _____
	• Start-up (seed) capital secured
	• Accountant hired and payable obligations
	• Terms of management team remuneration stabilized
	• Credit history established
		• Sales revenue continue to increase
		• Volume projections reached
		• Gross and net margins stabilized
		• Retained earning
		• Cash flow meets debt obligations
		• First round expansion capital obtained
		• Proforma statements completed
		• Fixed and operating expenses detailed
		• Other _____
			• Development capital needed for second generation product modifications and refinements
			• Equity through retained earnings used as equity and collateral
			• Break-even reached Banking relationship stabilizing (ie., personal lines of credit may not be required)
			• Other _____

As noted earlier in Chapter 2, the likelihood of securing any outside capital, including bank debt, is dependent on several factors. These include the maturity of the product concept and the management skills resident in the firm. The following chart illustrates the often-cyclical process of growth by stage of product and management development. With it, owners can gauge their own firm's evolution against product development, management, and financial growth thresholds. A clear understanding of these product and management thresholds can help allocate scarce resources and provide insight into your own financial management priorities.

MANAGING START-UP IDEAS

Like all other aspects of business, ideas must be managed. Evaluating start-up concepts, products, and service ideas are tasks best undertaken in the early phases of planning your business. Critical assessment can save financial hardship and long-term disappointment. In the famous words of Thomas Edison, "Invention is 1% inspiration and 99% perspiration."

It sounds so easy. Find a good idea, develop a business plan, and be profitable. First the idea. We are frequently asked, "Where do most successful new venture ideas come from?" Regardless of business size—from small Canadian home-based enterprises to large American Inc. 500 Companies—most new venture ideas come from previous employment, hobbies or skills, friends, acquaintances, or family.

Given the time, energy, and family demands of small business ownership, it is not surprising that successful businesses are often based on owner's interests. Further development of the idea, however, depends on intentional and deliberate actions.

Top Five Sources of New Venture Ideas

Home-Based Business Owners[6]	Small Business Owners[7]	US Inc. 500 Founders[8]
• Previous employment • Hobby or personal interest • Friends, relatives, or aquaintances • Personal observations • Business magazine	• Previous employment • Hobby or personal interest • Chance event • Someone else's suggestion • Education or course	• Working in same industry • Hobby or vocation • Someone else could do better • Systematic research • Can't Explain

[6] W. Good, "Home-based Business: A Phenomena of Growing Economic Importance." *Journal of Small Business and Entrepreneurship*, Vol. 10, No. 1, 1992.

[7] K. Vesper, *New Venture Mechanics*. (New York: Prentice-Hall, 1993).

[8] *Ibid.*

- **Personal networking** is critical to glean first impressions of market acceptance of the concept. Approach, meet, and interview potential bankers, partners, collaborators, suppliers, and clients. Business is about servicing other people's needs and providing customers with real product advantages. Thus, sharing ideas and information are significant steps in enterprise development. During the start-up phase these networks can be invaluable, particularly when self-doubt is high and the workload looks endless.

MENTORING MICRO-BUSINESS OWNERS

A mentoring relationship can start with a phone call to an old friend. You might learn more than anticipated. When Savitri Galardo of Toronto decided it was time to turn her artistic talents and interests to the commercial market, she picked up the phone and called a former board member from her yoga training centre. Luck had it that at the other end of the line was Rena Blatt, a well respected business consultant with the Ontario government. Rena Blatt also happens to volunteer with the Step Ahead Mentoring Program. This program links female volunteers with budding female business owners. Rena was able to provide Savitri with an immediate network of enthusiastic business owners, and a circle of women that she could draw upon for specific expertise. While her graphic arts business is in early commercialization, Rena's mentorship also provided Savitri with a bigger perspective on her initial business start-up idea.

- An important attribute of successful ideas is that they are **market-driven**. Growing firms provide products, services, and activities based on what the market needs. This is very different from firms that are **product-driven**—firms that try to commercialize an idea or innovation that the market may or may not need. In other words, successful new firms innovate; they "listen to the market" thereby providing customer products and services with a competitive advantage.

When new idea and product failures are studied, patterns emerge that demonstrate the importance of differential advantage.[9]

---

[9] *Ibid.*

- Customers do not recognize the need for the new product or service. Poor financial performance can be an indication of either weak ideas or poor communication of good ideas. The solutions afforded by new products are often not well communicated.

- Customers also criticize developers for inadequate market analysis and product testing—start-up activities that require investment capital.

Start-up ideas require investment of capital if they are to grow. But, investors and lenders want a clear sense of what it is that makes an opportunity innovative and where the competitive advantage lies. They want to know the anticipated growth and financial earning potential of an idea.

UNDERSTANDING THE FINANCIAL MERITS OF A START-UP IDEA

Evaluating new ideas is not easy. Often, start-up ideas, particularly special interests and hobbies, have strong emotional value. Try to put these passions temporarily aside when evaluating the merits of all start-up ideas. Take an objective approach: gauge ideas according to their profit potential. To assist with this, it is useful to draw on research that has established patterns.

Certain types of small businesses or ideas consistently demonstrate low profit margins. As a generalization, then, businesses that have limited interest for lenders and investors are those with:

- low levels of work complexity, technology, and innovation;

- little client or supplier autonomy; and

- repetitive or routine work.

As such, if you are considering self-employment as an artisan or clerical administrator, a very small retailer, or a low volume, low margin manufacturer, your business is (again) not likely to catch the attention of investors. Hence, low growth, low earning firms are most likely to financed through personal funds and love money.

CHARACTERIZING SUCCESS

Successful firms tend to be those that offer differential advantage. Typically, they have high levels of **work complexity** and **task autonomy**.

Work complexity refers to the level of a firm's sophistication and innovation. For example, simple clerical, middle administration, and non-professional skills are characteristic of low work complexity. These activities also constitute the fastest growing segment and the poorest income prospects for the self-employed.

Conversely, technically trained professionals that bring to the market innovative ideas and the ability to draw on others with complementary skills constitute the other side of the remuneration continuum. They are also far more likely to find the financing required to expand.

Client and supplier **autonomy** refers to the number of potential suppliers and buyers of the products or services. Businesses with a limited numbers of suppliers are vulnerable to competitor's pricing and material shortages. Businesses with few major buyers are also vulnerable to changes in demand and unanticipated competitor activity. Multi-level marketing opportunities, contract selling, piece-rate employment, and leased employment are formalized work arrangements that can limit small business "owners" opportunities to expand a client or supplier base.

Based on these concepts, the on Small Business Opportunity Grid on page 85 provides a visual guideline for evaluating earnings potential. The outcome of this visual mapping is to help position your business ideas against those of competitors. It may warn you about launching business concepts that in the long-run may offer few financial rewards. The Grid is divided into four market segments:

- **Low Task Autonomy/Low Complexity**, for example: piece-rate cottage trade work, clerical trades, artisans, and crafts;

- **Low Task Autonomy/High Complexity**, for example: software programmers, lawyers, accountants, and contract professionals such as sales agents;

- **High Task Autonomy/Low Complexity**, many service providers, simple manufacturing operations, retailers, and wholesalers; and

- **High Task Autonomy/High Complexity**, such as biotechnology, computer software, sophisticated manufacturing, and robotics.

Outlined on the horizontal axis is the Degree of Management Autonomy that owners hope to achieve in their business. Degree of autonomy ranges from simple, piece rate or hourly fee work to the management of work forces that require sophisticated human resource skills. The ability to delegate and communicate are key factors.

The vertical axis depicts the Degree of Product or Service Innovation. On this axis estimate the level of product (or service) complexity, including the amount of technology used to create or deliver the product or service. These factors may ultimately determine competitive advantage and likelihood of growth.

Having located your start-up ideas, position those of your competitors. A number of sample businesses are illustrated. For example, at one end of the continuum are piece-rate cottage traders, businesses that typically rely on a few clients and are therefore vulnerable when their clients find cheaper sources or move their operations offshore. Many one-person operations face such threats: firms that rely on one or two clients for the bulk of their business, enterprises such as telephone marketing agencies, data processing, insurance claim operations, fast food order takers, and/or some "consultants." Similarly, simple, "me-too" manufacturers, businesses that use a low price entry strategy, may be vulnerable to competitors with multiple supplier relationships, and which operate in both local and international markets.

For example, if you have been "downsized" and now contract back your time (now lower-cost labour) to former employers, be wary of the longevity of such a relationship. Consider ways of improving levels of service innovation to compete more effectively and to attract other clients. Potential investors and lenders undertake similar analysis.

PLANNING THE FINANCING OF YOUR BUSINESS START-UP

Even sophisticated businesses can falter without the planning necessary for seamless execution, and the key to that is is the firm's business plan. The importance of a business plan cannot be overstated. In this section we provide several tools to assist with the financial planning section of the business plan. Direction about

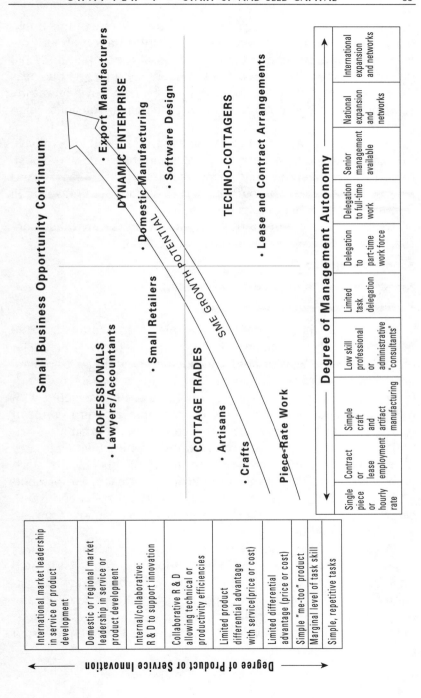

how to prepare a business plan is beyond the scope of this book, but there are many excellent sources of information about how to prepare one, some of which are listed in the Appendix. Most universities and colleges also hold frequent seminars on business plan preparation. Banks and consulting firms have literature, templates, and computer programs that help in business plan preparation.

As a word of caution, it is not necessarily a good idea to have the plan prepared by a consultant unless, in the process, the business owners become fully conversant with it. Lenders and investors will expect the owners to have a complete grasp of all that the business plan contains.

The planning of any start-up requires owners to manage concurrently three demanding management tasks:

- idea refinement,
- customer and market development, and
- design of the firm's infrastructure.

Something that might seem simple on the drawing table (such as picking and packing tomatoes) may actually require a lot of thought. Detailed thinking and back-up planning are integral to successful start-up. Many would-be business owners and start-up operators underestimate the time and costs associated with this phase of business formation. For example, a common rule of thumb among small business consultants when evaluating start-up business plans is to take the business owners own estimates of time and costs and double them! A sample checklist of start-up activities and the financial implications of each, are presented below. Being able to anticipate the required tasks communicates to investors and lenders a degree of management acumen, an attribute they prize.

Apart from your specific business financing needs, investors will be looking for personal information regarding your own financial situation and profile. If you intend to use assets that are jointly owned by a partner or spouse, you will also need a statement of your partner or spouse's debt obligations and assets. Independent financial advice for this individual will be requested by your lending officer.

☑ CHECKLIST

SAMPLE START-UP TASKS AND FINANCIAL IMPLICATIONS

Sample Activities	*Financial Implications*
Idea Refinement	
❏ Scale or size of the idea or concept	Field or market research expense
❏ Product development	Prototypes, modelling, tooling, production, and testing expenses
❏ Image of product or service	Advertising agency retainer required
❏ Advertising and product image	Up front cost of media purchase and creative production
❏ Build preliminary inventory	Parts, services, and other materials required
❏ Determine technology required	New supplier payments often based on COD terms
❏ Engineering resources and standards	Engineering fees, and software development
❏ Legal affairs	Patent registration, copyright, joint venture agreements with associated licensing and legal fees
❏ Packaging	Design, cutting dyes, production of inventories, and design expenses
❏ Insurance	Product and premise liability insurance
Customer and Market Development	
❏ Determining customer buying methods	Negotiated terms of sale, i.e., delivery schedules and inventories with approved financing required
	An understanding of industry or trade discount required
	Need to assess customer credit worthiness
❏ Market development	Promotional pricing may erode intended margins, i.e., rebates
	Advertisement and sponsorship expenses
	Sales force contract agreements required with ensuing legal fees and retainers
	Travel and communication expenses associated with market development by owner and key managers
	Samples required
❏ Community visibility	Business association and club fees

Business Development

❑ Secure appropriate premises	Lease, purchase, or rental expenses
❑ Equipping office	Supplies—furniture, invoices, cards, etc.
❑ Complete banking arrangements	Fees of service including loan fees, cheque clearing costs, etc.
❑ Books and record keeping	Office administrator, bookkeeper fees payable, computer and filing system set-up, management information procedures, and invoicing procedures established, manage activities that require professional assistance and associated expenses
❑ Contract arrangements with employees and/or partners	Legal retainers for associated legal advice
❑ Firm structure	Stock offering, draw on cash, salaries determined
❑ Process of government reporting	Articles of incorporation, board of directors composition, and associated legal fee.

ESSENTIAL ELEMENTS OF PERSONAL INFORMATION

A clear understanding of the owners' personal net worth and financial health, includes:

- cash accounts;
- savings accounts;
- securities (GICs, bonds, stocks, options, etc.);
- life insurance policies;
- house, car, and other major assets; and
- RRSPs and other retirement savings vehicles.

Personal liabilities, include:

- loans outstanding;
- mortgages or rent payable;
- credit card debts;
- lease payments;
- short-term and long-term notes payable; and
- pending legal payments such as divorce settlements and child support.

Family household expenses must also be quantified in order to calculate the owners' draw on the firm's anticipated revenue stream. Armed with a business plan a personal financial profile, with a formalized idea evaluation, backed up with alternative start-up scenarios, securing additional start-up capital can be initiated.

SOURCES OF START-UP FINANCING

You are likely familiar with several traditional sources of start-up capital—personal savings, love money, credit cards—but there are alternatives to financing start-up without dipping into your retirement nest egg or placing demands on personal relationships.

Sweat Equity

Sweat equity refers to the creativity, skills, time, and effort that a business owner must expend during start-up. While sweat equity is not bankable, time and efforts should be documented. For example, the owner's time commitment, if documented can be a selling point to investors. Hours worked, notionally paid at reasonable wages comprises an important starting point for determining owners' equity. It also provides the owner with a more accurate estimate of the cost of doing business. In-kind contributions made by friends and family should also be documented and valued to inform potential lenders of the scope of support for the business owner. For example, if a family member is an expert on computer information systems and has agreed to help set up your computer operating system, document their time multiplied by an estimated rate as an in-kind component of equity in the business.

Personal Savings

The use of personal savings is the most frequently-used source of start-up capital. Use a little caution to ensure that the tax department and future investors are aware of your personal investment in the start-up operations.

First, for sole proprietors and partnerships, personal savings can become easily lost in operations of the firm and everyday life. Establish a commercial bank account to minimize the risk of losing track of early start-up expenditures. A separate account into which all savings are committed and through which business-related cash flows are tracked, can document early-stage activities.

START-UP FINANCING

T I P

• Formalize personal equity contributions with documentation. Provide your accountant with written statements indicating the day, amount, and purpose of each cash transaction.

• Within an incorporated business, cash is generally advanced to the firm in return for shares. When structuring the firm's shares, discuss with a qualified and experienced accountant or financial advisor the advantages of various share offerings (i.e., common shares, Class A shares).

T I P

Second, start-up expenditures usually exceed budgeted expense. As a result, personal savings can be depleted quickly. This may mean having to dip into savings committed to retirement or targeted savings plans such as an education savings account. Beware of resorting to these funds for extra financing. Using this money now can have serious implications for your personal situation in the future.

Recent government measures allow business owners to use part of their RRSP funds for arm's-length business purposes. Given the reality that so many start-ups fail, using retirement funds for investment in small firms should be thought through very seriously. While manufacturing operations have assets at the time of the owners' retirement, many small service firms do not. Most micro service operations have little goodwill or tangible assets to provide an owner with a retirement fund. So short of depleting your own retirement nest egg, what other kinds of financing are available?

Love Money

Love money, money from family and friends, is the second most frequently used source of start-up capital. This type of equity brings its own costs and benefits. Leveraging personal savings with those of friends and family provides additional financial resources and allows owners to tap a larger group for expertise, advice, and capital. But it also brings with it the stress associated with spending the savings of loved ones and friends. You may want to consider extending to family and friends the same professional courtesies a traditional lender would seek. Documentation that spells out the anticipated return and interest on funds borrowed can clarify assumptions of the financial relationship and help to avoid miscommunication and damage to relationships with friends and family. Documentation is also important in the event that the firm is sold or the owner changes marital relationship.

An example of a popular method of providing love money is in the form of a demand note, a written agreement that the lender can demand payment from the business owner at any point in time. This type of agreement ensures that the lender's risk is at least partially covered.

Government Funding

In general, governments are moving away from cash assistance and towards information access. The challenge is to find the information. Two of the best places to start hunting are:

• The Canada Business Service Centres (CBSC), a network of federal and local, regional and provincial small business support agencies. Each CBSC offers a variety of products to help clients obtain quick, accurate, and comprehensive business information, minimize telephone run-around and the duplication of services.

• Industry Canada complements federal and provincial programming with an interactive web site for small business owners called **Strategis**. The web site location includes a data resource, chat line, information server, reference library, and listings of government programs and other relevant points of contact. This site is a excellent small business contact for those familiar with the Internet. Strategis can be located on the Internet at: **http://strategis.ic.gc.ca** or e-mail: **Contact@ic.gc.ca**

CANADA BUSINESS SERVICE CENTRES

A sample of services include:

- a toll-free telephone information and referral service;
- data bases containing information on services, programs, and markets;
- a collection of interactive diagnostic software;
- videos;
- publications;
- business directories;
- how-to material;
- CD-ROM products; and
- external database access.

ON-LINE INFORMATION FOR SMALL BUSINESS OWNERS

Strategis is an on-line information resource for Canadian small business owners, students, and support intermediaries. One of Canadian's largest web sites, it provides easy, direct access to Industry Canada's extensive information resources, such as statistical data for benchmark comparisons, hot links to small business chat groups or magazine articles, industry reports, and other information such as:

- Markets, Trade and Investment News;
- Industrial Perspectives;
- Technology and Innovation Reporting;
- Micro-economic Research and Analysis; and
- Marketplace Services.

Credit Cards

Personal credit cards are frequently used for short-term financing during the start-up phase of operations. Recognizing the potential value of the very small business market, at least one bank has also introduced a commercial charge card targeted to micro and new business owners. One-page application procedures, 24-hour turnaround on decisions, and statements that provide spending breakdowns are more suited to the lending needs of start-up businesses. The overall package of fees and rates assumes high risk so applicants are cautioned to review the actual terms of credit card lending as commercial rates are high. Charge cards are therefore best considered as a short-term, high cost source of capital.

Micro-lending Programs

Non-government and community-based agencies have recently originated several innovative micro-lending initiatives to aid very small companies. Micro-lending models were originally introduced in the 1980s to service the needs of the poor, the self-employed, and those unable to secure traditional credit. Such agencies as the Women's World Bank, the Badan Kredit Kecamatan (BKK), and the Gremeen Bank have successfully pioneered informal financial systems and social lending networks. The Calmeadow Foundation of Toronto, working with the support of Canadian banks, have piloted similar innovative programs in Vancouver, Toronto, Nova Scotia, and several native regions. There are essentially two types of micro-lending models: the lending circle (also known as peer lending), and very small loans with no group affiliation.

James Brown of Nova Scotia knows the benefits of micro-lending. When his doctors told him he would never work again as a fisherman, he was able to secure a (micro) loan of $500 from Calmeadow Nova Scotia, based on his character "not collateral." As the business grew, he borrowed a total of $16,000 including supplier credit. He now has two employees and operates year-round.

"Growth in the Grassroots" PROFIT, October-November 1996

A lending circle is made up of five or more business owners who share in the task of screening loan applicants before they accept the applicant into the group. The basis of assessment is often judgement of subjective criteria related to a loan applicant and loan structure, and not the traditional collateral-based method of assessment. Subsequently, if one member of the group defaults, the other members must make good on the loan.

The group, or "circle," therefore has incentive to approve loans prudently and to monitor each other carefully.

OBJECTIVES OF LENDING CIRCLES

- To provide start-up capital at reasonable market rates to members of the community.
- To enhance the financial management skills of program participants.
- To allow would-be business owners to commence operations quickly and easily.
- To empower individuals to help themselves.
- To encourage community members to build businesses and spend locally.

SNAPSHOT OF MICRO LENDING[10]

- A "micro" business refers to a very small business with five or fewer employees and gross revenues of less than $500,000. Most businesses are considerably smaller; most have no employees.
- Most loan applicants have been turned down for traditional debt lending.
- Loans are generally less than $15,000 for new businesses and $25,000 for existing businesses. The average loan is between $500 to $5,000.
- A key to application is a good business plan, although not all lending agencies require written documentation.
- The rate of interest charged ranges from prime +1 to 1.5% to rates that are competitive to those charged on credit cards.
- Applicants range in demographic profile and level of business sophistication.
- Some loan circles and lending institutions require participants to attend ongoing business training and mentoring programs.
- Historically, loan circles source funding from not-for-profit community organizations and private donors.

---

[10] B. Orser, and M. Foster. "Lending Practices and Canadian Women in Micro-based Businesses," *Women in Management Review*, Vol. 9, No. 5 (1994): 11-19

In other community-based micro-lending programs, loans involve some form of security rather than peer pressure. Calmeadow, for example, plans to initiate a new program that will provide loans for the purchase of fixed assets for as much $15,000. These loans will not depend on peer pressure; rather, they will require some form of security.

Loan applications, approvals, disbursements, and collections are stripped down to the bare minimum required to effect the transactions. While a rigorous assessment of micro-lending initiatives has yet to be completed, they have been well-received by communities and targeted small business groups. However, the Calmeadow program operating in the Greater Vancouver area has loaned more than $250,000 to more than 100 clients, with a 96% repayment rate.

ATTRIBUTES OF MICRO-LOAN PROGRAMS[11]

Simplicity. Programs are streamlined and commensurate with loan size. Applications, approvals, disbursements, and collection activity is stripped down to the bare minimum. Loan applications are often no more than one page.

Risk Assumption. The micro-loan is recognized to have increased risk and is treated as a separate class of product by lenders. While Canadian research on rates of default rates is lacking, international anecdotal research on female lenders in developing countries suggests a failure rate that is lower than that for traditional lenders.

Accessibility. Lender outlets are located near the customer to a greater degree than are formal commercial lenders. Community accessibility is a hallmark of these programs.

Active Participation. Many lending circles require participants to take an active interest role in each other's businesses and in the administration of the loan. Some also require participation in training and mentoring programs.

Lending Principles. Programs rely as much on motivation as on information. Motivation to repay the loan is based on social pressure and the promise of continued access to services. Motivation to repay is based on techniques such as group guarantees or pressure, the promise of repeat loans, and in increasing amounts or savings requirements.

[11] *Ibid.* Also see Dawn Ringrose & Associates, "Micro Loans and Micro Loan Circles, "How to Manual," prepared for the Alberta Economic Development & Tourism, (March 1993).

Ideally, micro-lending programs are a social program that could operate at little or no public expense. Community-based groups raise loan circle funding from financial institutions, businesses, and non-profit organizations. Once established, loan circles can not only sustain themselves, but they can even earn a profit.

T I P

CREATING A MICRO-LENDING PROGRAM IN YOUR COMMUNITY

Many programs rely on government subsidies to cover operating expenses, however, some are self-sufficient. If you are interested in establishing a micro-loan fund in your community here are several tips:

- Check to see if there is already a lending program operating locally. A good starting point is the Chamber of Commerce or the area economic development officer.
- Review municipal zoning by-laws as they may prohibit or restrict micro enterprises from establishing operations in certain areas, for example, on residential property.
- Ensure that all business applicants meet standard provincial health and safety standards.
- Establish early in the development process the requirements of participation, i.e., all participants must understand each other's business situations, meet on a monthly basis to discuss progress, etc.
- Call on the expertise of the growing number of resource agencies (see Appendix). Most also provide a listing of additional resource materials.

T I P

Business Development Bank of Canada

As noted in Chapter 3, The Business Development Bank of Canada also offers a "Micro-Business Program," which targets loans to start-up firms and enterprises with fewer than five employees and revenue of less than $500,000. The focus of the Micro-Business Program is to foster start-ups and early-stage expansion by helping to finance the acquisition of fixed assets, start-up costs, market research, or product development expenses. Both capital (up to $25,000 for start-ups and $50,000 for established businesses) and mentoring are part of the program.

THE BUSINESS DEVELOPMENT BANK OF CANADA
MICRO BUSINESS LENDING PROGRAM

This program offers more than debt. It also affords participants an initial assessment of their management skills and a diagnosis of the business' needs. Management skill shortcomings are identified and a training program designed to address these deficiencies. Bankers and consultants also assist in the development of a business plan. Follow-up management support is continued.

Criteria for the program are that the proposals must be innovative and management must already be committed financially to the business. The firm must be either in the start-up or growth phase, be able to demonstrate market potential, and owners should be experienced.

The Small Business Loans Act

The *Small Business Loans Act* (SBLA), as mentioned in Chapter 3, provides loan guarantees on term loans for firms too small to qualify for traditional bank lending. This includes business start-ups. Of more than 180,000 loans made since 1989 under the terms of the SBLA, more than one-third were to start-up firms, defined as firms that were less than one-year old at the time of borrowing. Loans may be for as much as $250,000 and borrowers can expect to pay the bank lender prime rate plus 2.75%, an initial fee to the SBLA administration, and an annual fee for the loan guarantee.

The SBLA is a useful means of financing for small firms. The government guarantee provides the lender with comfort that would otherwise have to be provided through collateral security. For many small business owners, the SBLA provides an alternative to pledging the family home.

Community Programs

The Saskatchewan and Manitoba governments have also initiated community based "pools" of capital. Grassroots programs and government agencies are drawing on community members to support indigenous economic development. While there is no clearinghouse for programs, a call to your economic development department or

Chamber of Commerce, e-mail to Strategis, or contact with an accountant, are starting points. For example, the community of Perth, Ont., helped launch Knudsen Engineering Ltd.

COMMUNITY FUNDING

In 1995, owners Donald and Judith Knudsen were drawn to Perth, Ontario, a community of 5,500 after community members organized local potential investors. Backed by an objective technical and market assessment by the Innovation Centre in Waterloo (Ontario), Perth community members were able to raise the investment capital required to lever funds from other financing agencies. Shareholders are now beginning to see the benefits of their investment as Knudsen Engineering is selling 30% of its products, digital marine electronic systems, domestically with contacts to defense companies, universities, and government agencies. "Venture capital doesn't have to come from institutions, labour funds, or wealthy individuals. It is possible to tap pools of small investors in a single community if the company has the contacts and a credible technology."

"How a Small Town Funded a High-Tech Hopeful"
Shaun Markey and Gayle MacDonald
Reprinted with permission from *The Globe and Mail*, Monday, March 3, 1997

Employers

A current or former employer might well be an unrecognized source of start-up capital. Traditionally, the financial rewards of successful product development and idea generation have been to the sole benefit of an employee's firm. This model is changing, particularly within emerging industries such as software development, communications, and biotechnology. Employers are increasingly realizing the mutual employee-employer benefit of profit centres, spin-off operations, and stock option programs. Such firms are no longer spurning ideas generated by employees that do not fit the corporate plan. In the past, such rejection often led to the loss of valuable and creative employees who had no choice but to leave the firm if they wanted to pursue their ideas. Instead, traditional pyramid or hierarchical structures of organization are giving way to organizational forms such as virtual or mutual organizations.

Mutual organizations are financial networks, supplier linkages, and small firm technology networks grouped to share risk capital, information, and rewards while maintaining independent asset bases. Joint projects, alliances, subcontracting, technology and information sharing, and research consortia are all examples of this emerging form of small firm organization, most which have been initiated and managed by former employees.

Capitalizing on a new business idea while providing financial incentives to keep employees may also take the form of employee stock options and ownership plans. The chart that follows provides a preliminary checklist for business owners contemplating stock ownership as a vehicle for financing.

INVOLVING EMPLOYEES

Employee stock ownership plan. Under this arrangement a firm provides shares of stock or sufficient cash to purchase shares for its employees based on a predetermined formula. Employees cannot sell the shares until the expiry of a predetermined retention period, usually one to two years.

Stock option plan. Employers can grant key employees options for the purchase of company stock at a fixed price for a designated time. Options are vested—or owned by the employees—after a specific period of time.

A Checklist for Developing an Employee Stock Ownership Plan

❑ A willingness of the employer to share ownership with employees in a meaningful way.

❑ Strong management belief that employee involvement and participation can add value for the corporation.

❑ Effective communication with those who are eligible to participate in the plan.

❑ Clearly defined strategy: Who will benefit? What percentage is required to make employees feel like true owners?

Hurbert Marleau, PROFIT Decision Board
PROFIT, September 1996.

START-UP CAPITAL ON THE SME RISK GRID

In this section, we continue with the SME product-management risk grid introduced in Chapter 2. In Chapter 3, we focused on bank borrowing, debt capital accessed mostly by well-developed firms—those in the top right corner of the grid. This chapter relates to the other extreme early stage firms, found mainly to the bottom-left of the grid. Here, we reviewed a variety of ways of finding hard-to-get start-up capital. However, diversity is present even among start-ups and so we locate several forms of start-up funding on the grid because not all the sources we identified are equally applicable for all new firms.

Stage of Product and Market Development	SME Risk and Growth Grid				
Second stage production and new competitive entries					
Product or service line expansion and market development	Employers Micro Loans Community Funding	Employers			
Prototype stage of product or service	Savings Love Money Micro Loans	BDCs Micro Loans, SBLA			
Concept stage of product or service	Savings Credit Cards Micro Loans	BDCs Micro Loans, SBLA Community Funds			
→ **Stage of management development**	Technically trained owner-founder	Multiple owners. Few experienced or trained managers	Multiple owners with a financial professional involved	Multiple owners with marketing and management abilities	Fully developed management team

MANAGING THE FINANCIAL MIX: WORKING WITH PROFESSIONALS

What is the optimal capital structure for your firm? How can a business owner maximize the availability of capital, while minimizing commercial and personal risk? One solution to these questions is to seek the knowledge of professionals. In Chapter 2 we noted that the presence of a financial officer is a distinguishing attribute of high performance firms. Many small businesses understand this. Others, however, perceive professionals as an unnecessary expense (or even a waste of money) at a time in the business when funds are extremely tight. Our experience has taught us that spending money on accounting or legal fees at start-up is money well-invested. These professionals can help situations that have long-term negative consequences, such as exploiting suppliers, and they provide suggestions for structuring the firm that are likely to save money in the long-run.

The following chart indicates the breakdown of various types of professional services reported by a survey of Ernst & Young small business clients. While these results are not typical of all small business, they provide a ranking of the types of professional services favoured by many small business owners. We'll take a closer look at the two most frequently used types of professional assistance, financial advisors, and lawyers.

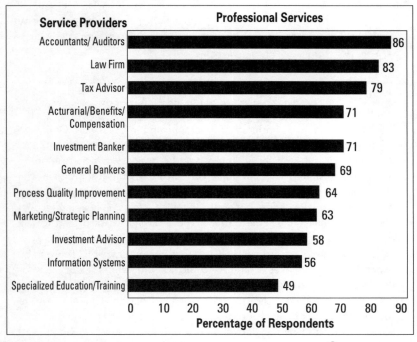

Reprinted with permission from Ernst & Young, The Entrepreneur of the Year® Institute, 1984.

Why Use Financial Advisors?

Financial professional services is the largest category of expertise sought by small business owners. Service providers include accountants, auditors, tax experts, actuarial benefits and compensation officers, commercial and investment bankers, and general advisors. While few start-up operators require the use of all these services, several are key. An accountant and tax advisor can play a critical role in the management of the firm. They provide:

- time-saving advice on how to create and maintain the firm's accounting records;

- networks with other small businesses;

- an informed and objective sounding board for owner-managers;

- important tax advice, even at the early stages of start-up, including information on current and intended changes in tax regulation; and

- assistance with costing the product or service. This is particularly important in the service sector where new business owners tend to underestimate and undervalue the cost and time required to service customers.

T
I
P

FOR WOULD-BE BUSINESS OWNERS

Jamie Ingram is a chartered accountant living in Unionville, Ont., who has an active practice with professionals and very small business clients. He suggests that before would-be business owners rush out to buy a computer, they invest in a filing cabinet! "My biggest problem with most micro-business owners is that they don't file properly. They may have a lot of market knowledge, but most show little interest in keeping records and getting their filing done on time. These businesses also tend to mix personal and professional expenses. As a result many clients end up paying for my time to track down and sort invoices and receipts. This can be expensive. It also makes it difficult to provide different types of information to users such as the bank, creditors, or Revenue Canada. A second tip is to use a commercial charge card. Revenue Canada does not want to see toy and family holiday receipts unless they are directly related to your business. This also avoids throwing up a red flag to Revenue Canada at audit time."

T I P

Financial professionals help present the firm in its best light to potential investors and lenders. Even an informal relationship with an accountant or financial officer demonstrates some degree of fiscal responsibility by the business owner. As we mentioned earlier, research shows that firms that retain financial advisors are turned down less often for loans and receive financing on better terms, compared to Canadian firms with no associated financial officer.[12]

Why a Lawyer?

Legal assistance is cited as the second most frequently-used professional service of small business owners. Many owners postpone seeking legal advice until the time of incorporation. But early advice, even before incorporation, is warranted. Legal assistance can provide:

• expertise on managing the firm's legal and regulatory paperwork;

• assistance in establishing the ownership structure of the firm. For example, many new owners are not aware of the tax benefits of establishing a family trust at the time of incorporation; and

• a network on your behalf with potential investors, partners, suppliers and customers, and other small businesses.

During the start-up period, initial legal discussions might also focus on:

• how to protect personal and commercial assets;

• potential customer and supplier liabilities;

• commercial and personal insurance requirements;

• contract obligations with potential suppliers, employees, and customers; and

• tax implications and a preferred corporate structure.

---

[12] L. Fabowale, B. Orser, A. Riding, and C. Swift, "*Gender, Structural Factors, and Credit Terms Between Canadian Small Business and Financial Institutions*," Entrepreneurship, Theory and Practice, Vol. 19, No. 4, Summer 1995.

MEETING THE FINANCIAL HURDLES OF START-UP

Here are several more tips to consider when managing the start-up process and meeting the hurdles of small firm growth.

When dealing with professionals. The growing small business marketplace has ushered in a boom market for quasi-professional "experts." The quality of professional advice is highly variable and as yet, there is no system of accreditation. Anyone can set up shop as an advisor to small businesses. Even among the larger service providers, quality is not guaranteed. Owners should shop around. This is where networking can play an important role in securing quality professional advice.

Don't underestimate the time required for securing start-up capital. Many start-up owners underestimate the time required for and obstacles to securing start-up capital. Securing your start-up finance, like any other management task requires thoughtful, time-consuming effort. Start the process early. Your financial backers, accountant, lawyer, tax expert, and lenders can be a sounding board for your ideas. They can also serve as mentors as the organization evolves.

Balance short-term and long-term capital. A mixture of start-up capital can provide flexibility and more realistic payment terms, than relying only on an owner's savings, an operating loan, or charge cards. Plan for the provision for future equity in the form of retained earnings and explore other alternatives. The Business Development Bank of Canada has introduced several innovative debt instruments.

Take the time to investigate bootstrap programs—you may qualify. A number of government and non-governmental organizations and agencies provide micro or "bootstrap financing." Contact your local Canada Business Centre Office (Industry Canada) for a listing of the provincial and federal programs. Non-governmental assistance is a little harder to find. Try contacting your local Chamber of Commerce, or small business consulting services located in many universities and community colleges. Knowledgeable staff should be able to point you in the right direction.

Don't fall too far behind on your paperwork. Nothing is as certain as death and taxes...and in the case of small business...an unreasonable amount of time to pay the tax bills! Keeping ahead of paperwork is a challenge for all business owners. Unfortunately the tax department doesn't wait. Budget your time and make provision for administrative assistance including a bookkeeper at the earliest point possible.

CHAPTER FIVE

FINANCING EARLY STAGE GROWTH
Where Angels Don't Fear to Tread

During the heyday of New York musicals, "angels" were people who provided financing for new plays or musicals on or off-Broadway. Today, "business angels," also known as "informal investors," are important sources of early-stage capital for businesses. These individuals, who invest their personal capital directly in businesses owned by others, are business angels. In addition to individual informal investors, the market for informal capital comprises corporate angels (businesses that invest in other businesses), archangels (lead investors who assemble a syndicate of angels), and immigrant angels (individual angels from other countries). While almost invisible in terms of media coverage and research, informal investment accounts for the largest, oldest, and most frequently-used source of external equity finance for small businesses.

Collectively, informal investors represent a large pool of capital directed primarily to early-stage firms. Estimates of their importance vary. Yet, even the most conservative assessments suggest that business angels in Canada invest of the order of

$500 million annually in Canada, usually at the early stages of enterprise development.[1]

As impressive as their investment record is, research indicates that the potential of the informal investment market remains largely untapped. Among individuals who report levels of financial wherewithal similar to that of angels, fewer than five percent—one in 20—are active informal investors. Put a little differently, out of every 100 people who have sufficient personal capital to be angels, 95 are *not* active informal investors. Therefore, the pool of potential informal investment funding is enormous and remains largely untapped. Why, then, are so few wealthy Canadians not taking an active part in the financing of entrepreneurial ideas and innovation?

There are two main problems associated with access to informal capital. First, it is a fragmented market. There is no central meeting place at which those who seek capital can interact with suppliers of capital. Second, informal investors are often unimpressed with the managerial skills of the owners of early stage businesses. These two problems contribute to what some call a "gap" in the market. Closing this gap requires information about how to overcome the fragmentation of the informal market to find angels, and information about how to deal with informal investors. These are issues this chapter addresses, issues such as how you can tap into informal investor networks, what investors are looking for, and how to win them over. Over the last five years we have been asking these questions to informal investors across Canada. Our research through one-on-one interviews and surveys with almost 300 informal investors, provided much of the information presented here. We explore these questions through the following topic headings:

- investment patterns of informal investors;

- how angels make investments;

- motivations of informal investors;

- a psychological profile of investors and what makes them tick; and

- legal considerations when dealing with informal investors.

---

[1] Survey research conducted by the Canadian Labour Market and Productivity Centre documents that twice as many businesses have relied on investments from angels, at some point in their development, as on any other form of external equity investment, including institutional venture capitalists.

INFORMAL INVESTORS:
A PROFILE OF INVESTMENT PATTERNS

Informal investors play an important role in financing businesses in many economies, not just in Canada. Researchers are learning more about who these investors are and how to mobilize the
untapped pool of potential risk capital. The profile of these individuals is consistent, regardless of country of origin. For example, the average informal investor has previous small business
experience, is about 50 years old, is male, and has secured adequate net worth to be able to now invest in others' endeavours.
We show some of these common themes in the following table.

Attributes and Investment Patterns of Informal Investors Around the World

	United Kingdom[2]	Sweden[3]	USA[4]	Canada[5]
Age	53	54	47	47
Gender	99% male	—	95% male	98% male
Annual Family Income	$100,000	60%> $1,000,000	$120,000	$177,000
Net Worth	$700,000	57%> $1,000,000	US$750,000	C$1.36m
Previous Entrepreneurial Experience	57%	96%	83%	89%
Investment rate	2 every 3 years	1 per year	2 every 3 years	1 per year
Rejection rate	7 of 8	7 of 8	7 of 8	97%
Average investment	$23,000	$100,000	$70,000	$110,000
Location (%<50 mi.)	54%	—	72%	53%

[2] UK data from Harrison and Mason (1991, 1992), as reported by Mason and Harrison, "Closing the Regional Equity Gap: The Role of Informed Venture Capital," *Small Business Economics*, 7:153-172, 1995.

[3] Data from Sweden from Lundstrom (1993), as reported by Mason and Harrison, 1995.

[4] US data from Gaston (1989), as reported by Mason and Harrison (1995).

[5] Canadian data from A. Riding, Haines, G., Duxbury, L., DalCin and Safrata. *Salient Characteristic of Informal Investors*, Industry Canada and the Ministry of Economic Development and Trade of the Province of Ontario, 1993.

Typically angels are late career investors. They report high incomes and wealth. On average, they report annual incomes in excess of C$150,000 and personal net worth of at least C$1 million. They are also well educated. Most are university graduates and a high proportion have advanced degrees. Most angels are people who have succeeded as entrepreneurs and are looking for their next success. While certain tax incentives might catch the interest of these investors, they did not become angels because of tax benefits alone. They prefer to focus on the fundamental merits of growing firms.

Of course, not all angels conform to this "average." However, we can learn from this prototype. Angels are usually people who have had previous experience as an entrepreneur. For them, the process of building a business is not a mystery. They know what to expect and understand the tasks that face business owners. They have also made money in the process. Having been successful before, angels are willing to accept the risk that attends new business ventures.

Perhaps this is part of the explanation as to why so few wealthy Canadians are active informal investors. Those who have gained their wealth through inheritance or by means other than small business ownership, may view small business investing as beyond their risk threshold. Many people simply may not "know the ropes" of small business investing. Alternatively, the demands of monitoring the firm's performance and providing advice and direction are too onerous for the potential rewards.

Fortunately, those who do invest are willing to do so across all sizes and sectors of businesses. Typically, however, they invest in businesses that they have experience in. For example, the "new economy" does not intimidate them. After all, many angels

ANGELS AND HIGH TECH ...

In the Ottawa-Carleton area, our research found that 50% of informal investments were in the technology sector. In the Cambridge, Mass., region, new technology-based firms, far from having to search for capital, were approached by local angels hoping to get in early on the next Microsoft. In both regions where technology-based firms are emerging, so are technology-focused informal investors.

are themselves products of the new economy. Most angels invest near their home or office. Therefore, angels tend to be at ease with the nature of local industry.

The average investment made by Canadian angels is slightly more than $100,000; however, angels often invest as little as $10,000. To take advantage of larger investment opportunities, angels frequently form syndicates among themselves. This allows a group of informal investors to invest much larger amounts, often of the order of $500,000. Syndication also spreads risk and allows individual angels (and the owners of the firms in which they invest) to gain the expertise and contacts of a larger group. Of course, angels are not a homogeneous group of people, but we can discern several different types of informal investor.

TYPES OF INDIVIDUAL ANGELS

Encouraged by the prospects of generous return on investment or government programming that provides incentives to would-be immigrant angels, the profile of informal investors complements the diversity of the small business sector.

Independent Angels. Individuals who provide equity capital to small businesses, most often entering into participation during the growth phase of maturation.

Immigrant Angels. Second only to family members and refugees, business immigrants have been given a high priority for entry to Canada. Business immigrants include:

- Entrepreneur immigrants, people with the ability to establish, purchase, or make substantial investment in a business.

- Investor immigrants, or people who can demonstrate a business background and high net worth. They must invest a minimum amount in a business, a privately administered investment syndicate, or a government-administered venture capital fund. The minimum investment varies by province, with lower levels of investment required in the six smallest provinces.

- Self-employed immigrants are people who intend and are able to establish or purchase a business that will create an employment opportunity and contribute to the Canadian economy.

The goal of the immigrant investor program is to attract financing that provides capital for Canadian small business. Quebec, which administers its own version of the program, has attracted $1.5 billion of immigrant investor capital since 1986.

Archangels are individuals who marshal informal capital by establishing syndicates of other investors. Often, archangels play a primary role in commercialization of product ideas and technology. They contribute to economic development far beyond their own personal investments by creating the informal network infrastructures that facilitate informal capital.

Corporate Angels

In addition to individual informal investors, some large firms provide both financial and logistical support for new businesses. For example, Newbridge Networks has established a remarkable record of backing innovative ventures. Most of these ventures arose from creative people within Newbridge but who have pursued—with Newbridge financing and support—separate business entities. Naturally, many corporate angels focus on investments that are complementary to existing activities.

Luda Tovey was almost in business. Armed with a $150,000 sales order to produce corporate videos for a major pharmaceutical company, she and her former partner approached some banks for start-up financing. Banks, however, declined financing and Luda and her partner had to look elsewhere. Their search led them a Kaleidoscope Entertainment Inc., a distributor of television programs. In exchange for one-third of the company, Kaleidoscope provided approximately $400,000 in start-up equity capital. Luda's firm, Oberon Productions Inc., was born. Kaleidoscope not only provided capital, they also acted as mentors to Ms. Tovey. Five years later, Oberon's billings had increased eightfold over their first year in business. Last year Oberon had developed 13 multimedia programs, each worth $50,000 to $200,000 and the firm was looking to continue its expansion.

"Angels Go WHere Bankers Fear to Tread" by Marjo Cusipag. Reprinted with permission from *The Globe and Mail*, April 27, 1996, page B27.

Corporate angels are a growing phenomenon in Canada. In the past, employees with an innovation typically had to leave employment with a large firm if they hoped to commercialize their creation. More often, now, employers realize that by providing support to these innovative ideas, they are creating a "win-win" situation. The corporate angels retain, if not the employees, the fruits of their creativity. The innovative employees do not have to dilute their efforts seeking logistical or financial backing. Finally, the support of the corporate angel enhances dramatically the chances of successful commercialization.

HOW ANGELS MAKE INVESTMENT DECISIONS

Canadian investors are a discerning group. They reject 97% of the proposals they encounter. What is more telling, however, is that angels reject three out of four opportunities *at first sight,* before even reading the business plan. To get a sense of why angels are so selective, we trace the process by which investors make their decisions.

If business owners could look over the shoulder of informal investors as they make their decision, owners would have a better sense of what turns investors on and off an opportunity. This section does just that. Here we trace the process and the thoughts of investors from the first moment they see an investment proposal, to their decision to invest—or not. To organize this process, we identify four steps by which investors make decisions:

• first impressions, or, rejection at first sight;

• inspection of the business plan, or initial screening;

• meeting business owners (or getting to the bottom of the principles of the principals); and

• due diligence and negotiations.

First Impressions: Rejection at First Sight

There are two main reasons why informal investors reject almost three-quarters of business opportunities at first sight. First, they do not perceive that the product or idea has market potential. Second, investors reach rejection decisions because they lack faith in the business owner(s)' managerial abilities.

These two reasons relate to each other. The investor wants to earn a substantial return on investment. Business plans that are unprofessional or incomplete speak volumes about the (in)ability of management to commercialize successfully the idea or product. Investors do not even bother to read such business plans, and in the eyes of many investors, too many business plans are simply not well-prepared.

An additional factor at this step relates to how the business plan came to the investor's attention in the first place. Some business owners send proposals directly to angels in the hope of finding investment capital. In other cases, business associates and friends refer business opportunities from the owner(s) to the potential investors. Opportunities that business associates or friends refer to investors stand a far higher chance of surviving beyond the first impressions stage than others. This makes sense. To the extent that the investor respects the intermediary, they also respect business opportunities referred by them.

Reviewing the Business Plan: Initial Screening

Investors reject 60% of the opportunities that survived their initial impressions. By the end of the first two steps in the decision process—first impressions and initial screening—investors will have rejected nine out of 10 proposals! Again, the professionalism connoted by the business plan is paramount. From that plan, the investor makes an evaluation of the principals of the firm. A negative impression leads to almost certain rejection.

Seeking informal capital, then, can be discouraging. To run this gauntlet, business owners must accomplish two tasks by means of the business plan. First, they must capture the *attention* of the investor. Presenting the investor with a challenge that appeals to the investors' motivations is helpful. We will examine patterns of investors' demands as well as investors' motives later in this chapter; however, catching the investor's attention may mean that the business plan needs to be tailored specifically to each investor! Second, and perhaps most importantly, business owners must convince the investor of their *management* abilities. The angel investor is considering entrusting thousands of dollars of personal funds to a business in its early stages. To do so, the investor must perceive that the owners of the enterprise will not only treat the investment with fiscal responsibility but that they are able to transform the product or idea into a successful business. This takes management skills that do not necessarily come with either technical competence or engineering brilliance.

Meeting the Business Owners: The Principles of the Principals

For the 10% of opportunities that survive the first two stages of review, in the third stage of the decision process the investor meets with the business' principals. Investors reject half the remaining proposals at this step, usually because investors have doubts about one or more of these three factors:

• investors will try to confirm their initial impressions about the capabilities of the owners, especially the *management capabilities;*

• investors will form impressions about the integrity of the owners; and

• investors will test for the *compatibility* that a close long-term relationship entails.

Investors demand integrity. Any sense that the ownership of the firm is not forthright, is attempting to conceal relevant information, or is being less than honest ends the decision process. In addition, investors want to test that they will be able to work closely with the principals and that the principals of the business understand the values, needs, and motives of the investors (more on these later).

Closing the Deal: Due Diligence and Negotiation

The final step comes when the investor and business owners get serious about making a deal. Investors will carry out a detailed examination of the firm, called "due diligence." Due diligence involves a thorough examination to confirm that the business plan accurately and fully describes the enterprise. This process

☑ CHECKLIST

A Checklist of Information Requirements

The building block for any deal is the business plan, including the firm's financial statements, anticipated return on investment, description of the management team, and product offering. Additional information will vary depending on risk, level of need, negotiating position, etc. Here is a checklist of points to consider when drafting a proposal and negotiating terms of agreement with angels.

❑   **Summary Statement of Intent:** A statement summarizing why the investor is investing in the firm. This provides a clear summary of what the investor anticipates will be her or his financial returns and involvement in the company.

❑   **Exit Scenarios:** Statements including when and how the investor will exchange ownership of the firm for payment, for example, stock purchase options; when/if the firm will go public; provisions for the sale or buyback of the company; provisions for finding new investors; consequences of liquidation of the firm; and/or penalties.

❑   **Summary of the Firm's First Financial Profile:** Scenarios of the future detailing potential debt and equity financing, use of subordinated debt, and venture capital.

❑   **Collateral Provisions:** Details of all secured assets of the firm, subordination to bank financing.

❑   **Use of Proceeds:** A summary statement of how and where the firm will use the proceeds from the investment. This may also include specific provisions of ways in which the firm cannot use the funds. For example, the firm may not use the funds as working capital, to pay down outstanding debt, to purchase capital assets, pay salaries or bonuses, finance product development, research, etc.

❑   **Risk Factors:** Summary of risk factors associated with the firm's financial projections. These statements should include "what if" scenarios, projections that anticipate major changes in the operating performance of the firm.

usually involves site visits, reference checks, and detailed examination of all elements of the business. Details vary depending on the nature of the investment and maturation of the firm (start-up, first or second stage financing, turnaround, buyout, etc.).

Once satisfactorily completed, the investor(s) and owner(s) engage in negotiations about the investment and the structure of the deal. The proportion of ownership the founders are willing to cede in exchange for the needed capital is very often a stumbling block at this point. Again, investors reject half the investment opportunities that survived the three earlier decision stages, usually because the two sides simply cannot reach a mutually acceptable agreement.

WHAT IS A REASONABLE RETURN ON INVESTMENT?

Angels' investments are about the most risky investments around. In most cases, the firms are at very early stages of development, with unproved products or services and an incomplete management team. Investors could, alternatively, invest in the stock market and get, on average, a 10-15% rate of return. Institutional venture capitalists invest at later stages of development of the firm, stages that are less risky, and still expect rates of return in excess of a 30% annualized rate. Angels also expect compensation to reflect their risk, but they are patient investors. On average, for each dollar invested informal investors expect to take seven dollars out of the firm six to seven years later.

To inexperienced business owners, this may seem high. However, angels' experience is that only 2 out of 10 investments are profitable. To keep active in the market, investors' losses on the majority of investments that do not work out must be made up by the minority of investments that succeed.

POSITIONING INFORMAL INVESTMENT

In terms of the product development-management development risk grid introduced earlier, informal investors are active across a wide range of risk levels. In general, their role is complimentary to institutional venture capitalists and supplementary to seed financing. Their positioning on the risk grid reflects their contributions of management expertise, experience, and contacts as well as their propensity to invest at the early stages of enterprise development.

WHAT ANGELS LOOK FOR
IN AN INVESTMENT OPPORTUNITY

If owners and investors are to reach agreement, both sides must understand and trust each other fully. Therefore, it is worth learning about what motivates angel investors, what they want, and their underlying psychological needs. Three primary factors motivate informal investors:

• their desire to make more money (financial gain);

• their decisions also reflect their level of comfort with the risk of the enterprise; and

• their socio-psychological motives for investing.

Stage of Product
and Market
Development

SME Risk and Growth Grid

Stage of Product and Market Development						
Second stage production						
First stage production						
Early commercialization stage of product or service		INFORMAL INVESTORS				
Prototype stage or product or service						
Concept stage of product or service						
→ Stage of management development	Technically trained owner-founder	Multiple owners. Few experienced or trained managers	Multiple owners with a financial professional involved	Multiple owners with marketing and management abilities	Fully developed management team	

Financial Motives

Economics 101 was right. Investors prefer more wealth to less wealth. In the case of informal investors, they understand that by investing in businesses with potential they can make a lot of money. This is especially true if they can get in on the ground floor by investing while the firm is in the formative process. Informal investors also understand that success seldom comes overnight. They are patient, willing to wait. They expect that it may be as long as seven years before they see any return on their investment. To yield their required return over a seven year holding period means that investors require a sevenfold return from their investment, net of taxes. For example, for each $100,000 investment, angels expect that after seven years, they will be able to take out $700,000 after taxes.

Angels' expectations about financial returns bear implications for negotiations between investors and business owners. Suppose, for example, your business plan projects the value of your business' equity to be $7 million seven years from now. As noted, each $100,000 invested by an angel implies that the angel will want $700,000 in seven years. This amount is one-tenth of the future equity of your business. Therefore, for each $100,000 invested now, the angel in our example will want a 10% stake in your firm.

Risk Aversion

Economics 101 was right again. Investors are very aware of the riskiness of early-stage businesses and they want to minimize risk. Typically, they have been through the process of business development themselves and have seen businesses fail. They are also aware that not everyone is honest. For these reasons, investors will want to check out a business before making any investment. Investors are simply seeking to protect themselves by learning as much about you and your business as they can. This usually involves site visits and inspections; credit and reference checks; references from bankers, suppliers, and customers; in-depth reviews of your financial statements and business plan, and other steps. Due diligence is also a process by which the investor gets to know you and other principals of the business. This is a crucial part of the process. The honesty and competence of the business owner is central to informal investors.

Social Goals

Angels also have social goals. These include the desire to affiliate with like-minded individuals; the urge to be involved with a successful growing firm; and the desire to enjoy the process. Investors consider group interaction to be an important and attractive attribute of informal investing. It is to your advantage to cooperate with investors' due diligence efforts, no matter how difficult the questions they ask. A trusting, confident, and fully informed investor may well prove your best friend later in the process.

THE IMPORTANCE OF PEOPLE

One investor we interviewed required that the business owner "Survive the Toledo test: I ask myself if I would be willing to spend a rainy weekend in Toledo with the business owner. If not, I don't invest."

A Note About Control of the Firm

There are many small firm owners who are unwilling to accept equity investment in their firm. Frequently, such owners base this reluctance on their unwillingness to dilute control of their business. Loss of control of the business that an owner has founded and nurtured is very often an emotional issue. Without acceptance of external equity, however, significant incremental growth is unlikely. It is rare, even with high margins, that a firm can generate sufficient cash from normal operations to finance a material expansion. For reasons explained in Chapter 1, reliance on debt is also unlikely to provide the financial resources necessary to enable a material expansion of the firm.

There is a trade-off. If equity capital is important for substantive growth, then an openness to external equity encourages bankers and other investors to see the firm as a viable opportunity for real growth. The corollary is that if owners declare an unwillingness to accept infusions of equity capital they are thereby communicating disinterest in substantive growth. This makes the firm less attractive to bankers and investors.

In summary, informal equity offers the best of both worlds. If angel investors provide equity capital, they should expect—and receive—a reasonable share of the firm for the risk they are undertaking. However, informal investors also bring to the business their experience, their personal energy, their contacts, and their drive. The issue need not be loss of control if the investor(s) and the founder(s) are compatible with each other and if a mechanism for dispute resolution is in place. Very often, owners can retain effective control, even with less than 50% of the voting shares; and 40% of a large firm can be much more valuable than 100% of a small business.

WHAT MAKES ANGELS "TICK"? A PSYCHOLOGICAL PROFILE OF INFORMAL INVESTORS

Understanding psychological attributes of informal investors can be helpful in terms of designing business plans that attract angels' attention. When reading through this section, think about how you can use this knowledge to your advantage. How can you appeal better to an investor's social needs? How can you put your own situation and business opportunity to the investor, in terms that satisfy his or her needs for achievement, involvement, and recognition of ability?

This information is more important with independent angels than with corporate investors. To an extent, the entrepreneur is appealing to personal taste and personality, not simply to a corporate policy or monetary "logic." In what follows, we outline a psychological profile of the prototypical angel investor. We use some psychological terms, but we explain these terms and how to interpret and use the information presented. It is important to remember that this is only a profile of a *typical* investor.

Our research on Canadian informal investors finds that:

- Angels feel that they personally can influence outcomes through their own ability, skills, or effort.

- They have very high needs for achievement and dominance. That is, they seek to do things better or more efficiently, to solve problems, or to master complex tasks. People high in need for achievement like to put their competencies to work and will take moderate risks in competitive situations. High need for dominance means that angels like to control other people and external events.

- They possess moderately high needs for affiliation or the desire to establish and maintain good relations with other people. Yet they also require autonomy and the desire to be able to work independently.

• They are motivated by subjective feelings that result from performing well; hence, they are highly involved in their work and their investments.

• Finally, relative to other people, angels report high levels of perceived stress and they cope with this stress by working harder.

Informal investments are attractive to investors because of the high expected returns, but also because such investments cater to their own psychological needs. Angels undertake investment strategies that allow them to cope with risk by indulging their needs for dominance and autonomy. The other side of this profile is that unless an entrepreneur is willing to permit the investor partner this scope, there is less likelihood of a successful partnership.

It is not just the finances that spoil many deals. Rather, business owners may be unable to obtain sufficient capital because investors and entrepreneurs are unable to come to an accommodation over control and independence. To obtain informal capital, then, entrepreneurs must appreciate investors' needs to reduce their risk exposure through personal involvement and personal control. This involvement is a double-edged sword for the business owners. Entrepreneurs may forego some control; however, investors can contribute much more than capital to the business. They add personal energy, skills, experience, contacts, and they strive for success. Here are some tips to help make the best of your chances of attracting informal risk capital.

Investments that offer angels the opportunity to satisfy these needs will be more attractive than those that do not. When owners and investors reach the point of negotiating an investment, it is essential to articulate clearly the respective levels of control of the contracting parties. A well-articulated process for dispute management is also useful. This may involve input from your lawyer, banker, accountant, or from other financial professionals.

Investors' needs for affiliation and risk aversion also suggest that entrepreneurs should expect investors to syndicate their investments. Syndication involves a group of investors who

---

TIPS ON SECURING INFORMAL RISK CAPITAL

T
I
P

- **Spell out expected returns.** After all, investors want to make money.
- **Show investors that the firm is well-managed.** In particular demonstrate fiscal responsibility and emphasize that managerial skills are in place.

  If your ownership team does not yet have management capability, either obtain it or seek out angels willing to take a leading management role themselves.

- **Present the opportunity as a challenge to the potential investor.** This provides angels with the opportunity to exercise their need to achieve.

- **Expect investor partners to take active roles in the organization.** The business will likely benefit from angels' high levels of confidence in their own abilities to succeed and from their high need to equate successes with their own efforts.

T I P

---

come together to finance and otherwise support a particular opportunity, and also share with other investors the risk of the deal. Syndication can be useful to the business owner as it spreads exposure of the firm to future, perhaps larger, investors. Finally, angels invest in businesses because they like involvement, to be part of the action. Therefore, keep even passive informal investors engaged by advising them fully of developments on an ongoing basis.

FINDING ANGELS

The pursuit of compatible investors is an important part of the financing process—finding the right person is half the battle. Undertaking an intelligent and well-organized hunt helps prove that you deserve the money. But even with a better understanding of how angels make investment decisions, locating them remains a problem. Finding angels is not straightforward. Unlike banks or venture capital companies, angels do not list themselves in the yellow pages. Indeed, most wealthy people, including angels, do not want to be easily identified. Nonetheless, there are several indirect routes to informal investors.

FINDING INVESTORS TAKES TIME

Rick Norland, partner with the investment intermediary firm Thorington Corporation, Ottawa, suggests you plan carefully when seeking informal financing. Often consuming 85% of the CEO and CFO's time over six to twelve months, it is important to plan who will oversee the business in that period and to minimize the time in the market. "Entrepreneurs should prepare a detailed financing plan showing how much capital they need, when, and from what kind of investor—for the next three rounds. Time is wasted approaching venture capitalists for less than $1 million. Go straight to informal investors. Start looking when you have a strong balance sheet—you will have more time and avoid taking a bad deal. Most importantly, prepare answers for expected investor questions in advance so as to maintain your momentum." Here are Rick Norland's recommended tasks and timelines.

❑ **Organization of Team: 3-4 weeks**
- Includes management, legal, and accounting advisors, and intermediaries

❑ **Preparation of Financial Plan: 2-3 weeks**
- Starts with projections and includes analysis of risks and opportunities
- Estimates capital required over next three years: amounts, types, sources, terms

❑ **Writing Offering Documents: 6-8 weeks**
- Business plan (250 to 350 hours) developed to support projections, in legal phrasing
- Other preparations (in parallel)
- Document answers for investor questions (due diligence material)
- Prepare investor presentation and identify prospective targets
- Housekeeping matters including stronger board membership, key employment contracts, options plans, etc.

❑ **Marketing Initial Interest: 6-8 weeks**
- Selling of "opportunity concept" to prospective investors, and distributing
- Offering documents

❑ **Due Diligence Process to Closing: 6-8 weeks**
- Mitigate investor concerns, negotiate terms, finalize legal documents
- Collect cheque

TIP

The importance of informal capital is being increasingly recognized by economic developers. As a result, many communities maintain services that attempt to facilitate entrepreneur-investor linkages. Such offices also provide advice about preparation of the business plan and introductions, when warranted, to potential investors.

THE SPECIAL INVESTMENT OPPORTUNITIES (SIO) PROJECT

The Ottawa-Carleton Economic Development Corporation (OCEDCO) has maintained, for several years, an office tasked with linking businesses with informal investment capital. SIO staff maintain working relationships with a large number of local investors. This SIO project works with emerging businesses to help develop business plans that are attractive to investors. Once properly qualified, businesses list in SIO's periodic publication of opportunities and SIO staff introduces them to likely investors. For each of the past several years, the SIO project has facilitated millions of dollars in informal investment. In 1995, the SIO project was instrumental in arranging early-stage financing of almost $5 million for Ottawa businesses.

The SIO staff works hard to maintain a cadre of potential investors. They follow leads through syndicates and are proactive in offering seminars, meetings, and other events that are of value to investors. This helps them keep local investors engaged in the program.

A second route to informal investment is less formal. It lies through local Boards of Trade, Chambers of Commerce, or other business associations. The informal investment market is both **local** and **personal.** Angels seldom invest more than 100 km from home base. Other business owners, usually members of business associations, may have worked with angels. These individuals can help plug you into the network. Once there, remember that angels frequently syndicate; therefore, finding one informal investor typically provides several leads.

A variation of this approach is to meet with as many local business owners as possible. First, recall that many angels are themselves successful business owners. Second, it is likely that angels have invested in many of these enterprises. In time, these owners might also be willing to refer you to the investors they know. We have already mentioned that referred deals have a much better chance of success than cold deals.

ANGEL SYNDICATES AND CONTRACT FINANCING

The chief information officer of Canadian Enterprises, a large public company is reading *Wired* magazine at home. He reads about a new program, which he thinks is relevant. He goes to work the next morning and asks the director of computing whether anybody can design this program and the answer is negative. He tells the director to find someone. They find two recent graduates of Brock University's Computing Science department who have incorporated a new firm with $2,000 in the bank and $50,000 in sales. Canadian Enterprises awards the pair a $500,000 contract to design the software.

To do the work, they need financing. One alternative is to look for some angels who, of course, would provide the funds but take an equity stake in the firm and expect a 30-35% rate of return. Instead, they get help from Contract Financiers, a syndicate of investors (primarily angels) run by Sharwood and Company. Satisfied that the newly minted engineers could carry out the project and realize its high margins, Contract Financiers lend the fledgling firm $250,000 for three months at an interest rate of 40% per year. Since it is "lent equity" the new graduates have to pledge their shares, but they will get them back with a good profit on fulfillment of the contract. According to Gordon Sharwood, of Sharwood and Company, this type of "virtual corporation" and the attendant contract financing is going to become very popular.

Adapted with permission from an example cited by Gordon Sharwood, Sharwood and Company, Toronto

Finally other bridging programs are becoming available. For example, in an effort to promote informal investment, the federal government has recently announced the Canadian Community Investment Program (CCIP). This program subsidizes local governments or institutions that form facilities for investor-entrepreneur matchmaking. It is just getting underway. Such facilities draw on CCIP funds to support mentoring of fledgling firms, linkages with investors, identification of investment communities, and post-investment advisory services. Under the terms of the initiative, 20 such new facilities, each similar in spirit to the OCEDCO SIO program, will be operational across Canada by the end of 1997. Contact the Minister of Industry, (613) 995-9001.

To be successful, local matchmaking facilities require integrity, independence, and credibility. Two British researchers have reviewed a variety of international implementations of computerized investment matchmaking services. They outlined four factors critical to their success.[6]

REQUIREMENTS FOR SUCCESSFUL MATCHMAKING FACILITIES

A critical mass of investor clients. Private investors are a diverse, hard-to-reach group. They usually need convincing as to the value of the service. It is essential in this process to established standards that will winnow out the investments that are likely to be "lemons." Poor quality opportunities will drive investors away and investors must benefit from being associated with the facility.

Financial support. Business introduction services must be well-resourced. It is not possible to run a business introduction service on the basis of fees. Such facilities must rely on public and private sector support.

Proactive management. Matchmaking must not be limited to passive efforts. It is a hands-on, pro-active process that requires involved professionals who can provide initial vetting of the businesses.

Credibility. This demands that the service be housed and managed by respected, independent, third parties with broad community support. Ideally, the host organization should also have a high profile in the community and be free from the perception of vested interests.

LEGAL MATTERS

And now some bad news. Securities regulations in most Canadian provinces specify that businesses engaging in a distribution of securities to investors must provide a prospectus for potential purchasers. A prospectus is a document that discloses all salient and pertinent information about the business. It typically includes audited financial statements and other documentary evidence about the firm to ensure that, for their protection, investors are fully informed about the firm. A firm selling shares, even to a syndicate of infor-

---

[6] Mason and Harrison, 1995.

mal investors for a relatively small amount of capital is nonetheless engaging in a distribution of securities. The Securities Act normally requires a prospectus for most public distributions. Preparing a prospectus is a costly process. If it were not for several legal exemptions from the prospectus requirement, most informal investors would be breaking the law.[7]

Fortunately, there are several exemptions, which, if followed, allow entrepreneurs to get around having to do a formalized prospectus when seeking financial help from angels. Three are most common. The first is the "private placement exemption," according to which the issuing firm is exempt from the prospectus requirement if a single purchaser (in Ontario) is investing a minimum of $150,000.

According to the second common exemption, the "seed capital" exemption, issuing firms are exempt from prospectus requirements if they solicit from fewer than 50 potential buyers and end up selling securities to no more than 25 investors. This exemption is difficult for a regulatory body to police. Except for sales of securities on organized markets, identification of potential buyers is not straightforward.

The third exemption—and the one used most frequently by small firms—is the "private company" exemption. Securities regulators exempt from prospectus requirements private companies so long as the securities "are not offered for sale to the public." Here, law defines a private company as one for which the right to transfer common shares and the number of common shareholders is limited under the terms of the company's charter.

Given the uncertainties in terms of the legal interpretation of these exemptions as applied to specific cases, most deals involve legal counsel. Normally, a legal document known as an offering memorandum accompanies an investment agreement and essentially replaces a prospectus. The cost of preparation of an offering memorandum, however, is significant. For this reason, the average investment made by Canadian angels exceeds that of informal investors in other countries.

---

[7] For a more detailed and comprehensive review of these issues, readers are referred to Jeffrey Macintosh, *Legal and Institutional Barriers to Financing Innovative Enterprise in Canada*, (Toronto: University of Toronto Press, 1994).

The good news is that a task force of the Ontario Securities Commission is re-examining its security laws as they pertain to informal investment. In June of 1995, the task force, chaired by Susan McCallum, advanced a series of sweeping recommendations towards reform of *The Securities Act*. The need to remove barriers to capital formation by informal investors led to recommendations that would reduce the costs of compliance that currently faces small firms that attempt to raise equity capital.

SAMPLE RECOMMENDATIONS OF THE MCCALLUM TASK FORCE

- "The creation of a new prospectus exemption for issuances of securities by closely held business issuers. A lifetime limit of securities sold under this proposed exemption of $3 million was proposed."

- "Establishment of a new exemption...for a class of 'accredited investors,' investors that fit the profile of typical informal investors and that would include the issuer's management."

- A series of recommendations that, together, would facilitate small public offerings.

- Exemptions for trades in securities of "private companies."

If the securities commission acts on these recommendations informal capital may suddenly become far easier to access.

SUMMARY

Informal investors like to keep a low profile. Because of this, they are often hard to find. In keeping with the local and personal nature of the informal market, angels learn about potential investments mainly through business associates. However, angels reject most proposals. Yet they do invest!

On average, informal investors reject three out of four opportunities at first glance and another 60% after an initial perusal of the business plan. Angels reject almost nine out of 10 investment proposals within the first few moments of consideration. Overall, investors finance an average of one deal in 40. Most angels reject investment opportunities because they lack confidence in the

managerial abilities of the principals. Specific criteria employed
by informal investors include:

- the likelihood and amount of financial gain;
- the management abilities of the principals;
- the abilities of the entrepreneurs to succeed; and
- the nature and perceived market acceptance of the product or service.

Angels are patient investors. They expect to hold their investments for six to seven years over which they expect to reap an
after-tax capital gain of $6 per dollar invested. It is not far wrong
to say that investors operate on the basis of a "7-7 rule": they
expect to make a seven-fold after tax return over (almost) a
seven-year holding period. Finally, informal investors usually
involve themselves actively in firms in which they invest. They
bring to the deal their contacts, experience, and enthusiasm.
They are looking for ways to use their considerable skills...all to
the benefit of the entrepreneurs with whom they work. Our work
has shown us that while venture capitalists are concerned about
their clients, angels believe in them.

T I P

FINDING AND WORKING WITH ANGELS[8]

Study Your Own Local Networks. Angel investors in your neighbourhood
have varying interests and personalities. Your job is to meet as many as
possible and get all the referrals you can so that you can locate those
potential investors who will be compatible with you and comfortable with
your business. Part of the search for capital is working your way through
the network.

Customize Your Pitch. Go to people in the angel community and learn
about the investor before you approach him or her. Find out what motivates
them most: working in a specific industry, helping others, personal challenge, financial return, etc. Then personalize the business plan to emphasize how your business opportunity reflects the angel's goals. If your
business is not consistent with the angel's goals, move on to other angels.

---

[8] Adapted from the research findings of Riding, Haines, Duxbury, DalCin, and Safrata. *Ibid*,
1993.

Stress the Creative Elements of Your Project. Angels want to build and create. Your task is to show the angel exciting and unique elements of the opportunity you offer. You are not applying for a business loan. Show to advantage those elements of the opportunity that will excite an investor.

Emphasize Your Competence as a Manager and Your Integrity. Angels reject 39 out of 40 opportunities, mostly because they lack confidence in the management. In the business plan, stress your track record, ability, and honesty of your management team. Have a professional third party conduct your market research to lend independence and credibility. Don't try to hide weaknesses, show the angel how he or she can complement your team.

Target Lead Investors. Most angels prefer to invest in groups. Every investor community has prominent individuals whose judgement others esteem. Target these lead investors as a way of attracting and reassuring other potential backers.

Get in to Meet Potential Investors. Angels reject 75% of opportunities before even meeting the principals. If you can get the investor's personal attention, chances of making a deal increase dramatically.

Be Prepared to Give Up Something to Get Something. Most angels do not want to control your company, but they want equity (not debt) and they require high returns. Most will insist on a formal shareholders' agreement and two-thirds will require frequent updates and a big say on salaries and major decisions. Angels bring a wealth of experience and commitment to helping the business prosper. Heed what they say.

Be Persistent. Most angels are happy to refer a business owner whose proposal they have turned down to other potential investors. If an angel rejects your project, press for referrals to other angels and sympathetic business associates. Finding an informal investor is hard work, but that work is telling investors about your abilities.

TIP

VENTURE CAPITAL
Equity Financing
for Growing SMEs

"The first rule of venture capitalism should be Shoot the Inventor."

Sir Richard Storey (b. 1937), British
newspaper publisher and venture capitalist

The venture capital market embraces institutions, governments, and individuals who invest funds in risky enterprises. In the previous chapter we examined the investment activities of informal investors, angels. In this chapter, we continue our review of risk capital, but we now turn our attention to the formal side of that market: the institutional market for venture capital. The distinction between angels and institutional venture capitalists is important. On the one hand, professional venture capital fund managers are usually employees of a financial institution. Only by exception do they invest their own personal funds in businesses. Angels, on the other hand, connect more directly with the enterprises in which they invest. It is, for them, personal money at stake. However, beyond angels, there is a large and dynamic Canadian market in which institutional investors operate.

In this chapter, we redefine venture capital as funds invested by institutions that are members of the Canadian Venture Capital Association (CVCA). These investments reflect the decisions made by professional venture capital managers. Members of the CVCA account for the majority of venture capital activity in Canada, but not all of it. In addition to members of the association, merchant banks and, occasionally, institutions such as insurance companies will invest directly in small firms.

The recent growth of the Canadian venture capital industry, much of which is attributable to tax-subsidized labour-sponsored venture capital funds, ranks as one of the most exciting developments in SME financing. There is more venture capital available to SMEs now than there has ever been. As a result, venture capital is an increasingly visible and therefore legitimate investment activity. This is good news for small business owners in itself. Further good news is that the supply of investment capital continues to increase. Increased availability of venture capital has implications that extend across all aspects of SME finance. For example, linkages between the informal investment market and the formal venture capital industry allow early stage informal investments to access the larger pools of institutional venture capital. Moreover, increased availability of venture finance implies that the supply of capital is larger than before—SME financing, to some extent, becomes less of a "seller's market."

THE INCREASING SUPPLY OF VENTURE CAPITAL

In 1996 Canadian institutional venture capital companies made 881 investments in 525 companies placing $1.1 billion. This was up from 1995 activity of 455 investments in 364 businesses ($669 million). Although the 1995 and 1996 investment levels were both record volumes for the industry, the supply of venture capital increased by even more during 1995—by $1 billion! At the end of 1995, the venture capital industry held $2.3 billion available for investment. In spite of the investment of $1.1 billion during 1996, the industry continues to hold huge reserves.

Moreover, the industry has grown quickly. In 1980, the industry managed a total of $400 million. By 1985, institutional venture capital companies managed $1.4 billion. This had grown to almost $3 billion by 1990 and $6 billion in 1995.

The amount of capital going to early-stage firms has increased by threefold since 1994 with $344 million going into 204 early-stage companies in 1996. Moreover, two-thirds of venture capital investments were in technology-based enterprises.

Source: Canadian Venture Capital Association; Macdonald and Associates Limited, Toronto, 1996.

In spite of the abundance of venture capital, institutional venture capitalists continue to invest in fewer than three out of every 100 potential opportunities. Why, with so much capital available, are so few firms able to access these funds? In this chapter, we try to explain this apparent incongruity and we provide guidance as to how to maximize the likelihood of closing a successful venture capital deal. To do so, we first trace the recent history of the Canadian venture capital industry. Then, we document the process of making a venture capital deal, describe the expectations of venture capital investment managers, and examine common sources of conflict between venture capitalists and business owners. We use this information to show what to expect when dealing with a venture capital firm and to develop advice about how to maximize your chances of obtaining venture capital.

THE CANADIAN VENTURE CAPITAL INDUSTRY

Macdonald and Associates Limited is a firm that monitors activity of the members of the Canadian venture capital industry. Macdonald and Associates Limited group venture capital companies into five categories.

- **Private independent funds** are those investor firms that raise the capital they invest from institutions such as pension funds and insurance companies. In turn, the venture capital firms invest the funds in risky enterprises. These venture capital firms are accounting for a declining share of the industry.

- **Corporate subsidiaries** are branches of industrial or financial corporations that receive their investment capital from a parent business. Recently, several of the major participants have withdrawn from the industry (for example, Noranda). Corporate financial funds, on the other hand, are becoming more active.

These are firms that are divisions of financial corporations. Banks, in particular, are active in the industry through their venture capital subsidiaries such as Royal Bank Capital Corporation.

- **Labour-sponsored funds** draw their capital from public solicitations. Individuals who invest their capital in labour-sponsored funds receive significant tax benefits. Prime examples include Fonds Solidarité and Working Ventures. The former, located in Quebec, is the original, and largest, of the LSVCCs. Working Ventures, based in Ontario, is the second largest of these funds and is the only national fund.

- **Public sector funds** are established by federal and various provincial governments. The venture capital investments of the Business Development Bank of Canada are in this category.

- **Hybrid funds** are supported by government, but administered privately. For example, this type of venture capital firm includes, among others, those venture capital funds established specifically as a result of immigrant investor programs and others set up by provincial governments, but managed at arm's length. The Saskatchewan government established the Saskatchewan Government Growth Fund, for example, some of it is capital coming from immigrant investor funds.

The chart that follows shows the funds under management by firms in each of these categories for three selected years.

The structure of the Canadian venture capital industry has otherwise changed in two major respects over the last decade. As noted earlier, for the last few years, the emergence of labour-sponsored venture capital corporations fueled much of the growth of the Canadian venture capital industry. In addition, most of the major banks have established venture capital subsidiaries. These both represent fundamental changes to the industry.

Historically, the main sources of funds to the venture capital industry have been institutions such as pension funds, financial institutions such as insurance companies and mutual funds, and industrial corporations. Labour-sponsored funds, however, now provide a medium by which individuals can invest in the venture capital industry indirectly. Individuals who invest in LSVCCs also receive material tax benefits from federal and provincial levels of

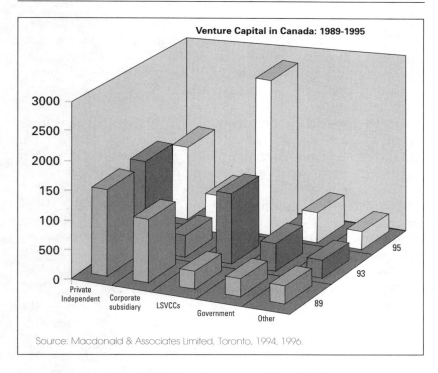

Venture Capital in Canada: 1989-1995

Source: Macdonald & Associates Limited, Toronto, 1994, 1996.

government. A result of this practice is that individuals are a primary source of funds to the venture capital industry. Investing in labour-sponsored funds is like making an investment in a mutual fund. A second result is the substantial growth in the pool of capital administered by labour-sponsored funds. In terms of the size of the pool of capital under management, labour-sponsored venture capital funds are now the dominant venture capital category.

Sales of shares in labour-sponsored funds have created a capital pool of billions of dollars, approximately equal to one half of the pool managed by the entire Canadian venture capital industry. The rate at which LSVCCs have been investing this capital, however, has disappointed the government, fund shareholders, and those businesses unable to raise growth financing. Of the $2.9 billion under management at the end of 1995, $1.2 billion was not invested as risk capital in young firms, even though the pool of capital continued to grow. Consequently, government reduced the tax benefits associated with individuals' investment in

LSVCCs for 1996. Until early 1996, investors in LSVCCs received a 20% tax credit from both the provincial and federal governments on a maximum investment of up to $5,000. Moreover, the investments are eligible for RRSPs. In spring of 1996, federal and some provincial governments reduced the tax credit to 15% and the maximum to $3,500.

These tax subsidies are significant in two ways. First, they are costly to cash-strapped governments: lost tax revenues to Ontario alone increased from $6 million in 1991 to $130 million in 1995. Second, the LSVCCs' cost of funds is lower than those of its competitors: the tax subsidy means that individual investors can be satisfied with lower returns. This distortion of the marketplace also reflects the fact that the uninvested pools of venture capital are chasing the same basic set of opportunities. As a result, returns to the industry in general will decrease. It is hard to say how the rest of the industry will react.

Private independent companies have maintained their absolute size; however, they are losing market share to the LSVCCs. Venture capital companies that are corporate subsidiaries have declined in both relative and absolute terms. These institutional investors traditionally obtained their investment funds from parent firms but one of the largest such venture capital firms, a subsidiary of Noranda group, withdrew from the business. Others are cutting back.

Venture capital programs administered by provincial and federal governments remain relatively minor players in the market. This is also true of the fifth category, "other" funds, a category that includes hybrid venture capitalists and funds specially created under the terms of immigrant investor programs.

THE IMMIGRANT INVESTOR PROGRAM

The federal Department of Immigration created the Immigrant Investor Program in 1986 to encourage foreign nationals to invest in Canada. In its original form, individuals were offered landed immigrant status if they invested a minimum of $150,000 in Canada (increased to $250,000 in 1990) for a period of three years. The program allowed an immigrant to use the investment to start a business or to purchase existing operations. In the first two years alone, approximately 6,000 immigrant entrepreneurs entered the program, creating more than 8,000 jobs. It was also a means of attracting talented and highly educated people to the Canadian business environment.

To ease access of Canadian companies to this source of capital, the program also allowed Canadian businesses with less than $35 million in assets to set up funds and for syndicates to manage a portion of these funds, subject to the approval of both federal and provincial governments. By 1990, more than 270 immigrant investor funds resulted, administering $1.1 billion invested by 5,000 immigrants. Unfortunately, in its original form it was too easy for fraudulent investment brokers to relieve new Canadians of their funds. Complaints that brokers charged exorbitant administration fees, directing money to their own businesses, and stealing resulted in suspension of the program in 1994. It was then redesigned, and reintroduced in early 1997.

According to its new provisions, immigrants must invest at least $350,000 in the six smallest provinces or $450,000 in Quebec, Ontario, Alberta, or British Columbia. Immigrants must invest at least 60% of the capital in SMEs. In addition, the redesigned program provides for regulation of the brokers who assist immigrants.

In spite of an apparent surplus of risk capital, venture capital companies remain discriminating. They do invest, but only a relative minority of Canadian SMEs have benefited from infusions of venture capital. The next section provides a sense of where venture capital fund managers are investing.

PATTERNS OF VENTURE CAPITAL INVESTMENT

Within the venture capital industry investments are made in firms at most stages of business development. However, individual venture capital firms usually specialize according to particular stages of development, by industry sector, or by other guidelines. We can make some generalizations about these tendencies. Private independent firms, given their profit motive, are most likely to prefer larger investments; that is, investments at the "higher" end of the market—usually in excess of $1 million. Government funds, on the other hand, are more likely to make smaller deals. Certain funds specialize along industry lines, focusing, for example, on biotechnology or communications.

STAGES OF VENTURE CAPITAL INVESTMENTS

Seed financing is an investment made very early in the development cycle of the business. Typically, little more than a prototype of the product exists at this stage and additional product and market development work remains.

⇩

Start-ups relate to those firms exhibiting few, if any, commercial sales but in which product development and market research are complete. Management is in place and the firm has a business plan.

⇩

First stage financing occurs when the firm has begun commercial production but requires additional financing to materially increase production.

⇩

Second stage financing relates to additional expansion of both productive capacity and markets.

⇩

Mezzanine financing is investment intended to provide for further expansion or to bridge working capital and market expansion needs prior to a public offering of stock or prior to a buyout.

⇩

Buyout financing involves investments that might assist management or an outside party to acquire control of a firm.

Range of Investments

In addition to the increase in the size of the pool of funds, three further trends characterize the Canadian venture capital industry:

• a strong preference for technology-based firms;

• a propensity to invest in expansion stage businesses; and

• an increase in early-stage investment activity.

As shown on the next chart, the industry has a strong propensity to invest in technology-based firms. As recently as 1988, technology-based firms' share was only 27% of total institutional venture capital investment in that year. However, by 1995 technology-based firms were the recipients of a large chunk of venture capital—64%! This inclination is the result of a clear shift in thinking, possibly reflecting the emergence of a strong technology sector in Canada.

Most venture capital investment activity is for the expansion of established growing firms. This is good news for small businesses that wish to exploit growth opportunities. Venture capitalists usually make their investments incrementally; that is, they do not invest everything at once. Most venture capitalists expect that after an initial round of financing growing firms will require further rounds of capital investment to promote their continued growth. Three or more rounds of venture financing are not uncommon during the development of growing businesses. Future rounds of financing follow the accomplishment of specific performance milestones.

A third trend in the industry is an increasing rate of investment in early stage firms. The next chart demonstrates that commitments to early stage firms have increased significantly in recent years, in both absolute terms and in terms of the proportion of investments. The share of venture capital invested in early stage firms rose from 23% in 1988, to 37% in 1995. We expect that the rate of investment in both new businesses and in those with growth potential will continue to expand. Again, good news for SME owners.

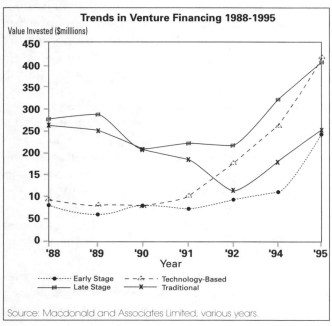

Source: Macdonald and Associates Limited, various years.

Scale of Investments

Traditional financial wisdom dictates that venture capitalists are reluctant to invest amounts of less than $1 million. The reasoning behind this adage is that evaluation and monitoring costs are high. It is not economical for venture capitalists to devote their scarce resources to "small deals." Venture capitalists do, however, make deals for less than $1,000,000. In recent experience, 46% of deals made in 1995 and more than half of venture capital investments made in 1994 involved amounts of less than $1 million. A majority of these small investments were "follow-ons" in which the investment was one that followed from an earlier deal with the firm.

Venture capitalists prefer large deals to small ones. While investors can earn higher rates of return on small investments, venture capitalists also value the absolute dollar value of the returns. A large rate of return on a small investment can yield fewer actual dollars of profit than a lower rate of return, but on a project with a large scale.

Normally, venture capitalists release funds to the firm in stages, or "rounds." This practice stems from the uncertainty that surrounds early stage businesses. At the outset of the deal, sales projections are not reliable. The two sides to the deal will typically disagree about such projections and about the level of risk of the firm. Staging the investment provides options for the venture capital investor as well as motivation for the principals of the firm. By staging the investment, the venture capitalist retains the option to abandon the venture if the future does not work. By the same token, the investor also gains the option to increase capital commitments if the project is more successful than the parties had anticipated. Staging the investment also provides the firm with flexibility should short-term problems arise or in the event of unexpected profit opportunities. This also provides the principals with the motivation to make good on their projections and encourages the parties to employ realistic scenarios in the first place.

The investment can take a variety of forms. Convertible debt and convertible preferred stock are vehicles that venture capitalists often use as securities behind early-stage investments. The debt or preference feature of the securities provides the investor with a higher-ranking claim on assets in the event of failure. The conversion feature allows the investor to participate in the firm's financial success.

With this background, we can position the role of venture capital in terms of the risk matrix introduced in Chapter 2. As shown, most venture capitalists concentrate at the expansion stage of business development. That is, the businesses in which they invest are more highly developed. Start-ups and early stage firms have recently received an increasing share of venture capital, corresponding to regions of higher risk. In addition, a small amount of venture capital finds its way to very early-stage businesses.

Stage of Product
and Market
Development

SME Risk and Growth Grid

Stage of Product and Market Development	Technically trained owner-founder	Multiple owners. Few experienced or trained managers	Multiple owners with a financial professional involved	Multiple owners with marketing and management abilities	Fully developed management team
Second stage production				INSTITUTIONAL VENTURE CAPITAL	
First stage production					
Early commercialization stage of product or service					
Prototype stage or product or service					
Concept stage of product or service					
→ Stage of management development	Technically trained owner-founder	Multiple owners. Few experienced or trained managers	Multiple owners with a financial professional involved	Multiple owners with marketing and management abilities	Fully developed management team

Coupled with higher levels of firm development or expansion, venture capitalists seek, on average, rates of return equivalent to 25 to 40%, expressed on an annualized basis. Naturally, they demand higher rates of return for riskier, early stage deals and lower rates of return for later-stage buyout and expansion-financing transactions. In spite of their careful evaluations the industry rule of thumb is that of every 10 deals, an average of two will be total losses and six others will not feature sufficient growth to provide a profitable exit opportunity. Accordingly, the investment in the minority of firms that grow rapidly must generate all the investor's profits and make up for losses. Venture capitalists therefore choose their investments carefully. We can better appreciate the reasons for venture capitalists' preferences of scale, return, and sector if we look over the shoulder of a venture capitalist as he or she makes investment decisions.

> In its six-year history, Techno POS, a screen printer and maker of marketing materials based in St. Leonard, Que., has raised more than $1 million in risk capital. According to Norman Lebeau, vice-president of Techno POS Inc., venture capitalists "invest on numbers but they invest mainly on the capacity of the individuals to really come across as winners who are going to turn the project into a reality."
>
> "Risk Capital—Down but not Out," PROFIT, December 1992, p. 60.

THE VENTURE CAPITAL INVESTMENT PROCESS

Throughout this book, we stress that raising capital requires perseverance and patience. This is certainly true for institutional venture capital. From initial contact to eventual signing, a typical venture capital deal can take several months to put together. The fact that assembling the deal takes so long is in itself important. Business owners who wait until the last minute before seeking venture capital face two problems. First, in the time it takes to put the deal together, the firm may have missed opportunities which it could have capitalized on had the venture capital already been in place. Second, by rushing to get the money, the firm puts itself at a disadvantage in the negotiations with the venture capitalist. In their desperation to land the deal, the business owners may have to give up more of the firm than they would otherwise. It is advisable, therefore, to start arranging venture capital well in advance, thereby demonstrating the firm's good management to lenders and investors.

The venture capital deal usually begins with a telephone call, either from the firm seeking capital or from another institution that is referring it to a venture capitalist. Following the telephone call, the venture capital investment manager examines the business plan. If the venture capitalist want to consider further the opportunity, he or she arranges a meeting between the principals of the firm and the staff from the venture capital firm. At this point, business owners should be aware that if the deal is to proceed, the venture capitalist will conduct a very thorough evaluation of the firm later on. During this "due diligence" any problems will eventually come to light. Therefore, the business plan should recognize any deficiencies right at the outset. Failure to do so, and any problems discovered later will damage the principals' credibility and integrity. The failure to disclose material problems early on can be a deal breaker.

Following inspection of the business plan and the meeting, the venture capital firm carries out follow-up work. For now, the venture capitalist takes much of the material presented in the meeting and business plan on faith, but will check out the information that is relatively easy to review. In doing so, the fund manager also gains a sense of the potential of the product and industry.

If the venture capitalist wants to pursue the investment, it sends a "proposal letter" to the firm. The proposal letter states that based on what the firm has presented, the venture capital company would consider further making a deal. In return, the firm must sign off an a promise not to shop the deal around to other venture capital firms and to provide some "earnest money." This payment covers the costs of further evaluation and demonstrates the firm's commitment to the process. It generally takes from two to four weeks to reach this stage.

Following acceptance of the terms of the proposal letter, the venture capital company conducts serious due diligence. During this process, the venture capital company checks out everything about the firm and its principals. This includes reference checks with suppliers, customers, bankers, and even competitors.

If, following due diligence, the venture capitalist remains interested, it prepares an offering memorandum that sets forth the terms of the offer. Once the firm and the venture capitalist negotiate the final terms, the venture capital firm's investment committee must approve the offer. There can be several iterations whereby terms of the offer that are not acceptable may go back and forth between the firm and the venture capitalist. Once the parties finalize the terms of the offer, the venture capitalist generates a commitment letter to the firm. On acceptance, there remain steps during which legal issues and documentation are completed. Overall, the process may take from three to nine months, or even more.

HOW VENTURE CAPITALISTS MAKE DECISIONS

The sequence of events we just described is typical of many venture capital deals. But how do venture capitalists evaluate a prospective investment? To understand further what goes on in the investor's mind, we will adapt the decision process we used for informal investors to the institutional venture capital situation. Like informal investment process, there are five readily identifiable stages through which venture capital investment decision proceeds. But while the institutional venture capital investment process is similar to that used by informal investors, activities at each step are more formal.

STAGES IN THE VENTURE CAPITAL INVESTMENT PROCESS[1]

Deal Origination in which potential investments come to the attention of venture capitalists.

⇩

Screening is a step in which the venture capitalist reaches an initial decision to investigate further the investment (or not). The initial screen is a cursory glance at the business plan to determine whether or not the proposal fits within the investor's areas of expertise. If warranted, the investor reads the plan more thoroughly as part of the generic screen to assess potential of the product or idea and obtain first impressions of management.

⇩

[1] A. Riding, G. Haines, and L. Duxbury, "Financing Enterprise Development: Decision-Making by Angels and Venture Capitalists," Working Paper, (Ottawa: Carleton University, 1996).

Evaluation, during which the venture capitalist conducts detailed analysis of the venture. Criteria that venture capitalists apply are:

- assessment of concept;
- assessment of the principals; and
- assessment of returns.

Due Diligence, if warranted, is the second phase of the evaluation step. This step may include formal market studies, reference checks, consultation with third parties. The investor outlines basic contract terms and discusses pricing.

Negotiation is a step in which the investor and the principals iron out the framework for a deal. The deal closes once the parameters are acceptable to both parties.

Post-investment activity relates to how the venture capitalist monitors the firm and takes part in major decisions. This phase largely involves monitoring, control, and intervention only as needed.

Deal Origination

Venture capitalists encounter prospective deals in many ways. As a business owner, you will find that your chances of success with a venture capitalist will vary greatly, depending on your first approach. The success rate varies substantially across these mechanisms.

- **Cold calls**. In terms of the quantity of proposals, venture capitalists receive most proposals "cold"—in the mail or through an initial interview with the business founders. However, very few investments result from cold calls. It takes an exceptional idea and an exceptional presentation to distinguish one firm's proposal from the many received this way.

- **Referrals.** Often venture capitalists receive referrals from existing clients and from financial intermediaries. Referrals from clients are an important source of investment leads. Clients know the investor's preferences and their investment practices. Their referrals, therefore, carry some weight with the investor.

- **Financial intermediaries.** This category of referrals covers a variety of firms. Banks are increasingly pointing clients to venture capital firms when the lender sees the need for additional equity capital. Lawyers and accountants who work with small businesses are often aware of the specialties of venture investors and can help match them with appropriate client businesses. Economic developers, working with small enterprises in the area, can also point the way to venture capitalists.

- **Matchmaking services.** Strategic alliances between venture capitalists and informal investor matchmaking facilities may become more common. In 1995 the Ottawa-Carleton Economic Development Corporation SIO Project (see Chapter 5) attempted such an alliance with Working Ventures, the major Ontario labour-sponsored fund. On paper, the joint venture seemed ideal. It potentially provided the venture capitalist with comfort because local informal investors would give investee firms their approval in a tangible manner—by investing their own money in it. The "deeper pockets" of the venture capitalist allowed leverage of early stage informal equity funds with formal venture capital.

- **Venture capital shows or fairs.** In some municipalities, local economic development agencies or universities organize periodic venture capital shows. At these events, the organizers invite venture capitalists to view one or more potential investments. Selected entrepreneurs get a chance to "strut their stuff" before the assembly of potential investors. Such fairs can be elaborate affairs, involving hundreds of participants, newsletters, electronic media as well as face-to-face presentations. At the other extreme, some are as simple as a dinner party, one to which a carefully selected entrepreneur is invited along with individuals who could potentially support the enterprise. Such support takes various forms, not just financial.

- **Proactive Solicitation.** By exception, some venture capitalists actively seek out investment proposals. Clearly, investments solicited in this manner stand a high chance of being financed.

THE TORONTO VENTURE GROUP

For several years, the Toronto Venture Group has organized monthly breakfast meetings. Each meeting featured a keynote talk of interest to individuals active in small business investing. Attracted by the keynote speaker, attendance included venture capitalists and informal investors. Each meeting, one entrepreneur has the chance to speak to the assembly, typically presenting the essentials of their business and their financial needs. Another benefit is networking. At the start of every meeting, the audience passes around a cordless microphone and attendees can stand up and introduce themselves. This gives investors a chance to say who they are and what they are looking for. Entrepreneurs have the chance to give a 10-second sales pitch to a very targeted audience.

For business owners seeking venture capital, it makes sense to take the time and effort necessary to avoid cold calls, an approach with a poor probability of success. Business owners can improve considerably their chances of securing risk capital by:

• learning about venture capital firms;

• nurturing contacts who could act as sources of referral; and

• emphasizing those aspects of the business that conform to each potential investor's areas of specialization.

Those firms that survive this initial first impression stage then face a screening step.

Screening

Experienced venture capitalists can readily identify proposals that they will not pursue. Venture capitalists reject most proposals almost as soon as they receive them. We can think of this initial screening step as having two stages: a "firm-specific" screen and a "generic" screen. Most venture capital firms are explicit about their specialties. There is little point approaching a venture capital firm that specializes in a different industry from that of your firm.

The "firm-specific" screen involves a cursory review of the business plan. Many venture capital firms specialize in one or more particular areas of investment and follow up on only those proposals that match their current investment objectives. Many venture funds focus on particular industries: for example, some only consider firms in the biotechnology sector; others concentrate on communications technology. Areas of specialization are readily available from the various funds. At this point, the venture capitalist investor looks for a "fit" between the attributes of the firm (such as stage of development, size, or industrial sector) and the venture capitalists' own eligibility criteria. If the proposal matches the venture capitalist's areas of interest, the venture capital fund manager gives the proposal a closer look.

VENTURE FUND SPECIALIZATION

Innovatech is a $300 million venture capital fund located in Quebec that specializes in high-tech deals. Between 1992 and 1995, the fund had made more than 100 investments averaging $1.5 million. As a result, firms in the technology sector in Quebec can attract earlier stage investors, investors who can look to funds such as Innovatech to provide future capital for successful enterprises.

In this second step, the "generic" screen, the investment manager ensures that the business plan embodies several important elements. This step is similar to an angel's examination of a business plan. Like angels, institutional venture capitalists pay attention both to the content of the plan and to what the plan says about the principals of the business. Venture capitalists require:

- a realistic valuation of the firm;

- financial projections of costs and revenues;

- information on the principals of the firm with particular reference to their capabilities as managers;

- credible marketing data, including booked orders, that can support financial projections;

- indications of means for profitable exit;

- historical data on the firm and principals; and

- the opportunity for good returns.

Inherent in these specific items is the potential of the product or idea behind the investment proposal. However, it is even more crucial that the principals have the management capabilities to transform the idea into a viable business opportunity. As in bank financing, venture investors make subjective judgements as to the principals' marketing abilities and sense of fiscal responsibility. Venture capitalists invest in the potential of the product or idea; however, they must depend on the principals of the business to realize that potential. Like angel investors, venture capitalists are backing the people as much as, or more than, the product. The extent of this reliance on the principals varies by the stage of the business. Early stage firms have no track records and forecasts about sales of new products often lack precision. In these instances, investors place yet greater importance on the principals of the enterprise. To reach these evaluations, the investment manager brings to bear the venture capitalist's knowledge and experience on the enterprise's business plan.

Evaluation and Due Diligence

For the minority of firms that survive the initial screening, the venture capitalist conducts more detailed evaluations. We can think of this third step as comprising two stages. First, the potential investor conducts an informal evaluation by reading the business plan and accompanying documentation, and from meeting with the principals. If the results of this evaluation are favourable, the investor then conducts more formal due diligence. The due diligence step conducted by institutional venture investors is far more formal and complete than that carried out by angel investors. Due diligence often involves:

• interviews with customers and suppliers;

• a compilation of audited financial statements (if they have not already been provided);

• interviews with bankers and other individuals or institutions with whom the firm has established financial obligations or relationships;

• an arm's-length verification of market research projections;

- credit checks including checks for unresolved litigation;
- an investigation of the principals' personal financial commitments to the business; and
- references on managers and key personnel.

Clearly, due diligence is costly for venture capitalists because it involves high-priced third parties (professionals such as auditors, lawyers, and market researchers). This is one reason venture capitalists prefer larger deals. The cost of due diligence can eat up the profits from small deals.

The due diligence evaluation assures the venture capitalist that:

- the business plan projections are realistic and attainable because there is verifiable evidence of demand for the product or idea; the product provides buyers with a demonstrable benefit over competitors; and
- the business has a viable marketing strategy;
- The investment opportunity has the potential for significant and material growth of revenues, earnings, and cash flows;
- the principals hold a material financial stake in the firm;
- the management team possesses the requisite background and skills;
- the principals are open to the potential loss of control associated with equity financing;
- the principals are willing to allow the venture capitalist to influence important decisions on strategy and finances; and
- a viable and potentially profitable exit opportunity exists, for example, going public.

Venture capitalists are patient. They recognize that businesses do not grow instantaneously. Most venture investors expect to wait four to six years before realizing returns on their investments. Venture capitalists focus on businesses that promise the rates of growth that allow a profitable exit. This type of growth usually entails several years of annual revenue increases in excess of 50% per year.

Negotiation and Valuation

For those firms that survive the due diligence process, the next stage is that of negotiation. During negotiations, investors seek to reach agreement with the business' principals about issues that include:

• valuation of the business;

• venture capitalists expected return on investment;

• form of the investment;

• post-investment involvement of the venture capitalist;

• form and frequency of reports; and

• employment status and draw allowed the principals and managers.

T
I
P

DON'T BE AFRAID TO THINK BIG

A friend in the animation business was in the process of securing investors for a children's cartoon concept. She sent out two unsolicited proposals, one to a small Canadian informal investor and one to a large, American multimedia production firm. Both said yes. The choice was not difficult. Financing for the launch now includes provisions for a television series and an international merchandising program. Don't be afraid to shoot high in your negotiations: you might be surprised by the response. Investors are looking for solid investment prospects, regardless of geographic boundary.

T I P

The valuation of the business usually follows directly from the business plan projections as verified through due diligence. Valuation is not an exact science. For firms on the stock market, financial analysts conduct valuation using a two-step procedure. The first step is the estimation of future earnings of the firm. The analyst bases the estimates on a thorough study of the fundamentals of the firm. In the second step of the valuation process, the earnings estimates are "capitalized" by multiplying them by a price-to-earnings multiple. Average price-earnings multiples are usually available by industry sectors, which the analyst then modifies to reflect the risk specific to the firm being valued. The result is an estimate of the firm's value.

Based on the firm's business plan, the venture capital investor will estimate the value of the firm. To respond, the owner also needs to value the firm and to be able to defend that value. The following insert outlines how to approach this task.

ON VALUING YOUR BUSINESS

T
I
P

Calculate **best-case and worst-case cash flow scenarios**. Start with several best- and worst-case scenarios of expected cash flows and earnings. For each estimate indicate clearly what assumptions were made to account for the different operating results. Margins should include room for financing expenses such as legal costs, administration fees, potential placement fees, etc.

Base expected cash flow(s) and earnings on historical earnings for two to five years of performance. If the firm experienced significant changes (new clients, loss of a major account, timing of a product launch, (re)financing equipment or facilities, etc.), provide a clear explanation of how and why company or market events affected performance.

Work with your accountant or financial analyst. A good accountant can refine your contingency scenarios using simple averaging methods or weighted averages of historical performance. The cost of this type of contingency analysis is low by using the initial data entered into the financial spreadsheets. More sophisticated proforma statements demonstrate a degree of flexibility and professionalism. This type of sensitivity analysis provides potential investors with a good basis for evaluating downside risk.

Base estimates on *realistic* projections. Prospective financiers need to know the value of your business. Providing an objective and realistic value estimate is not, however, straightforward. Inflating the value of the firm discredits an applicant by demonstrating lack of realism. Underestimating your firm's worth affects the cost and terms of capital. Not backing an estimate with reasonable explanation is a turn-off for prospective investors, right from the start. It's best to sit in the middle, with realistic estimates based on sound assumptions.

Reflect the revised cost of capital. Margins must reflect the costs of capital, associated fees such as legal and administrative expenses while providing room for competitive erosion. Gross margins that fail to reflect the expenses associated with financing a deal become suspect in an investor's eyes. Do not forget to deduct from your income statement all long-term financial expenses that are not part of the capitalization. Depreciation, interest, and amortization expenses should be replaced by the estimated interest on the new debt or equity.

Calculate risk. What is the risk level of your firm? Investors expect a clear understanding of the nature and degree of risks associated with the deal. Risk assessment should account for factors that will impact your firm's performance such as industry, market, technological, political, and environmental trends.

Use financial benchmark data to support your claims. Canadian small business financial data can benchmark your firm's performance, and are available on a fee-for-service basis through private services or free of charge on Industry Canada's on-line database **Strategis**. These data allow you to compare your estimated performance with businesses operating in the same industry or market..

Calculate net present value. With an estimated cash flow and earning projection backed by sound industry, market, and management risk assessment in hand, calculate the net return on investment based on your required rate of return.

Suggest the terms of agreement. Why wait? Structure the deal that you need! Be imaginative and present several scenarios that you believe both parties can live by. For example, the terms might consider performance milestones that fit your operating estimates. Or, stratify the terms of payment that allow for a degree of flexibility while meeting performance targets.

Present the bigger, long-term picture. Substantial growth, that excites most informal investors often entails geographic, market, and product expansion. Present the big picture. Lay out for the reader where the firm is at present, and where the firm will be in five years. Let the reader know what role he or she will play in the longer-term success of the business. This creates excitement about the deal and clarifies your perspective on refinancing and the long-term performance of the firm.

TIP

Firms that seek venture capital, however, are not on stock exchanges nor do they typically have track records that allow precise estimates of future earnings. Moreover, for very small businesses, earnings figures are sensitive to arbitrary decisions such as the extent of the owners' salary draws. Price-earnings multiples based on larger, publicly traded enterprises may not readily translate to smaller ventures.

Nonetheless, valuation of firms for venture capital purposes also follows a two-step process similar in spirit to that used for larger firms. Here, however, one should use estimates of the business' total revenues. These estimates are then capitalized by multiplying

them by a price-to-sales ratio that might be characteristic of the
industry. We use sales revenues because, for small businesses,
forecasts of revenues are more reliable than forecasts of earnings. The multiples are industry-related and reflect the risk of the
business. Alternatively, (especially for more established firms)
venture investors use industry multiples to value enterprises by
capitalizing earnings or cash flows. Frequently, investors employ
multiple valuation techniques.

Once valued, the venture capitalist and the business owners
need to reach accommodation about the structure of the deal. A
common format involves the firm selling a security to the
investor that has the characteristics of debt during the early years
and which then converts to equity. **Convertible debentures** or
warrants are common securities that provide for this conversion
of debt to equity. By using ratchets venture capitalists further
enhance the potential of their equity. Ratchets are provisions that
provide the investor with additional equity under pre-specified
conditions.

Post-Investment Monitoring and Mentoring

The apparent emphasis on growth and return can lead to conflicts between venture capitalist investors and owners. Business
owners need to extract a draw of income from the firm to
finance living expenses. Investors, on the other hand, usually
want to reinvest as much of the business' cash flow as possible
to support future growth. Accordingly, once the owners and the
venture capitalist reach an agreement, they ordinarily sign a contract. Among the common provisions of a venture capital contract are:

• restrictions on principals' salaries and compensation;

• restrictions on transfer and pledging of shares;

• the right to nominate directors;

• the right to participate, pro rata, in new share offerings;

• access to audited and interim financial statements;

• life insurance on the principals; and

• limitations on management stock option plans, etc.

Owners can usually count on the venture capital investors insisting on a say in important decisions, such as hiring officers, controlling costs, deploying other sources of financing (including bank loans), and introducing new products. Seldom do venture capitalists take part in such day-to-day decisions as staff hiring, product pricing, and advertising.

Exit

Exit is a crucial part of the investment process. According to one venture fund manager, "if I can't get out, I won't get in." Exit is also important for the business owner. The owner has usually given up some degree of control. In return, the business received an infusion of equity as venture capital. When the venture capitalist wishes to sell this equity, owners often want the opportunity to buy back control. Therefore, the investment contract usually specifies liquidity provisions that satisfy both the investor and the owners.

The most profitable means of exit for venture capitalists are initial public offerings (IPOs) of equity shares by firms in which venture capitalists had previously invested. We discuss IPOs in Chapter 8. Briefly, the IPOs give the venture capitalists the opportunity to sell their shares of the firm to the public. According to the Canadian Venture Capital Association (1996), 1995 venture capitalists sold $231 million of shares of firms in which they had originally invested $45 million via IPOs. This provided them with more than a fivefold return.

Other, less profitable, means of exit include:

- secondary sales of stock of investee firms that had previously had an IPO;
- liquidation of assets;
- the acquisition of investee firms by third parties; and
- company or employee buy-backs.

GUIDELINES FOR GETTING VENTURE FINANCING

The most important prerequisite for venture capital finance is a business plan, one that commands the investor's attention and that gets the investor to believe in the potential of the business idea. This means distinguishing the investment from the hundreds that the investor receives each year and demonstrating how the investor will achieve the required rate of return over a reasonable holding period. The business plan must show the potential investor how development of the product or idea and development of the management team will address the investor's objectives. In this vein, there are some "dos."

TO IMPROVE CHANCES OF VENTURE FINANCING

T
I
P

Do define the business clearly. In particular, identify the "competitive advantage" that the product or service embodies. This attribute is what makes the business opportunity unique and provides the edge over the competition. Exclusivity by means of copyright or patent is useful.

Do identify clearly the target market for the product or service and present the marketing strategy that supports financial projections. The marketing strategy should stress how the product will provide value added to purchasers. The findings of independent market research should provide further reasoned estimates of the market potential and penetration.

Do demonstrate a thorough understanding of the industry sector in which the product or service will compete. Show the investor that you have a position in the industry conducive to rapid growth.

Do outline the management abilities of the business' principals. These capabilities should demonstrate proven marketing expertise and fiscal responsibility.

Do outline a proposed financial framework for the deal. The business plan presented to a venture capitalist should specify the financial return, identify sources of risk, make provision for profitable exit, and propose how to structure the deal. Depending on risk, venture capitalists expect the value of their investment to grow from fivefold (for low risk firms) to twenty-fold (for high risk firms). The business plan should identify how to include other investors, if any, in the deal.

T I P

Overall, the business plan should convey to the investor that the management team of the firm is "market-driven" rather than "product-driven." Investors know that the key to business viability and success is to design a product or service that meets the needs of the marketplace. Conversely, investors do not want to associate themselves with "product-driven" businesses, firms that focus on development of a product whether or not there is market demand for it. In this vein, there are several "don'ts."

T I P

TO IMPROVE CHANCES OF VENTURE FINANCING

Don't advance market projections that are unrealistic. One reason venture capitalists specialize is to develop expertise in given sectors. Investors have a good sense of what constitutes a realistic market forecast. The best defence against this error is to provide forecasts based on independent market research.

Don't ignore sources of risk and uncertainty. All businesses are subject to external uncertainty and have internal shortcomings. Show the investor that you recognize such risks and that you have developed contingency plans to address them.

Don't use a business plan that is the product of consultants' template plans unless you are fully conversant with the contents. Other businesses use such plans. So to some extent, your plan will look like others and you will fail to distinguish yourself. In the course of the venture capital investment process, the investor will get a sense of the extent to which the principals of the firm are conversant with the plan. If they cannot rationalize elements of the plan, they will lose credibility. In the competitive environment for venture capital, such a loss may be terminal.

T I P

SUMMARY

In this chapter, we reviewed the investment practices of Canadian venture capital companies. In doing so, we have tried to convey a sense of the events and institutions that are shaping the industry.

This sector of the capital market is changing rapidly. It is unlikely that the emergence of LSVCCs can continue at the current pace. The apparent surplus of capital in the industry, while good news for business owners, will ultimately find a home in investments that, otherwise, deserve no financing. Inevitably, such investments are likely to sport lower success rates. This may drive down returns throughout the industry and discourage further entry. From this perspective, it is not clear that the distortion of the industry by the short-term tax-driven capital surplus will be beneficial in the longer term. In the meantime, Canadian small business owners have never had so much risk funding available.

CHAPTER SEVEN

A PORTFOLIO OF DEBT FINANCING

The information and stories that comprise this chapter are all about debt financing. This means sources of capital that will impact your monthly cash flow, but will not erode your equity stake. Though more obscure than high-profile sources of debt capital such as major banks, the sources of non-bank capital described here are vital to small business. For example, trade credit is not often thought of as debt financing. Financing obtained from suppliers, however, is one of the more important sources of capital for small firms, particularly for firms in start-up and early stage expansion. Other sources of non-bank debt financing for small businesses include leasing and other means of asset-based financing, secured commercial loans from institutions other than banks, commercial mortgages, suppliers, factoring, and other forms of receivables financing.

The frequency with which small businesses are employing these means of financing is increasing and is likely to expand significantly in the near future. We'll talk about some of the reasons the non-bank capital market is evolving so quickly in Chapter 9.

This chapter focuses on the portfolio of non-bank sources of debt, from both lender and borrower perspectives. What emerges is a marketplace that includes several disparate vehicles of financing targeted to the small business sector.

TRADE CREDIT AND WORKING CAPITAL: BURDEN OR BOON?

You've just cracked the export market. All your months of hard work have paid off in a huge order from south of the border. You order materials, book overtime. How do you manage your phenomenal growth and success to make sure that the increase in business does not actually cause your business to fail? The success or failure of many SMEs derives directly from how well they manage current assets and current liabilities—the elements of working capital.

> "Our biggest source of capital was our creditors. We'd work things out with those that trusted us. As long as they saw our product was still on our floor and we had orders to ship, they went the extra mile. So we probably had some nervous creditors, but that helped us get to a point until we started producing our own product ..."
>
> Fritz Winkels, vice-president,
> Finance, Excell Store Fixtures Inc., Etobicoke, Ont., PROFIT, June 1996

Poor working capital management practices can create daily management headaches and crises. More to the point, poor working capital management is an important precursor to business failure. Managing working capital items such as receivables, inventories, and payables usually takes up a large portion of managers' time. These items also account for a high proportion of your firm's assets and debts. As your enterprise grows, the need for additional receivables and inventories expand quickly, along with levels of payables. The expansion of these balance sheet accounts can lead to a cash flow crisis—working capital consumes cash. Good financial management is essential. Understanding the cash flow cycle is therefore an important concept in the management of working capital. Accordingly, we turn our attention to the management of working capital and cash flow before going on to other avenues of debt financing.

The Cash Flow Cycle

The cash flow cycle arises from the normal operations of your firm. Suppose your contract with your new US client requires your firm to begin production. You order raw materials—and your supplier requires payment within 10 days (this generates an account payable). However, it takes you 20 days to convert the raw materials to finished goods (work-in-process inventory). Then it takes five more days to store and ship the goods to the client (finished goods inventory). Once the client receives the goods, and the invoice, you extend credit to them for another 10 days (accounts receivable). For this sequence of operations, you must pay your supplier of raw materials in 10 days—but you don't get paid for the goods produced from these materials for $20 + 5 + 10 = 35$ days. You have to finance 25 days of production! The following example puts numbers to this situation to show that this can really add up.

AN EXAMPLE OF THE CASH FLOW CYCLE

Suppose, on day 1, the firm receives a shipment of raw material worth $8,000. The supplier requires payment within 10 days. The firm takes 20 days to convert the raw material to finished goods, incurring labour costs of $2,000. The finished goods remain in inventory for five days and then you sell them. According to the firm's credit policy, the purchaser has 10 days to pay for the goods.

In this example, the firm holds its purchased goods as work-in-process inventory for 10 days after paying the supplier. It then holds finished goods for five days before a sale is made, and awaits 10 days for payment of the receivable from the purchaser. Assuming the firm's production process is even and continuous (that is, the sequence described above is one that represents a daily occurrence for the firm), the business must finance a total of 25 days of production (at $8,000 + $2,000 per day). This amounts to $250,000 of working capital.

For many people, the financing requirement implied by the cash flow cycle is surprisingly high, even for the simple transactions described here. It arises from the time lag between the need to pay suppliers and the receipt of payment from customers. This time lag creates the need for financing the inventories and receivables that constitute "working capital." If the firm cannot arrange financing for its working capital requirements, suppliers will not sell any more raw material and employees will leave. The firm will fail. Moreover, the longer the cash flow cycle, the greater the need for financing.

It makes sense that the firm can reduce its financing needs by shortening the cash flow cycle. It can do this in two ways: lengthening the time before having to pay suppliers and shortening the time until collecting from clients.

The **cash flow cycle** can be divided into two cycles:

The **operating cycle** is the time it takes to produce the goods and collect from clients: the time taken to convert raw materials to cash (35 days in our example). Shortening this period reduces financing needs. It can be subdivided into two components:

• the **inventory conversion period** is the time it takes to convert raw materials to sales (25 days in our example);

• the **receivables conversion period**, or "days of sales outstanding," is the time it takes to collect cash from purchases (10 days in our example).

The **payment cycle** is the time the firm has to pay suppliers of materials and labour or employees (10 days in our example). Lengthening this period reduces the need for financing.

The **cash conversion cycle** is the difference between the operating cycle and the payment cycle. It represents the number of days of production that the firm must finance. Usually, the operating cycle is greater that the payment cycle, and the firm needs working capital financing. If the firm can somehow stretch its payables and expedite its collections, the cash conversion cycle can even have a negative value! That is, credit advanced from suppliers extends beyond the time when the firm receives payment from its own clients. This provides the firm with financing.

> ## TIP
>
> "**I** think vendors are the biggest source of unwitting investors. We still lean on the same policy we started, which is we receive in 30 [days], we pay in 60 [days]."
>
> Tylaine Nicholls, president, ISDN
> Wire Service, Toronto, PROFIT, June 1996
>
> T I P

Of course, factors beyond the firm's control also affect these cycles. Efficient management and good relationships with suppliers and customers can also provide the firm with financing. The financing requirements depend on:

- terms of purchase;
- terms on which the firm provides its own clients with credit;
- production technology;
- sales growth; and
- marketing strategies.

It is not sufficient to simply stretch payables and hasten collection of receivables. Working capital decisions are part and parcel of the firm's operational needs, financing, and marketing policies. These are decisions that affect the firm's goodwill with suppliers and customers. Smart firms therefore carefully nurture and manage these precious relationships.

These relationships, however, run both ways. A supplier will actively support the business. A printer might help a new magazine

> ## TIP
>
> "**I**t has really been people that have assisted us...it's been relationships we have established with our banks, with our vendors, with our customers that have all led to our success....I spent a great deal of time sharing the dream of the company with all of our vendors. Once I got them to buy into our vision, getting 90- or 120- or 180-day terms was relatively easy. Once you get those people on your side, I characterized them as my partner. And I treated them as a partner by keeping them informed and showing them financial statements, and treating them like a strategic element in my business."
>
> Raymond Simmons, chair and CEO,
> CRS Robotics Corp., Burlington, Ont., PROFIT, June 1996
>
> T I P

trying to get off the ground by offering more time to pay or by buying advertisements; a manufacturer might offer special terms to a retailer during start-up. Suppliers recognize that by providing a young firm with support they not only make additional sales, they also engender a loyal and long-term customer. This type of cooperation will not come if the business at an early stage of development simply ignores due dates for payments. Both parties must see some long-term value in the relationship.

The (Sometimes Hidden) Cost of Supplier Credit

Frequently, supplier credit comes at a cost. For example, a supplier may offer 120 days to pay, but the supplier may also offer a cash discount as a reward for early payment. At first glance, the discount may seem like little more than a courtesy. At second glance, however, the discount can reflect a substantial interest rate for slow payment. The additional amount is not so much the cost of the goods as "interest" that the supplier charges for holding on to the supplier's payment for the additional period. This interest cost can be substantial.

COSTS OF DISCOUNTS FOREGONE

A supplier offers terms of 2/10, net 60. If the purchaser takes the discount, it pays 98% of the invoice amount on day 10. Alternatively, the client can pay that plus the extra 2% on day 60. The 2% is what the supplier is charging for holding on to the 98% for the extra 50 (60-10) days. This is an interest cost for holding on to the money for the extra 50 days. The implied rate of interest is 2/98 for each 50-day period. This corresponds to an annualized implied interest rate of (2/98)(365/50), or 14.9%, considerably more than bank borrowing!

The extent to which a firm can make successful use of trade credit, and for that matter, all capital, depends primarily on the ability of the firm's management team. Few elements of SME finance make the case as strongly for fiscally responsible decision making as does the management of working capital. Sound planning and management of trade credit and receivables are day-to-day hands-on operations that require careful attention to both financial and human relationships.

> "Getting the business to around $5 million was very easy. [It was] $5 to $10 million [that] was the scary range, where you weren't really in touch with all your finances because you never had the financial infrastructure in place; you didn't have a CFO [chief financial officer] and couldn't afford all those people. That was hard. We grew through that, but I think that's where a lot of businesses fail."
>
> Brian Sernkiw, CEO of Rand Technology, a Mississauga value added reseller of CAD/CAM systems, PROFIT, June 1996

Working with Customers

The other key to reducing the need to finance working capital is by keeping the level of receivables as low as possible. First, the firm must choose a credit policy. Credit policy has four parts:

1. **Who gets credit?** Over time, the firm will come to know its regular customers. With new clients, however, it makes sense to check them out. Asking for references is one way to accomplish this informally. Alternatively, the firm could use credit bureaus to find out if the new client has a history of late or non-payment.

2. **How long will you give customers to pay their bills?** This, of course, is also part of the firm's marketing mix. The manager needs to do a little arithmetic to see if the additional profits associated with a long credit period make up for the incremental bad debts and the cost of financing the additional receivables.

3. **Will you provide discounts to encourage early payment?** Some firms provide customers with incentives to pay early by allowing a discount from the invoiced amount. Again, this is partly a marketing decision. A little arithmetic done in advance will tell if the reduced financing burden of carrying fewer receivables compensates for the reduced sales revenue.

4. **How tough will you be when it comes to collecting overdue accounts?** Inevitably, some customers cannot or will not pay. How tough or forgiving you are can make the difference between survival and failure.

> ## COLLECT WHAT YOU'RE OWED
>
> **T**
> **I**
> **P**
>
> **M**aurice Polard, as president of Accounts Recovery Corp. of Victoria offers suggestions for collecting delinquent accounts:
>
> - Letters get ignored. Phone debtors instead.
> - When you call, refer to the specifics of the case so clients know you have singled them out.
> - If they hang up, call back within the hour to show you are serious and persistent.
> - Try to get as much money as you can upfront. Offer terms only as a last resort. Debtors usually do not keep up installment payments.
> - Ask consumers for details of their financial situation. If they get huffy, remind them that they have money that is yours. Advise them that cooperation is better than a lawsuit or having a court garnishee wages.
> - If all else fails, settle for a lesser amount than the debt.
> - Grow a thick skin.
>
> PROFIT, March 1995, p.68.
>
> T I P

An alternative to managing your own receivables is that of factoring, or hiring a company that specializes in financing receivables, to take over the task.

FACTORING AND THE FINANCING OF RECEIVABLES

The accounts receivable on the books of your firm are an asset. As we noted in the previous section, the larger the receivables, the more working capital financing the firm requires. One way of reducing this need for capital is by selling the receivables or by using them directly as security for obtaining capital. Often, receivables form part of the basis on which banks calculate the lending limit of an operating loan.

As we noted in Chapter 3, banks often use accounts receivable as the basis for operating loans and will advance 65-75% of the value of the receivables. Such loans cost between prime and prime plus three percent. Alternatively, the firm can raise cash by selling receivables that it has not pledged as security for a loan. Factoring is the process by which the firm sells its accounts receivable. Factors are specialized finance companies that work with businesses in two ways. They provide financing and services.

Financing

When a factor provides financing, the firm and the factor contract to undertake a continuous process. As the business receives orders, the factor:

- evaluates the creditworthiness of the customer and approves (or not) the extension of credit.

- advances 80 to 90% of the invoiced amount to the business; the amount retained by the factor provides for a reserve for contingencies such as rejection of the goods by the buyer. The factor usually remits the balance to the business once they collect the account.

- assumes the risk of collecting on the receivable.

This traditional form of factoring provides the firm with both financing and services. Firms can also contract with factors on a services-only basis.

Services

Factoring firms offer a range of services. These include acting as the SME's credit department by carrying out credit assessments, making the credit decisions, and assuming the risk of bad debts for all receivables. When the client firm sells its product, it sends a copy of the invoice to the factoring company. The factoring firm then takes on the responsibility of collecting the account. Unlike traditional factoring, the SME retains title to the receivable, and can pledge them to a lender if desired. The factor handles credit and collection services, including generation of statements and follow-up notices to the businesses' customers. The factor can also handle paperwork and provides reports to the client. Factoring firms offer credit guarantees and will buy, sometimes at full value, clients' overdue receivables.

Factors charge fees that average one to two percent of the gross value of the accounts receivable for both services and guarantees. These fees vary by business size and industry sector, with smaller firms generally paying rates at the higher end of the range, but fees can mount up if the firm is not paid the receivables when due. For overdue accounts, the cost of factoring is approximately one percent of sales—per month. This fee level is significant, particularly for low margin businesses. However, fees can still compare favourably with the internal cost of maintaining a credit department.

FACTORING PROS AND CONS

The young owner of a West Coast running shoe company was considering ways to expand nationally. Demand for the firm's tennis shoe was exceedingly high and he felt timing was opportunistic. Given the firm's explosive West Coast growth, capital for expansion was limited. To help overcome limited cash flow, he hired a well-respected Toronto sales agency. Payment would be based strictly on a commission for goods shipped. All sales to eastern accounts would be factored. His factoring agreement included credit checks on all new accounts. This minimized the firm's bad debts among new accounts. It also saved time and resources for the inexperienced, one-person credit management department of the firm. On the downside, his sales agent was annoyed that some prospective buyers were reluctant to deal with the West Coast firm because of the factoring. For a number of prospective accounts the additional paperwork stemming from the requisite credit checks and payment to the third party factor outweighed the benefits of buying a new line of running shoes!

While factoring was historically centred in the garment trade in Montreal, it is now common in such industries as consumer electronics, furniture, sporting goods, and automotive aftermarkets. Recent deregulation of the financial services industry includes provisions that allow banks to act as factors. Factoring is therefore becoming more common and is likely to expand further.

ASSET-BASED FINANCING

Asset-based financing is a means by which a company raises cash by borrowing against a physical asset, often the particular asset for which the firm needs the funds. Leasing, term loans, and conditional sales contracts are among the financial services that comprise methods of "asset-based financing." For example, if you go to a bank for an operating loan or a term loan to acquire a new asset, the bank looks at your firm's ability to repay the loan. For an asset-based loan, the focus is on the value of the asset itself. It becomes the security for the loan you use to buy it. In Canada, many of the firms that specialize in asset-based financing include Newcourt, GE Capital, Commcorp Ltd., and others, most of which are members of the Canadian Finance and Leasing Association.

ASSET BASED FINANCING COMPANIES[1]

Specialized finance institutions comprise five categories:

Independent finance companies, such as Newcourt Credit Group, Commcorp Financial Services, etc., dominate the market for equipment leasing. Their ownership includes institutional investors, banks, pension funds, US parent firms, and the general public. These are firms to which businesses can look for a broad range of financing alternatives.

Other business finance companies include firms that provide a range of more specialized financing services to business clients. Such services include asset-backed term lending, bridge financing, mezzanine financing to businesses. An example of a business finance company is Bank of Nova Scotia-owned Roynat.

Automotive sales finance companies, such as General Motors Acceptance, Ford Credit, etc., tend to be Canadian subsidiaries of US parent firms and specialize in automobile leasing.

Manufacturers' capital finance companies include such firms as Xerox Canada Acceptance, IBM Credit Inc., and specialize in financing products sold by their parent firms.

These firms differ from **sales finance companies**, firms such as AVCO Financial Services Canada Limited, Beneficial Canada Inc. These are essentially consumer loan companies.

For several reasons asset-based financing arrangements are attractive alternatives to bank borrowing. First, companies that specialize in this type of financing are usually more willing than banks to structure payments that reflect clients' cash flow situations. For example, payments on assets often vary from month

---

[1] The Canadian Finance and Leasing Association has more than 100 member firms and, according to the Conference Board of Canada, these account for 80% of asset-based financing in Canada. C. Connor, "Alternative Sources of Debt Financing for Small and Medium-Sized Enterprises," Conference Board of Canada, 1995.

to month to mirror seasonality of lessees' cash flows. Second, traditional lenders base their lending decisions on the ability of the lender to service the additional debt, the borrower's track record, and the quantity and quality of the firm's collateral. Conversely, asset-based financiers place most emphasis on the value of the asset being financed.

CANADIAN COMPARISONS OF ASSET-BASED LENDING

According to the Canadian Finance and Leasing Association, asset-based financing accounts for 32% of all equipment purchases in the US., 19% in the UK, and just 13% in Canada.

Third, asset-based finance companies have expertise in the management of, and asset markets for, most of the property they finance. This expertise allows them to reduce the uncertainty regarding the liquidation values of assets, an uncertainty that non-specialist traditional lenders perceive as "risk." For example, one area in which asset-based financing companies specialize is that of leasing tractor-trailers or "rigs." By keeping abreast of trends and changes in the resale markets of the rigs, asset-based lenders know with some certainty what the value of a used rig will be for several years into the future. Traditional lenders, as generalists rather than specialists, are not nearly as able to tap into the resale markets at the end of the lease or in the event of default. Lacking this specialized knowledge, traditional lenders are less willing to finance such assets.

Fourth, asset-based financing firms have shown leadership in Canada with respect to raising capital internationally and by "securitizing" loan and lease cash flows. One way to envisage securitization is to think of it as selling packages of loan and lease accounts receivable directly to investors. Securitization can reduce the asset-based financing companies' costs of funds. Low costs of funds allow them to offer competitive terms of financing while still earning their investors acceptable rates of return.

The most frequent form of asset-based financing is leasing. Other financial products provided by asset-based financing firms include secured commercial loans, factoring of receivables, non-residential mortgages, and conditional sales contracts. Not all firms provide all these services. Greyvest Ltd., for example, specializes in leasing of computer equipment. This section will begin consideration of asset-based finance by reviewing leasing. To understand best how to make effective use of leasing, it is helpful to understand the position of leasing companies and why they act in certain ways.

Leasing

A lease is an agreement between the "lessor," who owns the asset and provides the right to use the equipment, and the "lessee," who makes periodic payments for use of the asset. The agreement involves a series of contractually specified payments for an agreed period of time. Leasing offers several important advantages, especially to small- and medium-sized companies.

ADVANTAGES AND DISADVANTAGES OF LEASING

Advantages:
- Leasing provides use of equipment without the need to pay for it at the time of purchase. Potentially, the firm can redeploy capital to finance working capital or other resources. If the firm does not have the capital, it does not have to borrow the capital needed for the purchase.
- Leases often provide flexibility in their terms. Up-front payment of the asset is not required. Future earnings offset the cost of the asset.
- Certain tax benefits may allow owners to write-off the full cost of leasing, compared to claiming capital cost allowance on the value of purchased assets.
- Lease terms usually reflect fixed interest rates. Knowing, with certainty, the cash flows associated with the lease facilitates planning.
- Reduced risk of obsolescence to the user.
- After-tax cash flows can be at least as attractive as borrowing to purchase.

Disadvantages:
- Lease contracts often specify purchase options or renewal terms, thus limiting the firm's flexibility.
- The firm does not own the asset, thereby eroding the value of fixed assets.

> • The per-dollar cost of lease financing often exceeds that of borrowing
>   funds to purchase the asset; however, this varies widely by type of
>   asset and also depends on taxation effects.

Motives for leasing vary and depend on each situation. For many small businesses, the cash flow considerations are often dominant. Leases allow firms to acquire assets that would otherwise require a considerable outlay of cash. In other instances, convenience or obsolescence risk are primary. Certain types of equipment such as heavy industrial or commercial equipment, medical instruments, and computers are more amenable to leasing. Where obsolescence is an issue, leasing may have an advantage.

EQUIPMENT COMMONLY AVAILABLE THROUGH LEASING

- computers, software, and computer systems;
- office furniture;
- telephone systems;
- photographic, printing, manufacturing, and construction equipment;
- health care and dental equipment;
- heavy equipment;
- vehicles, buses, trucks, and tractor-trailers;
- aircraft; and
- railroad rolling stock.

The Leasing Process

A typical leasing transaction proceeds through four steps:

1. The business owner (eventually the lessee) or manager chooses the specifics of the equipment.

2. The prospective lessee negotiates terms of a lease with one or more potential lessors. Leasing companies will usually conduct a credit check of the prospective lessee.

3. When the prospective lessee and a leasing company reach agreement, they sign a lease contract and the lessor orders the equipment.

4. On delivery of the equipment, the lessor pays the equipment provider and the lessee begins payments to the lessor according to the terms of the lease contract.

An important variation of this sequence is a "vendor lease program." Vendor lease programs arise when leasing companies work with equipment vendors to their mutual advantage. Typically, the leasing company develops a program for the vendor that provides the equipment vendor with the ability to offer lease financing to potential equipment purchasers. For example, asset-based finance companies furnish vendors of tractor-trailers with: leasing documents identifying the vendor as the lessor; training programs to help the vendor's staff use leases as part of the marketing strategy; account administration; and ongoing liaison with an account executive. This arrangement equips the vendor with a broader sales package. For customers, vendor leasing provides a convenient alternative means of financing.

A vendor lease program also provides for immediate full payment to the vendor from the leasing company and it minimizes administrative tasks. The vendor does not tie up capital awaiting payment from the equipment user. The vendor may also make additional sales that might otherwise fall through if the user is unsuccessful in arranging conventional debt financing. Equipment users need not purchase the equipment and instead make (usually) monthly payments. To the user, it sometimes seems as if they leased the equipment from the supplier instead of from the leasing company. Vendor-lease programs are usually transparent to clients.

Vendor lease programs are particularly important for SMEs. Small businesses are ideal target markets for vendor lease programs, which can be of valuable help if your firm is looking to establish creative financing alternatives for your own clients. Vendor financing is most often available for "small ticket" items (equipment valued at less than $25,000), particularly for such items as office equipment. You can approach leasing firms directly, but it's usually easier to go through your equipment dealer.

ON ASSET-BASED FINANCING

"...unlike a bank, which has general knowledge of a wide range of endeavours, an asset-based financier can precisely estimate the rate of decline of the asset's value, and set terms of confidence." Ron Purvis reaped the benefits of that specialization. As a part-time financial consultant to a small oil company in Calgary, he decided to add a sideline: developing computer materials to help accountants market their skills. When he found a $5,000 computer system to buy, he was told to wait several days while his lease was approved. In that time he discovered a second package of comparable cost with twice the power. When Purvis called he was referred to Newcourt for financing advice—and got a lease approved in minutes. "The response was almost immediate," he says. The lender was able to determine that Purvis was purchasing equipment appropriate for his needs, and that it could get its money back from the hardware if his venture failed."

In addition, Purvis found the cost of his computer package better than competitive. "Newcourt needed $30 per $1,000 of computer per month," he says. Other lenders quoted $35 to $45.

"Banking on Your Assets" PROFIT, October-November 1996

Terms of Leases

The specific terms of leases vary with the type of equipment. Leases are generally for three to six years. In financial terms, leases tend to be more expensive than bank loans after accounting for all fees and costs on a before-tax basis. Since the entire lease payment is tax-deductible (compared with only the interest portion only for term loans), costs on an after-tax basis may be better or comparable with that of asset ownership. Lease payments, however, can be suited to the lessees' situations. The lease contract can often be arranged at the point of asset acquisition, and leases do not require the full upfront capital cost of the asset. For many businesses, this level of convenience is important.

Types of Leases

Regardless of the nature of the equipment or the nature of the leasing transaction, there are two broad categories of leases: capital leases and operating leases.

LEASE DEFINITIONS

The Canadian Institute of Chartered Accountants qualifies a lease as a **capital lease** if any one of the following conditions holds:

- there is a reasonable assurance that the lessee will obtain ownership of the asset by the end of the term of the lease;
- the term of the lease exceeds 75% of the useful life of the equipment;
- the present value of the lease payments is more than 90% of the original cost of the equipment.

If there is no reasonable assurance that the lessee will own the equipment by the end of the term of the lease **and** if the other two conditions do not hold, the lease is an **operating lease**. In short, capital leases and purchasing the asset by term loan borrowing are almost indistinguishable. Therefore, the decision should rest on the relative costs of each.

Capital Leases

Capital leases usually provide for equipment financing that spans the useful life of the equipment. The lessee cannot normally cancel the lease. Hence, some people call capital leases "full payout" leases because the lessor structures the lease to recover the full original cost of the equipment, as well as a contribution to profit and overhead. Essentially, all the rights and benefits of ownership of the equipment rest with the lessee.

With a capital lease, the risk the leasing company takes is primarily a credit risk—that the lessee will not, or cannot, make the contractual lease payments. In the event that the lessee fails these obligations, the lessor can repossess the leased asset and resell it. For this reason, lessors often specialize in certain types of equipment. They become conversant with the market value of the leased equipment and are able to resell it at the best possible price.

To reduce credit risk, leasing companies investigate the credit worthiness of their potential clients. As in bank financing, this investigation frequently includes:

- an analysis of the lessee's key financial ratios (often using credit scoring systems);
- review of the client's track record; and
- reference to credit bureau ratings.

As in bank financing, the depth and breadth of the investigation varies with the amount financed. Small firms typically
lease relatively low-cost assets, and are not subject to the same
criteria as businesses seeking to lease costly assets. In assessing
SME clients, the most important factors are the firm's credit
record and the nature and value of the particular asset being
leased. Capital leases are typical for such equipment types as
tractor-trailers, medical and dental equipment, office equipment, and computers.

One common variation of the capital lease is the "stretch
lease." Under which, the lessee has the option to purchase the
leased asset after a specified number of payments at a given
option price. The intent of a stretch lease is to make sure the
lessor receives its full return even when the lessee need not purchase the equipment at the expiry of the lease. The price is such
that the lease payments to that time with the option price provide the full required return. If the lessee does not exercise the
option, the lease is "stretched" for an additional number of payment periods such that the value of the incremental lease payments is equivalent to the option price. At the end of the
extended period, the lessee may buy the asset at its then fair
market value or return it to the lessor.

Operating Leases

With an operating lease, the term is usually shorter than 75% of
the useful life of the equipment. Also, the present value of lease
payments is less than 90% of the original equipment cost. An
operating lease, then, finances equipment for only a portion of
its useful life. For example, a self-employed physician may prefer to regularly replace and upgrade his or her office's medical
equipment and furnishings. At the expiration of the lease, the
lessee can return the equipment to the lessor. At that point, the
leasing company must either sell or re-lease the equipment. Two
reasons why a lessee might want an operating lease is to transfer the burden of reselling equipment to the lessor and to be
able to lease new or up-to-date equipment prior to obsolescence. Most of the time, car leases are operating leases.

FEATURES OF A STRETCH LEASE

- The lessee is under no obligation to exercise the purchase option.
- There is no bargain purchase option offered to the lessee. Extra (stretch) payments equal the purchase option amount.
- The lessee treats the lease as a capital lease for tax purposes and can deduct 100% of the rental payments for tax purposes.
- The lessor assures itself of its full return and reduces its equipment risk.

"Basic Lease Categories," *Canadian Leasing Review, Asset Finance & Leasing Digest,* April 1995

For operating leases, then, the lessor takes on two types of risk. First, as with a capital lease, the lessor takes on a *credit risk* associated with the lessee's ability to make the contractual payments. The second form of risk is *uncertainty of the market values* for used equipment. Lessors deal with credit risk in the same way they do for capital leases: by careful investigation of the creditworthiness of the prospective client. This operating lease relationship works because the lessor is typically better able to cope with equipment risk than could either the lessee or a bank lender.

Lessors deal with equipment risk in three ways. First, operating leases are usually only available for equipment that has a ready resale market, such as automobiles. Second, leasing companies often specialize in particular types of equipment. For example, Greyvest Capital Limited focuses exclusively on computer leasing. Third, as experts in asset valuation, leasing firms are able to work with small business owners in their firm's asset management. This benefits both the client and the lessor: lessees can often obtain equipment upgrades or improvements because it is in the lessor's best interest to maintain the market value of the asset.

T
I
P

TAX TREATMENT OF LEASES

For tax purposes, lease payments are a tax-deductible expense for the lessee and the lessor, as owner of the asset, claims Capital Cost Allowance [CCA]. However, Revenue Canada deems a lease to be a sale if any of the following conditions is present:

- title to the equipment passes to the user automatically by the end of the lease;
- the lessee is required to purchase the asset; and
- the lessee has the option, during or at expiry of the lease, to acquire the asset on terms that a reasonable person would exercise.

If any of the above holds, the lease is a sale for tax purposes and the user of the asset claims CCA, but not the lease payments.

T I P

The Sale-and-Leaseback

The sale-and-leaseback arrangement is a useful means of raising expansion capital for firms that own certain types of assets. According to this arrangement, a firm that owns land or buildings (and sometimes equipment) sells the asset at market value, usually to an asset-based financing firm or to a financial institution such as insurance company. The firm thereby accesses an amount of capital equivalent to the value of its existing asset. Simultaneously, the firm executes a lease contract with the purchaser of the equipment, calling for periodic lease payments. Through the sale-and-leaseback arrangement the firm transforms an asset it already owns into a lump sum cash amount, a requirement for periodic lease payments, and continues to use the asset. The lessor invests capital in return for a contractual series of lease payments. This arrangement can be useful to both parties. When the lessor's cost of capital is lower than that of the firm, the lessor achieves a satisfactory rate of return while the lessee can potentially raise capital at a cost lower than that of borrowing.

Other Forms of Asset-Based Financing

In addition to leasing, specialized finance companies also offer secured commercial loans, conditional sales contracts, non-residential mortgages, and factoring of receivables, as we discussed earlier in the chapter.

Secured Commercial Loans

While the banks are the largest source of term loans, they are not the only source. Asset-based finance companies are also term lenders, with the loans usually being secured by the assets purchased by the proceeds of the loan. For the most part, however, asset-based financing companies and other specialized financing firms concentrate lending activities on larger firms.

Conditional Sales Contracts

A conditional sales contract is a means of granting credit whereby the vendor of the asset retains legal title until the purchaser has made full payment. Often, items that paid by means of an installment basis over several years (for example, medical and dental equipment) use conditional sales contracts. The advantage of a conditional sales contract is that, in the event that the purchaser cannot complete payment, having title to the goods facilitates repossession. Therefore, conditional sales contracts are a useful financing alternative when the seller doubts the ability of the purchaser to pay. Because they are a method of financing, conditional sales contracts carry an implicit interest rate, one that is comparable with rates on term loans.

Non-Residential Mortgages

In form, non-residential mortgages are very much like residential mortgages except that they finance the land or buildings used for business purposes. While specialized asset-based lenders have a presence in the market for commercial mortgages, this is a market dominated by life insurance companies; however, a recent study by the Conference Board[2] suggests that life insurance companies, for all their domination of the commercial mortgage market, lend disproportionately little to SMEs!

---

[2] Conner, 1995.

Commercial mortgages can finance the purchase or renova-
tion of real estate through debt that uses the property as security. They are usually of one to five-year terms, but with
amortizations of up to 25 years. Interest rates tend to be fixed for
the term and they reflect current levels. Fees are additional,
involving an initial negotiation fee and possible account management fees. Principal repayment is usually not permitted during the term of the loan.

MERCHANT BANKING AND MEZZANINE FINANCING

One of the recent developments in financial markets over the
last 20 years is the development of a merchant banking sector.
Merchant banks provide firms with financing, deal structuring,
and advice—a type of financing boutique. Hees International
Corp. of Toronto was probably the first merchant bank to operate in Canada during the 1970s. Other firms followed Hees, such
as Canadian Corporate Funding Ltd. and merchant banks linked
to such firms as Power Corporation, Brascan Ltd., etc. More
recently, most of the chartered banks also established merchant
banking divisions.

Unlike banks, merchant banks are not deposit-taking institutions. The "bank" part of the term relates to the fact that loans
are the major assets on their books. Unlike investment dealers
and investment banks, merchant banks are more than agents.
Often, merchant banks use their own money to buy a stake in a
company, then resell the firm at a profit. However, merchant
banks are particularly active as brokers in mergers, buyouts, refi-
nancings, and restructurings. For the most part, merchant banks
work with large firms; however, notable exceptions are Sharwood and Company and Roynat Inc., merchant banks that focus
more on SMEs. One of the financing tools that merchant banks
often employ is mezzanine financing.

Mezzanine Financing

"Mezzanine financing is money borrowed against projected cash flow instead of hard assets," says Dr. Jim Hatch of the University of Western Ontario's business school. "It's so-called because it falls between conventional debt secured or pure equity financing, both in terms of the degree of security expected against the loan, and in terms of costs. Most finance texts don't mention it, but it's becoming more popular as entrepreneurs get more imaginative about filling in the gaps in the financing puzzle."

"Taking Lending to the Next Level"
by Richard Wright PROFIT, September 1996

Mezzanine financing is a type of "venture lending" that usually accompanies a significant restructuring of a firm such as a change in share ownership, a management buyout, recapitalization, expansion, an acquisition, or simply to improve liquidity. Often, mezzanine financing *follows* institutional venture capital and *precedes* a buyout or an initial public offering. It almost always involves a long-term commitment and is debt financing that is secondary (senior or subordinated debt) to other existing long term debt. It is called "mezzanine" financing because it comprises a layer in the firm's capital structure below senior debt, but ahead of common equity. In most instances, mezzanine financing is essentially subordinated debt. Subordinated debt is a debt obligation bearing very high interest rates and often accompanied by "equity kickers" such as convertibility, warrants, options, or equity of the existing equity purchased at a nominal cost. Mezzanine financing may also involve royalty arrangements or even a fixed dollar bonus at maturity.

The debt aspect of mezzanine financing provides the investor with the protection of a debt instrument. The relatively high interest rate motivates the firm to eliminate the debt as soon as possible, ideally through an issue of shares on the stock market (see Chapter 8). The equity features allow the lender/investor to gain in the event that the firm performs well. Convertibility of the debt provides the best of both worlds, allowing the firm to "pay off" the debt by issuing shares. Debtors turned shareholders can reap the benefits of the firm's growth performance and financial

attractiveness. This combination of features provides owners of
the business with significant motivation to perform well and to
increase the value of the firm's equity.

SOLVING A FINANCING PROBLEM

Early in this chapter, we discussed how growth can consume cash and
bring a firm to the point of being unable to pay its bills. As an example, consider a designer of wine bottles who sells to the vintners and
contracts out the manufacture of the bottles to a large packaging company.
The designer's sales grow rapidly from $3 million to $6 million, then $12 mil-
lion, and $17 million. Yet, the total market for the designer is probably no
more than $30 to $35 million, so its growth will soon hit an upper limit. The
retained earnings are just not enough to finance the rapid growth in receivables and inventories. The result is that the designer becomes strapped for
the cash necessary to pay the packaging company for the bottles. Payables
to the packaging company get longer and the supplier gets worried.

Gordon Sharwood, of Sharwood and Company suggests a solution.
By arranging $2 million of preferred shares sold by the designer to the
packaging company, dividend payments and redemption of the shares
provides the packaging company with a high rate of return. In the meantime, the bottle designer can pay its accounts in 10 days, take advantage
of the trade discounts, and keep the packaging company collector at bay.
When growth slows down, the cash generated from freeing up the working capital will allow the bottle designer to retire the preferred share issue.

Example courtesy of Gordon Sharwood, Sharwood and Company, Toronto.

Subordinated debt is most common when collateral cannot
secure conventional financing, or when the debt-to-equity ratio is
too high, or when there are special needs, but cash flow is abun-
dant. Equity often supplements subordinated debt for emerging,
high growth companies that need to conserve cash flow for expansion and working capital. Firms use both when they need to recapitalize, make changes in share ownership, facilitate a management
buyout, expand, acquire another firm, or improve liquidity. The
term to maturity of subordinated debt is usually longer than that
of senior debt. Subordinated debt also generally involves restrictive covenants similar to those associated with the firm's senior
debt. The subordination agreement that accompanies mezzanine

financing typically specifies what happens in the event of default, so that control of the disposition of the firm rests with the senior lender.

THE LINGO OF MEZZANINE FINANCING

Convertible debt: debt exchangeable for equity by the lender at the lender's option on pre-specified terms.

Equity kickers: securities that provide the holder with the opportunity to share in appreciation of the firm's equity.

Warrants, options: contracts that give their owners the right to buy or sell a particular stock for a fixed price on or before a given date.

Recapitalize: restructuring of the firm's long-term sources of finance.

Restrictive covenants: terms of borrowing that restrict the borrower from specified actions.

Subordinated debt: debt placed in a secondary position with respect to other specific classes of debt.

Suppliers of mezzanine financing embrace various categories of firms. These include merchant bankers, bank venture capital subsidiaries, and venture capital companies. In addition, several specialized mezzanine financing firms syndicate capital from life insurance companies, pension funds, and other financial institutions. Mezzanine financing is primarily the domain of merchant bankers. Gordon Sharwood, CEO of merchant banker Sharwood and Co., estimates the total size of the market for mezzanine financing to be $5 billion annually. This amount compares with the size of the whole venture capital market.

A PROFILE OF A MERCHANT BANK

Roynat Inc. is a leading private lender specializing in term financing and merchant banking services. Here is a profile of the type of capital included in Roynat Inc.'s lending portfolio.

Subordinated Debt	Equity Capital
Preferred Size:	**Preferred Size:**
• $500,000 – $2,500,000	• $250,000 – $2,500,000
• 5 years	• 5 – 7 years
Purposes:	**Purposes:**
• Corporate acquisitions	• Corporate acquisitions
• Management buyouts	• Management buyouts
• Recapitalization	• Expansion capital for high-tech companies
	• Recapitalization
	• Special situations (early-stage technology and turnarounds)
Industries:	**Industries**
A wide variety, including manufacturing and distribution sector, *excluding* natural resources, retail, and real estate	A wide variety, including manufacturing and distribution sector, *excluding* natural resources, retail, and real estate
Benefits:	**Benefits:**
• Defined yield requirements, that is, bonus fees, cash flow participation	• Patient captial
• Quasi equity	• Lowers debt/equity ratio
• 100% equity ownership retained by owners	• Minority position only
	• Defined exit formula/price

Like other categories of investors, those engaged in mezzanine financing look for firms with solid management, a proven track record, and an established cash flow. This type of financing, then, is not for most small early-stage firms. Mezzanine financing is more for so-called "mid-market" firms in need of $3 to $12 million. Firms most likely to qualify for mezzanine financing must demonstrate good prospects for both the firm and the industry,

ample working capital, a prudent level of equity, and a strong
board of directors (or board of advisors).

MEZZANINE FINANCING: COMPARATIVE TERMS		
Costs of various types of long term investment in mezzanine-stage firms:		
	Underwriting and other fees (% of issue)	Investor pre-tax ROI (%).
Senior Debt	0-2%	Prime to Prime +2%
Subordinated Debt (Mezzanine)	3-5%	15 to 25%
Equity	3-5%	More than 25%

At the other end of the deal, mezzanine investors are typically patient, and do not expect an exit for five to seven years.
Exits typically take the form of an IPO, a buyout, or by means of
a refinancing through senior debt at maturity. While expensive in
terms of interest payment and fee requirements, subordinated
debt mezzanine financing is cheaper than raising public equity.
Mezzanine financing also provides flexibility in that the term,
coupon, and covenants can suit the issuer's needs. In addition,
the interest payments and fees are, unlike dividends, tax
deductible. Apart from cost, disadvantages are that the firm is
more highly levered and can appear more risky.

FINANCING INTERNATIONAL TRANSACTIONS

In the normal course of business, many firms engage in international transactions, either as an exporter (seller) or importer
(buyer). A variety of situations and reasons prompt international
business transactions:

- Local markets may be too small to sustain efficient or cost-com-
petitive sizes of operations. International transactions allow firms
to take advantage of economies of scale and market expansion.

- Firms are able to enjoy the flexibility of dealing in a variety of
currencies, interest rate settings, and economic climates.

- Firms can access wage structures and skills not available
domestically.

- Firms can avail themselves of government incentives such as export development initiates and tax breaks.

- Firms can establish research linkages and alliances with foreign firms.

- They can take advantage of market trends.

Obviously, when the buyer and the seller of goods or services reside in different countries, it is more challenging to effect a business transaction. Potential barriers include language differences, currency differences, and fluctuations in exchange rates, foreign exchange controls, legal traditions, customs and practices, cultural and philosophical backgrounds, and knowledge of each other. Unlike the situation where buyers and sellers are close to each other, it is more difficult to establish a business relationship between buyers and sellers separated by distance and other factors. Moreover, international transactions present several other risks. In addition to the normal sources of risk such as commercial failure, international transactions introduce risks that arise from political considerations (change of government, government policies, war, etc.), foreign exchange fluctuations, and differing levels and volatility of interest rates.

SOURCES OF RISK IN INTERNATIONAL TRANSACTIONS

There are three types of foreign exchange risk: transaction risk, value risk, and political risk.

Transaction risk primarily affects importers or exporters and arises when there is a time lag between contracting and the cash flows that result from the contract. Examples include both payables and receivables. If exchange rates shift in the interim between invoicing and collection, the dollar value of the payable or receivable changes.

Value risk is the effect that shifts in exchange rates have on the valuation of the whole firm. At an obvious extreme, if your firm sells all of its output abroad, an adverse change in exchange rates decreases the value of the business as a whole. To a greater or lesser extent, the values of all businesses are sensitive to exchange rate fluctuations. Even a firm that produces and sells domestically is sensitive to exchange rate changes. This is because the intensity and viability of competitors who are exporters and importers also change.

Political risk extends beyond the obvious dangers of insurrection, or political instability. Political risk also relates to the possibility that countries in which the firm does business change the ground rules such as when foreign exchange controls or protectionist policies are enacted. An extreme example is the controversial *Helms-Burton Act*, a policy enacted by one of the most politically stable countries in the world that affects the ability of enterprises, including Canadian businesses, to do business in both Cuba and the United States.

In view of these risks, a variety of financial techniques are available to assist international small business transactions.

Managing Transaction Risk

You have just landed a big contract with a distributor in Bradford, England. Under the terms of the deal, you have to deliver the goods within 30 days and the client then has an additional 60 days to pay. The client will pay you in British pounds, which you then will exchange for Canadian dollars. If, between delivery and invoicing, the dollar appreciates, the pounds you get from the client will purchase fewer dollars: your profit drops. How do you minimize this exposure? To answer this, we need to know more about how international transactions take place.

A Primer on International Transactions

In a typical trans-border sale the seller ships the goods to the buyer along with shipping documents. On receipt, these documents provide for release of the goods to the buyer. Exporters want to receive the correct amount of money for their goods, as soon as possible, in the currency of their choice. Importers want to ensure that the right quantity and quality of goods are received in a timely way, and at the right place. They usually want to pay as late as possible.

To support international trade, a well-developed international system of correspondent banking has evolved. This system entails relationships among banks of differing nationalities. Trust and mutual respect are the basis of these relationships. Correspondent banking is particularly useful when the importer is

THE LINGO OF INTERNATIONAL FINANCE

- **Bill of exchange:** a written order to pay a sum of money, sent by the seller to the customer's bank.
- **Correspondent banking:** the international network of financial institutions that deal with each other to make international payments on behalf of business clients.
- **Open account:** credit extended to low-risk customers that may consist only of a sales account entry and a signed invoice upon delivery.
- **Sight draft:** a bill of exchange containing an order to pay immediately.
- **Time Draft:** a bill of exchange containing an order to pay before a given date.

unwilling to pay in advance and the exporter objects to shipping on credit or through an open account. Four means of payment used in international trade are:

- cash in advance;
- letter of credit;
- bill of exchange; and
- open account.

Cash in advance provides the seller (exporter) with the greatest protection. Through this means of payment, the seller receives cash either before shipment of goods or on arrival of the goods at the foreign destination. This particularly strong term of payment is best when the buyer (importer) is in a country where political stability is problematic or when the buyer's credit is in question. While of great protection to the exporter, cash in advance does not provide the importer with much comfort. Therefore, when importers are unwilling to pay cash in advance, a letter of credit is one appropriate alternative.

A **letter of credit** is a letter to the exporter written and signed by a foreign bank, acting on behalf of the importer. Essentially, the importer's bank promises to honour drafts as long as the exporter conforms with the terms of the sale of goods set forth in the letter of credit. Through the letter of credit, the buyer's bank substitutes its commitment to pay for the buyer-importer. This is usually contingent on performance of the exporter. In other words, the correspondent banks hold ransom the shipping documents necessary for release of the goods until the exporter has met the terms of the letter of credit and the importer has either paid or accepted the draft.

A TYPICAL LETTER OF CREDIT TRANSACTION

1. At the request of the importer, the importer's bank issues a letter of credit. This letter sets forth the terms with which the exporter must comply including a description of the goods, delivery arrangements, and other aspects of the deal. The letter of credit guarantees payment based on the bank's knowledge of the importer so long as the exporter meets the terms. The exporter then knows that its domestic bank will guarantee payment.

2. Once the exporter receives the letter of credit and has shipped the goods, the exporter takes the letter of credit and the shipping documents to the exporter's bank. The seller/exporter's bank can expect payment from its foreign correspondent bank counterpart.

3. The seller's bank forwards the documents to its foreign (correspondent) bank along with an international draft requiring payment be made by a specific date. The draft may be a **sight draft**, one that requires payment before release of the goods to the buyer. Alternatively, the draft may be a **time draft**, according to which payment is to be received at some specified time in the future.

4. The importer's bank pays the draft (if it is a sight draft) once it has received evidence that the exporter has fulfilled the conditions set down in the letter of credit. Alternatively, if the draft is a time draft, the correspondent bank accepts the draft (by stamping it "accepted"). By this action, the draft becomes a **bankers acceptance**, a financial instrument that is negotiable and sellable at a discount in the money market.

5. Proceeds from the sale go to the exporter's bank and become credited to the exporter's account in the local currency.

Letters of credit are usually **documentary** letters of credit, meaning that the seller must accompany the draft with invoices, bills of lading, and other documents to demonstrate that it has complied with the terms of the letter. Letters of credit may also be either **revocable** or **irrevocable**. Revocable letters of credit may be revoked, without prior notice, any time before presentation of a draft to the issuing bank. An irrevocable letter of credit, on the other hand, cannot be revoked without the consent of all parties.

In addition, the exporter's bank might be willing to **confirm** a letter of credit received from the foreign correspondent bank. This occurs when the foreign banking institution is well-known and highly respected. In addition, the seller-exporter's bank may be willing to purchase, at a discount, either confirmed or unconfirmed letters of credit, thereby easing the exporter's cash flow. Letters of credit offer advantages to both buyer and seller.

BENEFITS OF LETTERS OF CREDIT

Advantages to Exporter	Advantages to Importer
• Reduces uncertainty by eliminating credit risk so long as issuing bank is of good standing. • Reduces danger that exchange controls, etc., might delay payment. • Can provide protection for cases where an exporter is manufacturing to buyer's specification. This allows for creation of bankers' acceptances, thereby facilitating financing.	• Bank bears responsibility if oversight occurs. Ensures exporter acts in compliance with terms of the deal and that goods are shipped. • Does not tie up cash as does cash in advance. • Expands sources of supply because some firms will only sell on letter of credit.

International billing can also employ **bills of exchange** (also known as a draft) without a letter of credit. A **draft** is a written unconditional order to the importer to pay on presentation (**sight draft**) or at some specified future date (**time draft**). The seller/exporter usually writes and addresses it to the buyer-importer. Again, the correspondent banking system plays a useful role. The exporter (or its domestic bank) forwards the bill to the importer, either directly or through the importer's correspondent bank. The bank also holds the necessary shipping documents and releases these to the importer only upon payment of a sight draft or on signed acceptance of a time draft. A time draft, once accepted, becomes known as a trade acceptance; if signed by the importer's bank, the draft becomes a banker's acceptance.

Besides these payment processes, exporters can always ship goods on **open account**. However, in doing so the exporter exposes itself to all the risks that are attendant on international business transactions: the commercial risk (that the importer will not or cannot pay), as well as the risks of dealing in foreign situations.

T I P

EXPORT FINANCE

Terms of credit need to be carefully and fully specified. Even sight letters of credit can be problematic. If payment is due on sight at the overseas end, documentation takes time to reach the foreign destination. Moreover, not all clients in all countries honour sight letters of credit the same way. For example, the term until payment is due can mean that the clock starts on receipt of the documents at the foreign end of the transaction; or the terms could specify the time as from the date of the bill of lading.

For particularly risky situations, the Export Development Corporation can provide insurance for small businesses on accounts receivable as well as other types of assistance. This normally comes at a cost. In addition, your banker probably has a master insurance agreement for overseas receivables under which you may be able to arrange coverage.

"Unfortunately," says Peter Dawes, senior partner of Warrington International Import/Export Trade Consultants Inc. of Toronto, "there is no government support for an import business and government money for an import/export start-up. The most accessible and visible federal program of export assistance, the Program for Export Market Development (PEMD) requires a track record of at least $250,000 in sales before applicants qualify for the subsidy for travel and/or participation at a foreign trade show." According to Dawes, "the good news is that governments are slowly beginning to understand that the economic benefits of international trade are not confined to exports only, but also to imports."

PROFIT, September 1995, p.54

T I P

These various international trade financing methods have different implications for buyers and sellers. As the terms of the sale and payment get progressively stronger (or demanding), seller's risk decreases while buyer's risk increases. At one end of the risk continuum, payment in advance is most advantageous to sellers. At the other extreme, an open account is most advantageous to buyers. The choice of payment method involves balancing marketing considerations (sales are more likely with more relaxed terms of credit), financial factors (shorter collection periods involve less financial burden), and risk associated with all international transactions, such as transaction, value. and political risk.

METHODS OF FINANCING INTERNATIONAL TRANSACTIONS: RISK RANKINGS

	RISKS	
Most Advantageous to Seller	Sellers'	Buyers'
Payment in advance	NONE	HIGH
Confirmed sight letter of credit	⇓	⇑
Confirmed time letter of credit	⇓	⇑
Unconfirmed letters of credit	⇓	⇑
Sight bill of exchange	⇓	⇑
Time bill of exchange	⇓	⇑
Open account	NONE	HIGH
Most Advantageous to Buyer		

The Role of Banks in International Transactions

The international banking system is central to financial risk management involving international transaction. Bills of exchange and letters of credit are both arranged and managed through the banking system. Given this involvement, firms involved in exporting ought to consult with their banker at an early stage of international trade. Canadian banks have also developed specialized departments that deal primarily with international transactions and many offer additional ways of effecting foreign trade to those mentioned here. All of these financial methods involve costs and risks, costs that sellers will want to build into their pricing structures in advance, otherwise they can substantially eat into profit margins.

Banks also perform roles beyond simply arranging the various bills and letters. For example, the strength of bills of exchange can vary by country. Laws and legal precedents in some nations are such that bills of exchange have very little likelihood of enforcement. Moreover, the buyer can avoid commitment simply by not taking up the documents, leaving the goods to accumulate storage charges. Most Canadian international trade bankers have sufficient experience to know which situations are most problematic. For dealings in most developed countries, bills of exchange are an appropriate method and they are less expensive to arrange than letters of credit. In addition, Canadian banks may be willing to buy an accepted draft, at a discount, especially if the collecting bank at the other end of the transaction has added its "avow" or guarantee. Therefore, it is important to confirm with your banker all the costs associated with bills of exchange and whether the bank will purchase an accepted draft from you and at what discount.

T I P

MANAGING THE RISKS OF INTERNATIONAL TRANSACTIONS

- **Invoice in Canadian dollars.** One way to manage transaction risk is to have invoices denominated in Canadian dollars. This shifts the currency risk to your overseas customer. A variation on this theme is to invoice for inputs such as imported raw materials or intermediate goods in the same currency as it sells its goods. This offsets foreign currency payables against receivables.

- **Hedge Your Risk.** In many instances foreign exchange risk can be off set by using forward contracts or "futures" on the currency involved. For example, suppose your firm must make a payment of £100,000 to a British supplier in 90 days. If the value of the dollar against the British pound decreases, this payable could cost you more dollars than you had been expecting. You can eliminate this risk by purchasing British pounds using a forward contract, a purchase that your banker can arrange. According to the forward contract, your bank agrees to exchange £100,000 for your dollars in 90 days—but at the exchange rate agreed upon now. These so-called "forward exchange rates" are listed daily in the financial sections of most newspapers. There are more ways of hedging foreign risk and your financial institution can provide more information.

T I P

Likewise, banks may also discount confirmed time letters of credit. As with drafts, the risk associated with letters of credit varies by country and, within foreign countries, by the collecting bank. Banks have considerable experience with respect to international transactions. They can advise as to the methods that make the most sense.

With international transactions, business owners have much to consider. Fortunately there is help close at hand. Most banks, the Export Development Corporation, and federal and provincial governments provide guidance, especially with respect to exporting, in the form of seminars, documents, and even on the Internet. In addition, the Export Development Corporation sells insurance on foreign accounts receivable, that may be available through your domestic banker.

SUMMARY

This chapter has reviewed a variety of financing methods that are available to Canadian SMEs. All represent forms of debt financing. Indeed, the financial marketplace continues to evolve. The role of asset-based financing firms, the growing trend to globalization, the rapid pace of deregulation, the movement to establish strategic alliances between suppliers and clients, and the creative financing methods being employed by merchant banks are all very recent developments on the Canadian financing scene. These economic forces are catalysts to change in reshaping the world of finance. Many of the financing vehicles reviewed here may soon be very different. Before exploring further the nature of the forces affecting capital markets in Chapter 9, the next chapter reviews the ultimate stage that constitutes a goal for many owners of small growing business—going public.

GOING PUBLIC

WHAT IS "GOING PUBLIC"?

This is every entrepreneur's dream. Going public. The pot of gold at the end of the rainbow, the bridge to future riches. Your firm has grown and prospered. So far, the firm has been financed to the stage where it has a fully developed product or service, a complete and competent management team, has established a good track record of sales and profits, and can look to the future with a realistic vision of more growth. To this point, the business has been financed at the early stages by angels and, more recently, by institutional venture capital. Your firm faces two tasks in the immediate future.

The first task is paying off the venture capitalists and early investors who have been the source of initial growth capital. Venture capitalists, for example, would have typically invested $2 to $4 million over the past five or six years and would like to make a profitable exit. At their required rate of return of 30 to 40%, this means finding $7 to $15 million.

The second task is to finance the expanded facilities necessary to take advantage of the growth opportunities that lie ahead. For firms in this enviable position, "going public," also known as an initial public offering (IPO), is the way to go. Until now the firm has been owned by a relatively small group of founders and investors (that is, it is "closely held"). For the first time, shares of the firm's common stock will be sold to public shareholders and will also be listed on one of Canada' stock exchanges.

> "We're in a very capital-intensive business, so we needed a sure-fire way of raising capital as the company continues to grow. We viewed our initial public offering as only the start of our public strategy for raising money."
>
> Raymond Simmons, chairman and CEO of CRS Robotics Corp., Burlington, Ont., a PROFIT 100 fast-growth company

The sale of the common stock will result in a firm that is owned by a wider group of investors who will be able to trade in these newly issued shares among themselves on the stock market. The proceeds of the sale of new shares will: allow the early investors and owners to "cash out" all or some of their equity stake, finance further expansion, and cover expenses incurred that are related to the IPO. Sounds perfect, and for many firms, this scenario is reality.

According to the traditional pattern of SME growth, most enterprises start small, as private businesses or partnerships. As growth occurs, and investors risk equity capital, firms usually incorporate so that ownership can be reflected by the proportionate holdings of common stock. Most of the time, the shares are not liquid. Owners, angels, venture capitalists, and others can only buy and sell shares through direct personal interaction. Many business owners hope that their firms will eventually "go public" and command a listing on a stock exchange. Not all businesses achieve sufficient growth to reach this goal. For those few firms that are highly successful, an initial public offering of shares can provide growth capital, share liquidity, and other benefits. For many business owners, going public is, indeed, the gold at the end of the rainbow.

FIRST, THE GOOD NEWS

DY 4 Systems Inc., based in Kanata, Ont., produces ruggedized computer systems for aerospace and military applications. Revenues in fiscal 1996 were $52 million with profits of $5.9 million. With 190 employees, DY 4 went public in 1993, selling its shares for $12. The proceeds of the sales allowed DY 4 to become the dominant source of advanced electronic systems that could withstand extremes of temperature, impact, and humidity. Since the March 1993 IPO, the firm split its stock three for one and sold at a split-adjusted price of $16.50 during 1996.

For many business owners, going public represents the culmination of their efforts: rewards, both financial and non-financial, for their vision, perseverance, and hard work. But not for all.

THEN THE BAD NEWS

A few months after DY 4's IPO, a nearby business, AIT Corporation of Nepean Ont., part of Ottawa's Silicon Valley North, also went public. AIT produces travel document readers and video surveillance and digital recording devices for security systems. AIT reported $16.3 million in revenues for fiscal 1996, on which it reported a loss of $13.4 million. Their share price, originally issued at $12 per share when it went public in September of 1993 was selling in the $3 range in early 1997.

While many growing firms hope to "go public," very few, perhaps one percent, will actually take the leap. Those that do provide the incentives for venture capitalists and other investors to get involved in entrepreneurial firms at an early stage. Business owners who seek a market listing and an IPO need to plan early for the event and to anticipate what is likely to happen. In this chapter we identify:

- the process of issuing shares, for the first time, on a stock exchange;
- the legal and regulatory framework surrounding sales of stock;
- costs and benefits of an IPO;
- listing requirements of Canada's various stock markets;
- alternatives to an IPO; and
- recent initiatives aimed at easing access to public equity capital for SMEs.

Taken together, the material we present in this chapter is geared to arm small business owners with knowledge that allows them to prepare, well in advance, for going public. In this chapter we describe the mechanism for the IPO process, myths and realities, and tips on how to flourish.

WHY GO PUBLIC?

We begin by outlining the terminology and the process of going public; that is, of issuing and trading new shares in public markets.

SOME TERMS

Authorized shares are the number of shares that, according to its charter, the firm may eventually offer for sale. Usually, firms issue a fraction of the number of authorized shares and these are termed, logically enough, **issued shares**. From time to time, firms can repurchase issued shares. For this and other reasons, the number of **outstanding shares** can differ from the number of issued shares.

With an initial public offering, common shares of a company owned by relatively few founders and investors are offered for sale to the general public for the first time. Normally, an IPO is accompanied with a listing on one or more Canadian or international stock exchanges. In the future, the firm may again raise capital through the sale of shares to the public; however, subsequent offerings are called *seasoned* offerings because the firm already has shares listed on the market. Following initial and seasoned offerings, investors can use the medium of the stock exchange to trade with each other in the shares of the firm. An IPO affords the firm several advantages.

The primary advantage of an IPO and the associated stock exchange listing is that it allows the firm to access a pool of capital that is much larger than it would be had the shares of the firm remained held by a relatively small group of original owners and investors. The firm is able to tap both into more investors as well as a broader range of investors. Thus, an IPO provides the

ADVANTAGES OF AN IPO

Owners of most companies have set going public as a long-term goal early in the life of the firm. Their reasons for doing so include:

- Going public provides the only means of accessing large amounts, usually more than $5 million, of equity expansion capital.
- It provides private investors and venture capital investors with a means of cashing out on their investment.
- It provides the founders with the ability to convert their equity into cash.
- It allows employees to take part in the success of the firm through stock options or employer-subsidized share purchase plans. Such arrangements are often used as a means of providing compensation and incentives to employees.
- It provides credibility to suppliers and customers.
- It means that the firm can use its common shares as a medium of exchange to acquire other companies.

firm with equity capital of a far greater magnitude than would ordinarily be available from other sources. For example, IPOs in excess of $20 million are not only common, but some investment dealers are unwilling to participate in deals of smaller value.

"As a high-technology company, our biggest challenge is to get lots of exceptional people. And those people are attracted to a chance to have equity, to create some net worth outside their pay cheque....The second thing is that it [IPO] gives credibility for your customers...Being a public company says your finances and the scrutiny that has been placed upon you have met a very high standard."

Brian Semkiw, CEO, Rand Technology, Mississauga, Ont., a PROFIT growth company

Once the shares of the firm trade publicly, the market participants get to know the firm's players and performance. Investment analysts, brokers, and other investors monitor the firm's
performance. This facilitates raising additional capital through
future seasoned offerings and through sales of debt or equity
securities directly to institutional investors, known as "private
placements."

From the point of view of founders and early investors, an
IPO reduces personal risk. Until the public offering, founders'
personal wealth is often concentrated in the firm. With a public
offering, founders can convert some of their holdings to cash and
use the proceeds to diversify their holdings. An IPO is also venture capitalists' favoured means of exit.

> "We had a...secondary financing from...Quorum Growth [a venture
> capital firm whose] philosophy is to be involved with businesses that are
> looking for funding to take them from just after the start-up phase to the
> next level...About two years later when we went public, they recognized
> about three of four times their investment."
>
> Brian Semkiw, CEO, Rand Technology, Mississauga, Ont., a PROFIT growth company

There are, of course, drawbacks to an IPO. These include the
significant investment of management time associated with both
the initial process of issuing shares as well as with the ongoing
requirements for reporting and shareholder relations. Moreover,
going public formalizes the management structure of the firm.
The owner-managers no longer have free reign: they must report
to the representatives of the now-public ownership of the firm,
the board of directors. While it is traditionally believed that loss
of control is a disadvantage, it is not unusual for founders to
retain controlling interest in the firm.

Considerable costs are also associated with an IPO. To provide a framework for understanding these costs, we turn now to
a description of the process by which a firm goes public.

THE PROCESS OF GOING PUBLIC

CANADIANA GENETICS INC.

Based in Carstairs, Alt., Canadiana Genetics is a new technology-based firm that uses embryo transfer technology to improve the genetic quality and productivity of beef and dairy cattle. Sales in 1996 are expected to reach $3.34 million with profits in excess of $1 million. The firm needed cash to support its rapid growth. Therefore Canadiana planned an IPO on the Alberta Stock Exchange for June 1996 to raise $2 million, half of which was earmarked for acquisitions, with the rest going to debt retirement and capacity expansion. The cost of the IPO will reach $80,000 plus an underwriter commission of six to 10% of the issue. According to Terry Gudzowsky, chairman and managing director of Canadiana, "This thing could be huge."

Canadiana Genetics, hopes to emulate successful IPOs such as Leitch Technology Corp. and Skyjack Inc. In both these cases share prices increased by more than 300% since going public in 1994.

"IPO Market Rebounding" by Paul Vieira Reprinted with permission from *The Globe and Mail,* April 23, 1996, p. B27.

Before your firm can begin the process of issuing shares to the public, it needs to find an underwriter willing to undertake the offering. In making a selection, factors to consider include: the underwriter's track record, especially with firms in your industry; the level of fees and commissions, which can differ widely across underwriters; and the size of the issue. The larger and more established your business and the larger the offering, the more choice of underwriters you will have. Such offerings attract the attention of the premier investment dealers who would like to underwrite large offerings of good businesses. For small firms with less of a track record, there may not be much choice. Underwriters differ in terms of prestige and areas of specialization. The larger and more established underwriters are reluctant to work with deals of less than $20 million. Moreover, before agreeing, underwriters will undertake due diligence, a detailed examination of the firm, to assure itself of the fundamentals of the enterprise.

Once an underwriter has been secured, the issuance process begins with the **pre-underwriting conferences**, meetings at which your firm and its underwriter come to agreement on the amount of capital to raise, the type of security to be sold, and the terms of the agreement between the firm and the underwriter. The pre-underwriting conferences culminate in the preparation of a **preliminary prospectus**. This document fully discloses all salient information about your company. The intent of the prospectus is to protect investors from misrepresentation. Therefore, it needs to include audited financial statements, complete descriptions of the terms of the issue, and identification of all potential developments that could substantively affect the firm. The preliminary prospectus does not yet, however, include the specific terms of issue price, size of issue, or underwriter commission.

Once complete, the preliminary prospectus is filed with the provincial securities regulatory body that acts as overseer for the jurisdiction of the stock exchange on which the shares are to be listed (for example, the Quebec Securities Commission in Quebec, the Ontario Securities Commission in Ontario, etc.). During this filing period, regulators examine the preliminary prospectus to identify omissions or misrepresentations. Regulators may then seek additional information from the issuer or its underwriter. This filing period is often set, by statute, as a minimum period that can be extended in the event that substantial revisions to the preliminary prospectus are required. If your firm has not done its homework and is not "market ready," amendments can be plentiful and time consuming.

Once satisfied, the securities commission clears the preliminary prospectus and, with the addition of the information on issuing price, size of issue, and underwriter's commission, the preliminary prospectus becomes the **final prospectus**. These additions are usually made late on the day before the final prospectus is submitted to the securities commission for final clearance. The final filing is immediately preceded by the signing of the underwriting agreement that details the sale of the securities from the issuing firm to the underwriter and the closing date on which the securities are purchased from your firm by the underwriter. The securities commission ordinarily provides final clearance of the final prospectus on this same day in order that the underwriter can begin to sell the securities to the public.

The underwriter sells securities either on a "firm commitment" or "best efforts" basis. In the firm commitment transaction, the underwriting agreement specifies the price at which the underwriter buys the securities from your firm and the underwriter purchases the securities from the issuer at that price on the closing date. According to this type of transaction, the firm is guaranteed receipt of the funds implied by the firm commitment price and the underwriter must resell the shares on the market. The underwriting risk is that the value of the shares will decrease between closing date and the date of issuance to the market. Under the best efforts approach, the underwriter conducts best efforts to sell the shares but it is the issuing firm that is exposed to market fluctuations and the impact of other events on the share price. Most IPOs carried out on the Toronto Stock Exchange are undertaken on a best efforts basis.

Under ideal conditions, an IPO can take as little as three months from inception to closing (one month for pre-underwriting conferences and preparation of preliminary prospectus; one month for filing and final clearance, one month from final clearance until closing). This period can extend considerably if the firm is not market-ready. Preparation of the preliminary prospectus requires additional time for lawyers and accountants to assemble the necessary information. It is also more likely that regulators will identify deficiencies and that such deficiencies will take longer to rectify.

Going public and listing on a stock exchange are usually undertaken together, but are actually separate decisions. A firm can issue shares without being listed, but its shares then trade on an unlisted, over-the-counter, basis. In Canada, very little trading occurs on the over-the-counter market and the liquidity of the shares is very low. For most firms, this eliminates one of the big advantages of going public. In practice, therefore, going public and stock market listing are almost synonymous.

The issuance process is costly, particularly with regard to the time commitments required of the business owners and senior managers. In the next section, we identify and estimate these expenses more specifically.

COSTS OF ISSUANCE

There are three categories of costs associated with going public:

- the immediate and direct costs of the issue;
- the immediate indirect costs; and
- the ongoing direct and indirect costs.

Direct and Immediate Costs of IPOs

Going public entails significant costs. The first major expense of an IPO are costs associated with preparation of the prospectus, a process that requires large amounts of professional time. Legal and accounting costs are a substantial component of the total cost of prospectus preparation, a total that can range from $200,000 to $400,000. In addition to the cost of the prospectus, the underwriter receives a commission in return for their involvement. The commission is larger, as a percentage, for small issues and decreases with issue size.

ISSUE AND UNDERWRITING COSTS

Accleading to Dr. Vijay Jog, of the School of Business at Carleton University, the expected cost of an "average" IPO is $340,000 plus seven percent of the value of the offering. For IPOs of the size usually issued in Canada, Dr. Jog shows that total cost has both fixed and variable components. Specifically, Jog finds that, on average:

- Issuing Expenses = $170,000 + 2% of IPO Value
- Underwriting commission = $170,000 + 5% of IPO Value, and
- Total IPO Expenses = $340,000 + 7% of IPO Value

Vijay Jog, "The Climate for Canadian Initial Public Offerings." In *Capital Market Issues*, edited by P. Halpern. Ottawa: Industry Canada, 1997.

There is yet an additional cost to going public, known as "under-pricing." Firms that issue an IPO are new to the stock market. As such, investors have no historical benchmark prices on which to base their valuation. Issuers and their underwriters attempt to put a reasonable value on the firm, but such valuations are prone to error. On average, it appears that the subscription price for new securities is set a little lower than the price the new securities fetch within the first day of trading. Underwriters appear to be "leaving a little on the table" to entice IPO buyers and ensure that the issue is fully subscribed. Underpricing shows up as an immediate increase in the selling prices of the IPO shares (often within minutes of the initial availability for purchase). For IPOs issued between 1984 and 1992, underpricing averaged 5.67%.[1] This means that issuer firms received less than their shares were actually worth. However, as the following chart illustrates, the amount of underpricing has decreased in recent years.

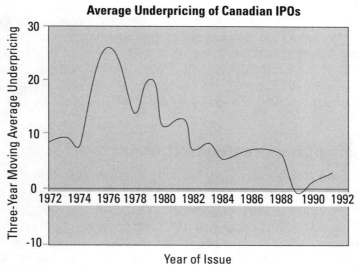

Data Drawn from Jog, 1997

Indirect Costs of IPOs

The financial expenses of going public are not the only costs. In addition, the firm faces indirect costs. These include:

• **Diversion of management time**. The task of prospectus preparation requires that company personnel redirect time and energy away from their usual work to cooperate in the accumulation of

[1] Vijay Jog, "The Climate for Canadian Initial Public Offerings." In *Capital Market Issues*, P. Halpern, ed. Ottawa: Industry, Canada, 1997.

the information necessary to prepare the prospectus. Top management spends significant amounts of time working with underwriters, lawyers, etc. According to the Conference Board of Canada, the cost of diversion of management time during the pre-listing period is equivalent to the full-time commitment of at least one senior executive![2]

- **Disclosure Costs**. One of the requirements of becoming a publicly listed company is the demand of the exchange and the regulatory bodies for full financial disclosure. This requires putting into the public domain information that was once private. This may entail both cash expenses as well as additional demands on management time and energy.

- **Loss of privacy**. The reporting requirements noted above place the firm under continuous public scrutiny. Professional security analysts will follow the firm and actively seek out private information. The disclosure requirement, intended to protect the public shareholders, mean that competitors can also more easily identify the firm's strategies and other information.

Ongoing Direct and Indirect Costs

Disclosure requirements are not only in effect at the time of listing. Once the firm is listed on the stock exchange, it must continue to abide by the ongoing disclosure requirements of the stock exchange, the securities commission, and other regulatory bodies. In addition, maintaining shareholder relations frequently represents a material financial cost. Some of these are obvious: the costs of preparing, printing, and mailing annual and interim reports; the costs of annual meetings and the attendant documentation; and the costs of maintaining careful records. Other costs are less obvious and less direct. These include: the significant quantities of management time dealing with the public and institutional investors, the costs of monitoring insider trading activities, and the indirect cost associated with diversion of management time.

[2] Andrews, Michael. *Initial Public Offerings: The Experience of Eight Canadian Growth Companies*, The Conference Board of Canada, Ottawa: May 1995.

SOME ADVICE FROM AN EXPERT

According to Douglas Hart, of Toronto's Hart & Associates Management Consultants Ltd., "Companies need to improve internally before they go public. There's a whole new accountability issue to deal with, a board of directors, shareholders. It can be quite onerous for a small company."

Reprinted with permission from The Globe and Mail, April 23, 1996, B27

T I P

In spite of the attractive features and the costs of going public, there remains always a significant possibility that the IPO process will not live up to its advantages. This is because many firms listed on stock markets do not trade frequently—some go months between trades. Thin trading, in fact, is the norm on Canadian stock markets. The result could be that the advantages associated with stock liquidity may not be realized. Stockholders seeking to sell their shares may be obliged to give up a substantial discount from the security's true value if they need to sell shares quickly.

A PROFILE OF A SUCCESSFUL IPO

What kind of offering can navigate today's cut-throat IPO market? They must demonstrate excellent, experienced management, screaming market need, a position of leadership and a dynamic business plan. The offer needs to be priced at the low end of what's fair. And investors are tired of new stocks that plunge in price, so expect all forecasts to go under a microscope. And if you're not yet a living saint? "You could find a merchant banker to buy the company, help you carry out your strategy and take you public," says Bob Calder of BMG North America Ltd., a stamped metal auto-parts manufacturer in Cambridge, Ont.

"The Tough New Market for IPOs" PROFIT, December 1994

T I P

MEETING THE LISTING REQUIREMENTS OF STOCK EXCHANGES

In addition to compliance with securities regulations, firms that go public and elect to be listed on a stock market must meet the listing requirements of the prospective stock exchange. Most trading in Canada takes place on one of four stock exchanges: the Toronto Stock Exchange, the Montreal Stock Exchange, the Vancouver Stock Exchange, and the Alberta Stock Exchange.

THE MAJOR CANADIAN STOCK EXCHANGES

The **Toronto Stock Exchange** (TSE) is Canada's primary securitied exchange, accounting for almost 80% of trading, by value. Approximately 1,400 securities[3] trade on the TSE, including common shares, multiple classes of shares, warrants, and other securities. Even though the firms listed on the TSE are among the largest in Canada, not all of them trade as frequently as might be expected. Many securities go days and weeks between trades. As a result, the prices seen for these securities in newspapers and other listings can be "stale."

Trades on the TSE are executed through a computer-assisted trading system (CATS), one that is being emulated on other international stock markets. In addition, the TSE is linked electronically to several US Stock Exchanges. This enables direct trading of inter-listed shares.

The **Montreal Exchange** (ME). Approximately 1,000 issues of securities representing about 500 companies trade on the Montreal Exchange Canada's second largest. Trading on the ME represented about 15% of trading in Canada, by value. During the 1980s a dramatic increase in new listing activity on the ME followed from the introduction, in 1979, of the Quebec Stock Savings Plan. This plan was an initiative of the provincial government, whereby tax incentives were offered for individuals who invested in Quebec-based companies. In addition, the plan reimbursed companies for a portion of their listing expenses. This, in turn, prompted many Quebec-based firms to seek a listing on the ME. Like the TSE, the ME has electronic links to US stock markets and trades on the exchange are facilitated by its own computer-assisted trading system.

The **Vancouver Stock Exchange** (VSE), accounting for less than 5% of the value of shares traded in the country, is the third largest in Canada. The VSE has a reputation as a speculative market for smaller companies,

---

[3] The precise number of listings varies over time.

often resource-based firms, sporting higher risks. Following "Black Friday" in 1984, when the prices of several VSE share issues fell almost simultaneously, provincial regulators have worked hard to improve its image. However, a tarnished reputation takes time to polish.

The **Alberta Stock Exchange** (ASE) is Canada's fourth stock market. The exchange is of particular interest to SMEs and policy makers because of its facility to allow listings of relatively small firms. The Junior Capital Pools (JCP) provides a mechanism whereby quite small firms can obtain an early infusion of equity capital, a provisional Alberta Stock Exchange listing, and the opportunity to raise additional capital. The JCP concept will be described in more detail at a later point in this chapter.

Listing confers several advantages to firms and allows investors to trade in the firm's securities among themselves.

ADVANTAGES OF LISTING AND TRADING IN THE MARKET

- Founders of the firm and early investors in the business can convert their share holdings to cash much more readily than they could by means of private transactions.
- Trading patterns of the share price provide the firm with important information. For example, the price at which shares trade reflects agreement among market participants as to the value of the firm's equity; variations in the price reflect investor uncertainty or risk.
- A liquid public market for the shares provides the firm with an additional means of attracting and compensating staff.

A stock exchange listing provides publicity and credibility for the listed firm because listed firms are required to provide ongoing and publicly available disclosure. To obtain a listing on any of these stock markets, firms must meet a variety of minimum conditions. These differ across stock exchanges and by industry sector. In addition, stock markets frequently update listing requirements. To provide a sense of the listing conditions, the table that follows illustrates the listing requirements for industrial companies as of late 1996.

Sample Listing Requirements for Canadian Stock Markets*

	Stock Exchange*			
Requirement	Toronto	Montreal	Vancouver	Alberta
Net Tangible Assets	$1,000,000	$1,000,000 tangible net worth	$900,000	$400,000
Working Capital	Adequate to carry on business	Adequate to carry on business	Adequate to carry on business	Adequate to carry on business
Earnings Record	$100,000 or more before taxes in fiscal year preceding listing	$100,000 or more before taxes in fiscal year preceding listing	At least $100,000 before income taxes in year preceding listing	History of profitable operations
Cash Flow Requirement	Pre-tax cash flow of $400,000 in year preceding listing			
Float	Public distribution of at least 1,000,000 freely tradable shares with aggregate market value of at least $2,000,000; 300 public shareholders each owning at least one board lot	At least $1,000,000 and 1,000,000 publicly held securities free of trading restrictions	At least 1,000,000 shares without resale restrictions of aggregate market value $1,800,000 held by at least 300 shareholders each with at least one board lot	At least 500,000 shares held by at least 300 public shareholders each holding at least one board lot. At least 20% of shares must be publicly held and free from trading restrictions

* These requirements are illustrative only. In each case, alternative requirements exist and, for some exchanges, exemptions are available.

ALTERNATIVES TO AN IPO

Businesses can make use of two alternative methods of going public: a so-called "back door listing" and the Junior Capital Pool Program within the province of Alberta. The back door listing provides a faster and less expensive means of obtaining a stock market listing. The JCP offers a means by which firms that would not otherwise qualify for a stock market listing (because they at early stages of development) can obtain both an initial injection of funds and a provisional stock market listing.

In addition to these means of raising capital from the public, many firms can raise capital by selling securities directly to institutions or individuals. We will also review these so-called "private placements" in this section.

The Back Door Listing

Also called a "reverse takeover," the back door listing occurs by means of the amalgamation of two firms: the private company seeking to go public and a so-called "shell" company. A shell company is a firm that, for historical reasons, has a listing on the stock exchange but which is now inactive.[4] According to the transaction, the two firms combine by means of the shell company's purchase of the assets of the private business. It effects this takeover by issuing shares to the shareholders of the private firm. As a result, the shareholders of the private firm now control the shell, which continues to be listed on the exchange. Once joined, the shell company continues to trade and the once-private firm can raise capital by a subsequent offering of shares of the erstwhile shell company. This process avoids prospectus costs and immediate disclosure requirements associated with an IPO. However, this saving is partially offset by the cost of purchasing the shell company.

Alberta's Junior Capital Pools

The Junior Capital Pool (JCP) program was initiated in 1986 with the explicit objective of providing junior start-up companies with "an enhanced opportunity to become listed on the Alberta Stock Exchange."[5] Under the current regulations, the founders of the firm must make a minimum cash investment of $100,000 in the shares of the firm. The firm can then make a JCP IPO on the Alberta Stock Exchange by selling additional shares to the public. The JCP listing differs from a regular Alberta Stock Exchange listing in that it is transitory. The listing expires within 18 months unless the firm makes a "major transaction." A major transaction

Seprotech Systems Inc. went public November 30, 1993 on the Alberta Stock Exchange with its shares selling for $2 per share. This Ottawa firm, which specializes in the manufacture and sales of water purification equipment, reported a loss in fiscal 1996 of $1.7 million on sales of $3.5 million. Its shares were trading in the $1.50 range in early 1997. Subsequently, a labour-sponsored venture capital fund injected $2.4 million into the young firm. Too small to list on the Toronto Stock Exchange, Seprotech obtained early capitalization through its listing on the Alberta Stock Exchange.

---

[4] For such firms, the price listed on the exchange reflects its potential value in a reverse takeover. This value prompts owners or trustees of firms that have ceased business operations to retain the firm's listing.

[5] Alberta Stock Exchange Circular No. 7, p. 7-1.

usually involves the acquisition of a significant asset purchase that is financed by a further offering of shares through the JCP market. Once a major transaction is completed, the firm's listing status changes from a JCP to a regular listing.

The Alberta Stock Exchange, in enacting the JCP concept, has also established a variety of regulations designed to protect public investors. These include escrow requirements that forbid the founders of the JCP firm to trade until the initial listing, and only one third of the escrowed shares may trade annually for the subsequent three-year period. In addition, the exchange places tight requirements on the firm for complete and timely disclosure. To maintain their listing, JCP firms must grow and establish themselves if they hope to access the funds to complete a major transaction. Firms that fail to do so, lose their listing.

SOME JCP PERFORMANCE RESULTS

According to Michael Robinson, a researcher at the University of Calgary:[6]

• more than $77 million has been raised in 405 JCP IPOs between 1986 and 1992;
• JCP firms have raised more than $475 million by means of post-IPO issues between 1986 and 1992;
• almost 86% of firms that used the JCP to go public between 1986 and 1992 had completed a major transaction by the end of 1992.

Private Placements

In a private placement, firms raise capital by selling securities directly to one or more investors, bypassing the process by which securities are issued to the general public. For a private placement, the investor(s) must have agreed to take up the entire offering of the issued securities as an investment (that is, not for immediate resale or redistribution). Investors who are eligible to

[6] Michael Robinson, "Raising Equity Capital for Small and Medium Sized Enterprises Using Canada's Public Equity Markets," in *Capital Market Issues*, edited by P. Halpern. Ottawa: Industry Canada, 1997.

LIMITED MARKET DEALERS CAN HELP

T
I
P

Finding capital is a process that is costly in the sense that it consumes a great deal of time that the business owner could other wise devote to managing the firm. Just as large companies can employ an investment dealer to help with issuances of common stock or bonds, there are agents available who can help smaller firms raise capital. Known as Limited Market Dealers, these intermediaries are accredited by the Ontario Securities Commission (in Ontario) to act as agents for small firms who are seeking private placements.

Limited market dealers are becoming more important as the markets for small firm finance become increasingly diverse and sophisticated. Limited market dealers specialize in knowing about the various aspects of small firm financing. Their business is to understand the preferences of venture capitalists, asset-based finance firms, mezzanine financiers, export financing alternatives, and other potential sources of capital.

T I P

buy a private placement of securities are usually institutions such as insurance companies or pension funds or existing significant shareholders of the firm. Securities regulators deem such investors "exempt" purchasers who, because of their level of knowledge, investment sophistication, or close relationship with the issuer, do not need the protection afforded by a prospectus.

In Ontario, purchasers may not usually resell the securities for a minimum holding period of at least six months. Although the buyer does not have to be protected by a prospectus, an offering memorandum is generally used. The transaction is arranged either directly between issuer and purchaser, or through an investment dealer that acts as the issuer's agent. Private placements can be either debt or equity securities and offer several important advantages over a public offering of securities.

In general, however, the advantages of a private placement outweigh the disadvantages. It is, therefore, no surprise that private placements are occurring more often.

PROS AND CONS OF PRIVATE PLACEMENTS

Pros:
- Because the seller is not making an issue of securities to the (relatively) uninformed public, prospectus preparation is not necessary and is replaced by the much less comprehensive (and less expensive) offering memorandum.
- Underwriter commissions are low relative to those involved in a public issue.
- Private placements can be arranged more quickly than a public offering.
- Public disclosure is minimized, although the private negotiations involved likely mean that the purchaser is intimately familiar with the issuing firm.

Cons:
- For the issuer, a private placement taps into a narrower range of funds than a public offering.
- In general, sale of the private placement is made at a discount to prevailing market price.
- From the purchaser's perspective, the holding period reduces liquidity and flexibility of the investor's portfolio.

GOVERNMENT INITIATIVES TO ENCOURAGE IPOS

Governments recognize that a viable capital market for SMEs requires a favourable environment for IPOs.

Without the potential for exit through an IPO, venture capitalists and informal investors are reluctant to endow SMEs with risk capital. Therefore, governments have undertaken several initiatives intended to stimulate IPOs.

WHY IPOs ARE IMPORTANT TO SMEs

IPOs are important to small businesses in general. An active IPO market:
- encourages individuals to start a business because they can envision a profitable exit;
- investors, such as venture capitalists and angels, are likely to be more active when IPO markets are lively;
- for knowledge-based and conventional firms IPOs provide a means of access to significant amounts of equity capital; and
- the climate for IPOs varies over the economic cycle. The owners of businesses that are not currently at the IPO stage can monitor the IPO market to learn when the timing is best to approach venture capitalists and angels.

Provincial Stock Savings Plans

Patterned on the Quebec Stock Savings Plan, several provinces have implemented or are considering stock savings plans. These plans have two objectives: to facilitate access to equity for local SMEs, and to encourage individuals to invest in SMEs. The plans allow individuals who purchase the shares of specified securities to receive (sometimes substantial) tax concessions on provincial income taxes. The write-off proportion varies by firm and over time. For example, investors could at one time write-off as much as 150% of the purchase price of the stock of small firms. By buying newly issued shares under the terms of, for example, the Quebec Stock Savings Plan (QSSP):

• issuing firms obtain investment capital;

• individuals who may not otherwise have invested in the stock market do so. Thus, stock market investing is demystified and new investors are more apt to invest further; and

• individuals receive the benefits of share ownership while enjoying a tax holiday on the costs.

Typically, the tax benefit is greater for small firms than for large. When the original Quebec Stock Savings Plan was introduced in 1979 it was hailed as an important innovation, one that encouraged both individuals to participate in new issues of small firms and growing businesses to issue equity. As a result, investors and lobby organizations pressed for similar plans to be undertaken in other provinces, with some success.

More recent evidence challenges the efficiency of these initiatives. According to Dr. Jean-Marc Suret, a Quebec researcher who has carried out an extensive study of the Quebec Stock Savings Plan, "listing securities on the stock exchange via tax incentives has been a very ineffective stimulant in the case of small companies [and that] ... the plan has probably had a perverse effect, driving many disappointed investors out of this market forever." Dr. Suret claims that the plan has not had the desired effect of financing small companies and that the only perceptible effect for large companies is that the plan has reduced the taxes paid by investors who participated. Given these findings and the budget deficits that face most governments, the future of tax-incentive stock purchase plans is dim.

SCORs: Only in the US you say? Pity.

SCORs are Small Corporate Offering Registrations. They enable owners of SMEs to raise equity capital by originating their own offering with their regular lawyers and accountants. Initiated in the mid-1980s in the US, SCORs are an attempt to remove regulatory burdens from small businesses and make acquisition of capital less costly. Only non-public companies are eligible to use SCORs.[7] Using SCORs, issuing firms in the US can raise up to $1,000,000 in a 12-month period.[8] SCORs must be filed in the particular state in which potential investors live. As of February 1995, 42 states accept SCOR filings and the Pacific Stock Exchange provides a secondary market in which SCOR stocks are traded.[9]

SCORs have two important benefits that prompt their consideration for adoption in Canada. First, the secondary market for SCOR stocks provides informal investors or venture capitalists with a means of trading in (and exiting from) their investments—even before the firm issues an IPO. This liquidity provides potential, but currently inactive, investors with liquidity. Second, SCORs provide an institutionalized instrument by which small firms can achieve many of the benefits of a public listing at a fraction of the cost of an IPO. In particular, SCORs provide firms not yet sufficiently established to go public by the traditional route with an early means of raising equity capital from the public.

Unfortunately, SCORs are not yet available in Canada (although JCPs on the Alberta Stock Exchange are similar in many ways to SCORs). SCORs may be an attractive means of facilitating access to equity funds in amounts that fall between amounts usually supplied by venture capitalists and commonly invested by angels. This is a gap that remains to be filled in Canada.

---

[7] Firms must be exempt from the reporting obligations of the *Securities Exchange Act* (1934) under Rule 504 of Regulation D. This is an exemption from prospectus requirements for which must non-public companies can qualify.

[8] The condition is that the firm has at least 10% equity capital equal to the amount of capital being raised.

[9] Listing requirements include a minimum of $500,000 in net tangible assets, $750,000 in net worth, and have a minimum of 150,000 shares and at least 250 shareholders.

IPOS AND THE SMALL BUSINESS LANDSCAPE

There are two conditions for successful IPOs. First, the market must be receptive, but the market for IPOs is particularly volatile. In 1986, more than 70 IPOs were registered on the Toronto Stock Exchange alone. In the year following the 1987 stock market crash, there were four IPOs on the TSE. In 1995 when interest rates were rising, dealers were reluctant to underwrite IPOs, but in 1996 some 64 IPOs hit the market.

Second, for an IPO the firm's "house must be in order." Clearly, traditional IPOs are for firms that have their product or service fully developed and a mature management team in place. This is less true for a listing through a JCP. For JCP businesses, neither the business idea nor the management team needs to be completely refined. Indeed, some JCP initial listings have not specified the industry in which the firm will eventually operate.

SME Risk and Growth Grid

Stage of product and market development

	Technically trained owner-founder	Multiple owners. Few experienced or trained managers	Multiple owners with a financial professional involved	Multiple owners with marketing and management abilities	Fully developed management team
Second stage production					IPOs
First stage production					
Early commercialization stage of product or service			JCPs		
Prototype stage or product or service					
Concept stage of product or service					
→ **Stage of management development**	Technically trained owner-founder	Multiple owners. Few experienced or trained managers	Multiple owners with a financial professional involved	Multiple owners with marketing and management abilities	Fully developed management team

In 1995, the Conference Board of Canada published a study that reported on the experiences of eight Canadian firms that had gone public. With their permission, a brief summary of their findings is provided at the end of this chapter. These experiences reflect a range of what business owners might expect with an IPO.

PREPARING FOR AN IPO

Taking your company public is a major milestone in the evolution of the enterprise. To prepare, Hubert Marleau makes the following suggestions.[10]

- "Prepare a comprehensive business plan. Underwriters are far more likely to consider a well-documented financial proposal than a "back of the envelope" presentation. Succinctly cover your objectives and strategies in addition to providing backgrounds on senior managers. Include your financial history for the past three years, and more importantly a detailed forecast. But don't exceed a 24-month period: underwriters are very sceptical about financial information that reaches out too far.

- Ensure that proper senior management is in place. It is my experience that young fast-growing companies usually need to professionalize their management before a public issue.

- Organize your house from a corporate and legal perspective. It's imperative that your corporate records are updated, operating permits are valid, you comply with laws to which you are subject, and outstanding litigation is under control.

- Finally, do your homework when selecting an underwriter. Speak to several firms to clarify what each offers, how they will manage the issue, fees, etc. There is great value in building a long-term relationship with your underwriter and their commitment to your firm should be the determinant factor."

Hubert Marleau's comments are a fitting way to end this chapter. They point to the need to ensure good financial management and good record keeping from a very early stage in the firm's development and they emphasize the importance of sound professional management. These are suggestions that relate to every phase of raising capital.

---

[10] Hubert Marleau is chairman and CEO of Marleau, Lemire Inc., a Montreal securities dealer specializing in the small-cap market. This section is based on his comments recorded in PROFIT, September 1995, p. 55.

Myths and Realities of IPOs

Myths	Reality
• IPOs are guaranteed winners	Not necessarily, selectivity is key. A recent survey of the Toronto Stock Exchange's 1994 IPOs by PROFIT magazine found that only 18 of the 39 stocks listed increased between 1994 and 1996. Twenty declined in value while one remained static.
• Size counts	One of the best performers from the 1994 IPO went public with an issue of $4 million. More important is the track record of management and the firm's profitability.
• Winners are those firms with innovative technology and price leadership	Again, not necessarily. Those firms that demonstrated consistent profitability, long-term owner-management, and diversity in their customer base were the winners. In other words, while technological innovation is important, a track record is critical.
• An IPO only benefits the brass	The majority of high growth IPOs used their stock to reward all or most of their employees. If employees bought early (and didn't sell), they were all much more financially secure than they were in 1994. Wolf Haessler, president of Skyjack Inc., a manufacturer of hydraulic scissors-style lifts on four-wheeled chassis, projects the win-win mentality into all his dealings. "I always try to leave a dollar on the table for the other guy. The next time he sees you coming, he'll be happy to see you instead of running for cover."

Myths and Realities of IPOs, PROFIT, Summer 1996.

Company Description	Date of IPO (Exchange)	Amount Raised	Issue Price (Price as at Sept 1, 1996)	Fees and Issue Expenses
Beamscope Canada, founded in 1982, is a distributor of computer equipment suitable for home use. It holds the rights for Canadian wholesale distribution of Nintendo and selected Sega products as well as numerous name brand and third-party software, accessories, and other products.	Nov. 1993 (TSE)	$16.65 million	$7.00	Underwriter: $1,082,468 Prospectus (est.):$450,000
Calian Technology Ltd. designs, manufactures, and integrates electronic systems for applications in the space, satellite communications and defence markets. Founded in 1982, this space and defence subcontractor provides space and communications ground systems to the federal government and internationally.	Sept. 1993 (TSE)	$12.9 million	$4.25 ($3.50)	Underwriter: $838,695 Prospectus (est.): $400,000
Computer Brokers of Canada purchases and resells to retailers computer hardware and accessories. The firm was founded in 1985. A portion of the proceeds of the IPO was used to repay shareholder loans to an investor in the firm.	April 1993 (TSE)	$16.1 million	$6.25 (n.a.)	Underwriter: $1,121,250 Prospectus (est.): $400,000
ID Biomedical Corp. is a commercial developer of medical products and technologies related to human infectious diseases. In part, it operates by licensing development activities to academic researchers with the goal of commercializing basic research findings. The firm was founded in 1991. It subsequently listed on the Montreal Exchange and then, late, on the Toronto Stock Exchange.	Nov. 1993 (VSE)	$2 million	$2.50 ($8.10)	Underwriter: $1,082,468 Prospectus: $450,000
Maxon Energy Inc. acquires, explores, and develops oil and gas properties in Alberta and Saskatchewan. The firm was rounded in 1981. It uses independent contractors to work properties in which it plans production.	May 1993 (ASE)	$1.2 million plus $0.68 million via option exercise		Underwriter: 8% of IPO plus option on future shares Prospectus (est.) : $40,000
Founded in 1949, **Mullen Trucking Ltd.** operates a fleet of more than 300 tractor units and 400 trailers. The firm has expanded into oil field services and has grown internally and through acquisitions.	December 1993	$9.56 million	$4.50 (10.50)	Underwriter: $573,750 Prospectus: $200,000
Royal Aviation Inc. was founded in 1979 as a firm that focused on aerial spraying, aerial forest fire-fighting and, related services. In 1992, the firm expanded into charter passenger airline services and as an air tour operator operating from Quebec City and Montreal.	December 1993 (TSE)	$13.46 million	$3.75 ($2.30)	Underwriter: $974,050 Prospectus (est.): $600,000
Originally a distributor of hardware and computers, **Sidus Systems Inc.** began to manufacture custom computers and workstations in 1988. It now produces Sidus-branded computer products, private-label products for OEMs, and also distributes computer-related products and peripherals.	November 1993 (TSE)	$32.5 million	$10.00 ($3.90)	Underwriter: $2,031,250 Prospectus (est.): $450,000

CHAPTER NINE

A LOOK INTO THE CRYSTAL BALL

In this chapter we speculate about how the financial marketplace for small-and medium-sized businesses might look in the near future. At the outset of this crystal ball gazing, keep in mind that there is no mystery to small business financing. The future of the market for capital reflects the sometimes subtle—and not-so-subtle—changes and forces that are operating now. We start with a simple conversation at a recent dinner party that epitomizes changes in the capital market, and then discuss some of these changes and suggest how these forces will affect financing small business.

A business associate called one evening to suggest dinner together as a mutual friend, Stephanie, was in town for the evening. As the dinner conversation unfolded, talk turned to this book. "I've got a story for you," said Stephanie, an Atlantic Canada-based entrepreneur.

Stephanie owns two thriving businesses and she has never before needed to borrow funds. Her lifestyle and businesses are such that she did not need much in the way of personal income.

However, the time had come; she needed to borrow $30,000 to bridge two transactions. "So of course I went to the bank. I approached the main branch in the town. First, they wanted this piece of information, then they wanted another piece of information, and then another." Her hands sliced through the air as she described how every time the lender got a new piece of information, it lead them down another road of inquiry. "At this point I asked why they needed all this material for a simple and relatively small loan. I was annoyed and I asked why they didn't lay out all their information needs at the beginning of the negotiation. They told me it was bank policy and that they had to keep discussing the matter with the Halifax office. The local loan account manager didn't have the authority to approve the loan. "Finally," said Stephanie, "they wanted information about a property I owned, but that is held in trust for my daughter. I'd had it! I called the loan account manager and told him to forget it. The deal was off."

"That's quite a story," said Mark, our acquaintance and an Ottawa policy maker who sometimes deals with SMEs. "I've been entertaining thoughts of leaving the civil service to start my own business. In this city there are lots of consulting opportunities for my particular specialty, but when I hear stories like that I have second thoughts. How do the banks expect businesses to thrive when they force creative businesses and people to conform with their mould?"

Why are we telling this story? Read on and see how this simple conversation illustrates changes in the markets that will affect how we do business in the future. We diverge from the dinner party temporarily to consider these factors.

THEN AND NOW: FORCES SHAPING THE CAPITAL MARKET

With apologies to Gordon Lightfoot, "there was a time in this fair land when the banks were all like one." Things were simple. The financial services industry stood on "four pillars": banks, insurance companies, trust companies, and investment dealers. Each brought a service expertise to the market. They were not allowed to compete across sectors. When we needed insurance, we went to an insurance company. When we needed a business loan, we went to a bank. No longer. With free trade, the globalization of financial services, deregulation of the financial services industry, and new technologies, we are seeing something of a financial free-for-all.

EVERYTHING OLD IS NEW AGAIN

"One thing that history teaches us is that financial markets react quickly to change. For example, in the first half of the 17th century, the people of Holland were fascinated with the development of new and rare blooms of tulips. So powerful was this force, that for a period of several years, tulip bulbs could be used as currency and were traded on the Stock Exchange of Amsterdam."[1]

The Macro Forces: Aging, Globalization, Technological Change

To appreciate what the future might hold for SME financing, we start by examining the forces that are currently shaping our financial futures. Three important forces that are evident in our daily lives are the demographic changes in the population, the trend to globalization, and the technological advances that seem to appear daily. Technological change is the most obvious of these. However, free trade agreements such as NAFTA and the European Union, and international business transactions are clear examples of events in the globalization of world economies. Less evident in its impact, but just as pervasive, is the aging of the population. These forces are reshaping both national and international financial markets and they will continue to effect change. Moreover, they, in turn, drive more specific dynamics that relate to how small businesses access capital.

---

[1] J.K. Galbraith, *A Short History of Financial Euphoria*. (New York: Whittle Books in Association with Viking Penguin 1993).

Population Aging

The aging of the population is part of an ongoing demographic shift. Part of it stems from advances in medical science, the scarcity of international conflicts of the scale of the two world wars, and increased attention to (and awareness of) health issues. We are living longer and older people usually accumulate greater wealth. In addition, the baby boomer generation is maturing, paying down their mortgages, investing in Registered Retirement Savings Plans, mutual funds, (and Labour Sponsored Venture Capital Corporations), and generally saving more money. The combined result is the establishment of large pools of capital.

In this book, we have already discussed the pools of venture capital that Canadians have invested in Labour Sponsored Venture Capital Corporations. These, however, are only a small part of the story. Mutual funds and pension funds have also exhibited immense growth. Imagine, for a moment, the problem faced by the manager of the pension fund of a large firm.

WHAT A PROBLEM!

Each payday, the employees contribute a portion of their earnings to their pensions; often the employers also contribute on behalf of the employees. Each payday, then, the pension fund manager must find somewhere to invest what might be millions of dollars. What do you do with all that money?!

As the population matures, pension fund contributions increase further and the pools of capital, each seeking investment alternatives, expand. We will see that the expansion of these pools of capital, in turn, are creating additional pressures on our financial structures.

Globalization

Globalization is also affecting our financial infrastructure. The movement to international trade of goods and services has brought with it the need to effect the attendant financial transactions. Banks follow their corporate clients overseas, or they risk losing them to foreign bank competition. The result is a global financial market that allows financial institutions to make large cross-border transactions that are virtually seamless.

A second result of globalization is the reinforcement of movements towards deregulation of the financial services industry. To be sure, deregulation of those markets has been underway for a long time. In part, deregulation arises from policy makers' initiatives to improve the efficiency of the market by removing unnecessary restrictions. In part, it follows from the move towards less government. However, deregulation also follows from globalization. Institutions and individuals use the international marketplace to circumvent restrictions that might arise due to national regulations.

US-BASED FINANCING FOR CANADIAN SMEs

With globalization, financing from US sources are becoming increasingly available in Canada, particularly mezzanine financing and venture capital. During the late 1980s and early 1990s the US venture capital industry expanded considerably to the point that there was more money, yet the quality and availability of deals in the US hand not kept pace. While the primary result of this was a shake-out in the US venture capital industry, a secondary outcome was the migration of US funds into Canadian venture capital pools. With free trade, the success of Canadian technology-based firms and the ongoing integration of capital markets, we can expect this trend to accelerate.

Impact of Demographics and Globalization

The basic demographic and globalization forces contribute to three of the more specific dynamics that are occurring in the financial markets:

- securitization;
- increased competition for savings; and
- disintermediation.

Traditionally, financial institutions have acted as the intermediaries between savers and borrowers. They have raised capital from bank deposits and then loaned them out, a process we call **intermediation**. However, institutions find it cumbersome to trade loans among themselves or with others: loans are non-liquid. With deregulation, savers and borrowers have less need for intermediaries such as banks. An alternative means of financing for institutions such as asset-based financing companies (and even banks) is through **securitization**, whereby institutional borrowers package liquid assets such as receivables from leases, secured loans, credit cards, etc. and sell these packages in national or international capital markets.

According to the securitization process, a specific set of assets are identified. These are, in effect, "purchased" from the original lender (or lessor) at an agreed price, thereby removing the receivables from the balance sheet of the original lender or lessor. Risk is partitioned among the original lender/lessor, agents in the market, and other stakeholders. The purchaser issues debt (as bonds, commercial paper, etc.) and uses the proceeds to pay for the assets. The cash flows from the assets are used to service the purchaser's debt obligations. The original lender/lessor continues to manage the assets and maintain liquidity. In short, lease or loan receivables (collateralized by the underlying equipment used by the lessee or borrower) are bundled into a portfolio which is then sold to investors (usually institutions such as life insurance companies) in the capital market. The portfolio can be designed to meet the needs of particular investors. This process of securitization allows the original lender or lessor to raise money from the public capital marketplaces to finance further lending or leasing.

Securitization boasts several advantages over borrowing. The process provides liquidity for previously illiquid assets. In addition, it allows the lenders or lessors to raise funds at market rates that reflect the reduced risk of the portfolio. This usually means that the cost of funds to an asset-based lender using securitization, can be less than the cost of funds involved in traditional lending.

Securitization is related to the large pools of capital created by our aging population. These pools in pension and mutual funds have to be invested somewhere. Asset-based lenders, or other institutions using securitization, provide institutional investors with an alternative (for example, to venture capital funds) in which they can invest the capital that they manage.

Moreover, with deregulation, and the large pools of savings, new, more specialized, firms are entering the financial marketplace to compete for these funds. Thanks to securitization, these new institutions may face lower costs of funds than bank lenders. They use their unique knowledge of the assets they finance to reduce risk (compared to banks) and they tend to be more customer-focused. Not only do they compete by taking the cash flows of their clients into account, they also have advanced a variety of innovations. For example, some asset-based finance companies lease photocopiers on a "per copy" basis. This "pay by usage" principle is being adapted to other classes of assets.

The additional competition for investment dollars, the accompanying innovation, and the emphasis on customer focus is good news for SMEs. It is likely that asset-based finance companies will become more prominent as sources of capital to small firms. As a result of these forces, traditional financial institutions face increasing competition. This process of disintermediation reflects the decline in the banks' share of the commercial credit market. In 1980, deposit-taking institutions held more than 51% of financial assets, a share that has now shrunk to approximately 44%! With increased competition from asset-based lenders, globalization, and the emergence of the pension and mutual fund industry, we can reasonably expect that the process of disintermediation will continue: that banks will become less dominant as lenders and sources of capital from beyond the banks will become increasingly important.

In addition to these factors, however, a third force is also at work: technological change.

The Third Force: Technological Change

Been on the Internet lately? If so, you have seen first-hand how easy it is to make a purchase from another country and pay for it on your credit card. In doing so, from the comfort of your home office, you have just effected an international financial transaction. International financial institutions are fully aware of this power. There may be a few kinks to work out, especially in terms of controlling security, but national and international banking across the ether is within technological reach. Canadian banks have all made their presence on the Internet clear to us. Nothing prevents non-Canadian banks from doing the same thing. Competition for business banking is not limited to Canadian institutions. Historically, only large multinational corporations were able to move capital on an international scale. With today's technology, SMEs will also do business, including lending and borrowing, nationally and internationally.

The following sections present a series of speculations about the future for various sources of capital for small businesses.

READING THE ENTRAILS[2]

Let's return to the dinner party we described at the outset of this chapter. The discussion illustrates a fourth force—inertia. Our primary banking institutions are large and often unwieldy businesses. The sheer human and institutional inertia that characterizes Canadian banks denied Stephanie a good banking experience. Bankers work hard to prevent the kind of experience that Stephanie faced; however, overcoming the established mechanisms of credit assessment takes time.

Meanwhile, banks' competitors are aware of this. They are moving to fill in the gaps and capture and retain a clientele of satisfied customers. Recognizing the aging population, financial institutions are focusing their efforts on high-net-worth individuals and scurrying to meet their needs—a customer-centred approach that is at odds with those policies of traditional institutions that serve the needs of those who fit the template, but which frustrate the creative, successful, high-net-worth business owners of the world, like Stephanie.

What do these forces hold for the various segments of the financial market? The following sections present a series of speculations about the future for various sources of capital for small businesses. To help summarize their impact, we present a schematic model of these market influences as follows.

---

[2] The high priest used to sacrifice an animal at the altar and examine the entrails to determine the hunt's direction.

Forces Shaping the Financial Markets

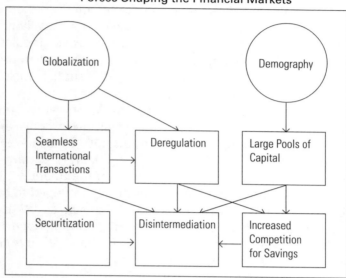

THE ARMADA AND THE ENGLISH FLEET

A recent advertisement by Newcourt Credit depicts their awareness of the force of inertia in the financial services industry. The advertisement describes the defeat of the Spanish armada by the English fleet. The armada out-gunned and out-manned the English navy. However, the larger but slower, heavily-armed Spanish galleons were unable to adapt to the force of the lighter, quicker English ships. The English tactics took advantage of the armada's weak points and the dominance of the Spanish navy was overcome.

The Informal Investment Market

The informal market is a local and personal market. As such, it is somewhat insulated from the effects of globalization. However, with the aging and maturing of the population there will be more high-net-worth individuals, potential informal investors. In addition, governments increasingly recognize that the informal investor sector is crucial to the early development of job-creating SMEs. As a result, we can look forward to a variety of developments intended to improve the climate for informal investment.

First, we anticipate that governments will ease current legal barriers to small-scale direct investment. As noted in Chapter 5, the securities acts of most provincial jurisdictions actually hinder informal investment. The recognition that securities regulations restrict economic development has been echoed by various lobbyists, development officers, and government studies, including that of the Ontario Securities Commission Task Force.

Second, we expect that governments at all levels will redouble their efforts to better mobilize informal investment capital. This includes establishing formal venture capital funds in regions where none exist. The Atlantic provinces took an important step in this direction recently with the creation of the Atlantic Investment Fund, a venture capital fund specifically intended to foster new business expansion in the Maritime provinces. With this fund, informal investors in the Atlantic region can hope for a profitable exit; with the potential of an exit, they are more likely to invest at the early stages of business formation.

The federal government's new Canadian Community Investment Program (CCIP) is another step in this direction. Under this program, the federal government will subsidize facilities located across the country that provide local marketplaces in which business owners and informal investors can assemble. CCIP sites aim to make the informal market less fragmented. To do so, CCIP facilitators will also work with local angels to ensure integrity to the process as well as the availability of informal investment capital. In addition to the federal government CCIP initiative, municipal governments and local institutions such as universities are also establishing programs to facilitate angel-entrepreneur matchmaking.

A BUSINESS MARRIAGE BROKER

The Business Introduction Service (BIS) at the University of Calgary offers benefits to investors, entrepreneurs, and other stakeholders. Investors may learn about pre-screened investment opportunities while maintaining anonymity. Business owners can take advantage of low-cost comprehensive business advice as well as access to informal investment. The program sponsor (the Royal Bank) establishes considerable goodwill as well as a destination to which they can refer clients not yet ready for bank financing. The university is able to provide education opportunities while enhancing its profile in the community.

Source: *In Search of Angels*, University of Calgary Informal Investor Project, 1995

Economic development officers, traditionally focused on attracting external businesses, will increasingly see the development of local firms as part of their mandate. They, too, will require education about informal investment. As a result, it seems likely that one of the important roles of the matchmaking facilities will be the continued education of new and current informal investors.

The Venture Capital Industry

The venture capital industry in Canada is facing competing forces. On the one hand, pension and mutual funds have traditionally been suppliers of funds for private independent venture capital firms. These sources of capital face considerable growth with the aging of the population. However, growth of the venture capital pool also implies the need for additional competent venture capital investment managers, as well as additional viable commercial opportunities. Otherwise, diminishing returns to venture investment will result. The supply of funds will then dry up as investors seek more attractive opportunities.

A second factor within the formal venture capital industry is the role of labour-sponsored venture capital corporations. On the one hand, these funds hold significant amounts of venture capital. On the other hand, their cost of funds, being tax-subsidized, introduces a distortion to the marketplace, one that needs to be resolved.

In Chapter 6, we reviewed the current situation in Canada's venture capital industry. In particular, we noted that labour-sponsored venture capital funds had undergone remarkable growth. Because of tax benefits to investors, LSVCCs have become the dominant category of institution in the industry. Most of the current supply of investable capital rests with LSVCCs. In the short term, this is good news for small business owners. In the long term, however, the picture is shadowed.

Why do we make this claim? Let us look at this situation from the point of view of the private sector, independent venture fund manager. To raise a supply of capital for investment in SMEs, the independent venture capital funds rely on institutions: insurance companies, pension funds, etc. These investors require the independent venture capitalist to provide a reasonable rate of return on the funds they advance. Given the risk of venture investments, it is reasonable for the institutional suppliers of capital to expect a high rate of return. To the independent venture capitalist, the rate of return demanded by the institutional suppliers of capital is the cost of those funds. With reason, then, the independent venture capitalist is investing funds that have a high cost attached.

This is not the same for the manager of a LSVCC. The individuals who supply capital to LSVCCs can do so, because of the tax breaks (for a few cents on the dollar the individual gets most of each dollar invested back through the tax benefits). Because of these tax breaks, the manager of a LSVCC gets funds at a much lower cost than does the manager of a private independent firm.

A LESSON FROM THE SOUTH

During the late 1980s, the venture capital industry in the United States experienced a material expansion. Encouraged by spectacular successes such as Microsoft, Apple, etc. more venture capitalist companies entered the US venture capital arena. The additional supply of funds, coupled with incrementally less experienced fund managers, with no increases in the supply of good prospects, led to poor returns. Each additional dollar of venture capital was chasing the same set of investment opportunities and was experiencing a lower incremental return. During the early 1990s a severe shake-out in the industry resulted.

The problem arises because the private independent funds are in competition with the LSVCCs for the same set of investment opportunities. In a competitive situation, the private fund is at a significant cost disadvantage: the labour-sponsored fund can offer better terms because its rate of return requirements are lower. From the viewpoint of a private independent fund, this makes competing an uphill battle.

In addition, another important economic force is at work. While the supply of capital has increased dramatically, the supply of viable, high-potential businesses has not kept pace. Therefore, each additional dollar of venture capital supply is chasing an incrementally less promising firm than the previous dollar of venture capital. Over time, this will drive down rates of return in the industry, discouraging institutions, and even individuals, from providing capital.

A CALL TO PULL THE PLUG ON LSVCCS

"Politicians...[seem] convinced that private capital systematically ignores small, innovative enterprises [and] labour-sponsored venture capital funds survive as one of the most wasteful by-products of this political blind spot....Until this spring, investors received a 20% tax credit from each of the federal and provincial governments on a maximum investment, generally of $5,000...and further tax sheltering if they put the investment in an RRSP....Several provincial governments...have just reduced the credit to 15% and the maximum to $3,500. They haven't gone far enough.

What have investors got besides the tax break? Generally, little more than a mediocre money market fund. The average return on Working Ventures...in the five years to April 30 was 4.1%, compared to the average money market fund's 5.7%.

What has small business gained from these funds? Precious little. As of Dec. 31, of Working Ventures $525-million in assets, just 24% was invested in business ventures; the remainder consisted of bonds and treasury bills....It is hard to argue that Canada is short of venture capital. Indeed, venture capitalists report that the flood of labour-fund money has created competition for a limited supply of investment opportunities....

If governments want to do something...they should pull the plug on labour-sponsored venture-capital funds."

Excepted from "Labouring under venture capital myths," Editorial, Reprinted with permission from *The Globe and Mail*, May 20, 1996, p. A10

One consequence of the large and increasing supply of venture capital is that institutional investors are withdrawing from the venture capital market. What has happened is that the once-attractive venture capital returns in the high 20% range have dropped to barely above zero. According to Mary Macdonald, president of venture capital adviser Macdonald and Associates, "Institutional investors are not particularly active. Many are sitting on the sidelines." Peter Forton, president of the Canadian Venture Capital Association, adds that, "The industry needs to generate the returns to bring institutional investors back," and that the amount of liquidity in the market, now $2.9 billion, stands in the way of higher returns.

"Deal-making is a Growth Industry" by Catharine Mulroney Reprinted with permission from *The Globe and Mail*, April 23, 1996, p. B29

Asset-Based Financing

The future for asset-based financing looks extremely encouraging. In the US, asset-based financing—primarily in the form of
leases—accounts for 35-40% of asset financing. In Canada, the
current market penetration lies in the order of 15 to 20% This is
a segment of the market in which changes are occurring quickly. Firms such as Newcourt have grown quickly and are now
among the largest asset-based financing companies in North
America.

In part, this growth is due to the ability of asset-based financing firms to raise capital at low cost, allowing them to offer business clients financing terms that are becoming more competitive. Asset-based financing companies raise part of their capital
from the large (and growing) pools of capital such as pension,
insurance, and mutual funds. It is these institutions that have the
task of managing the money being generated by the aging of the
population, a population that will augment further these pools of
capital. Traditionally managers of these pools have also looked to
the venture capital market as destinations for their investments;
however, the advent of labour-sponsored funds has distorted the
market for venture capital investments. Asset-based financing
firms probably look attractive to their funding institutions. Therefore, the asset-based financing industry can look forward to a
continuing supply of investment capital.

The opening of international financial markets provides a significant expansion of opportunities from which asset-based firms
can securitize the cash flows that emanate from their loans and
leases. Internationalization will allow such firms to sell their
securitized obligations for the best price, internationally. The
result will be leases, term loans, and conditional sales contracts
at costs to SME clients that reflect the lowest price of funds
nationally and internationally.

Banks and other Lending Institutions

Banks face two sets of demands. On the one hand, they face significant global competition from better-resourced international
financial institutions. To cope with this international competition,

Canadian banks would like to be able to expand, possibly through mergers, to take advantage of economies of scale and scope. Such growth could, however, exacerbate the inertia that is limiting their ability to be more responsive to SME clients. In this vein, the second set of demands faced by banks is the thrust of government policy aimed at enhancing competition in the marketplace for capital to SMEs. This market is now a battleground among banks, asset-based financing companies, credit unions, and caisses populaires. Waiting on the sidelines, for now, are more foreign institutions, that using electronic means, will likely enter the market without the need to establish a costly "bricks and mortar" presence.

NEW COMPETITION

US banking giant Wells Fargo & Co. is seeking the approval of the federal government to offer loans of up to $100,000 to Canadian small businesses. The loan transactions would be by telephone using a simple application form and a computerized credit scoring system that promises quick responses. The federal government faces a decision about how to deal with Wells Fargo's plan to offer loans without setting up offices in Canada.

Banks also lend to finance SMEs for a wide spectrum of assets. Unlike the case for asset-based financing firms, the margins on the small loans that characterize SMEs do not provide for the additional expertise that would be required for specialization. They cannot, therefore, mitigate risk by becoming expert in the aftermarkets for the assets they finance. Institutional lenders then, face a dilemma. On the one hand, demands for increased size and profitability push them towards additional competition and the provision of an increased variety of services. These initiatives oblige lenders to attempt, as best they can, to reduce the overheads associated with due diligence and monitoring. These trends are leading to increased reliance on automated "scoring systems," supported by technology, for loan evaluation. Products, services, evaluations, monitoring requirements, etc. will become more and more standardized. Examples of these early initiatives are the business planners/loan application forms available from most major banks on computer diskettes.

Owners of small firms must therefore be prepared to recognize the role of standardization. This scenario has both positive and negative attributes. On the one hand, the move to standardization will help ensure that loans are advanced based on the objective fundamentals of the business. This will reduce the effects of biases that might creep into the process due to gender, race, or other such attributes of the borrower. On the negative side, standardization may mitigate against the truly creative and idiosyncratic innovations who could be the real successes. Business owners like Stephanie remain frustrated. The institutional lender mill must either come to grips with this segment of the market or face losing it to the competition.

SO WHAT DOES THIS MEAN FOR SMEs? CLOSING COMMENTS

In this book, we have reviewed sources from which small firms can seek investment capital. As we go to press, five overall impressions stand out. First, Canadian SMEs have available to them a greater supply of capital, both debt and equity, than at any time in the recent past. We have provided evidence that the supply of capital is at historical peaks.

Second, with aging baby boomers and globalization, the future promises to be a period in which SMEs will continue to have available to them a broad and deep array of capital sources. New financial institutions such as asset-based finance companies, merchant bankers, and mezzanine financiers are stepping forward to provide a supply of both capital and creative solutions.

Third, Canadians are starting new firms at a faster rate than ever before. In part, this is because of our entrepreneurial spirit and the intentional initiatives of government to foster technology development and innovation. In part, new business formation is also prompted by the difficult period of economic restructuring that has been the hallmark of the early 1990s.

Fourth, there is no shortage of innovation. Our universities, government, and industry laboratories are generating new products and ideas at a breathtaking rate.

Yet, fifth, a very clear reality remains that businesses continue to express frustration by their experiences of attempting to finance their firms. The demand for alternatives is a very real economic force.

Taking these five points together, there is both a supply of capital and creative ways of deploying it and a widespread demand for these commodities. Economics tells us that supply and demand will meet. Making supply and demand meet, however, is not automatic. The people on both sides of the transaction have to communicate in the same financial language and to understand each others' needs.

Our hope, in writing this book, is to address this gap. Throughout, we have stressed the importance of management skills, especially financial management skills, in the quest for capital. In part, what appears to be a gap in the capital markets for SMEs is not so much a shortage of capital as the scarcity of managerial abilities, particularly financial. These skills are also needed if entrepreneurs are to convince investors and lenders of their fiscal responsibility. Such abilities are needed to convert innovations into a viable business opportunities, the proceeds of which reward inventors, investors, and lenders for the risks they must undertake.

Incidentally, Stephanie did solve her problem She shopped around. A telephone call, a few faxes, and a courier package provided her with the bridge financing within 48 hours. For Stephanie, Sounds Enterprising, and other creative firms, the unusual opportunities, the innovative thinkers, and the competent managers, it is indeed fortunate that there will be an increasing supply of capital within and...beyond the banks.

GLOSSARY

Acquisition: the purchase by a firm of part or all of another commercial operation.

Amortization: the scheduling or breakdown of amounts based on equal monthly, quarterly, or annual periods in time. Can refer to the amortization of debt or depreciation of assets.

Angel: an individual who invests personal capital directly in a business owned by others. Also referred to as an informal investor.

Archangel: an individual who marshals informal capital by establishing syndicates of other angel (informal) investors.

Asset-based financing: lending in which the risk assessment is based primarily, but not exclusively, on the value of the asset being financed. Includes leasing, term loans, and conditional sales contracts.

Bill of exchange: a written order to pay a sum of money, sent by the seller to the buyer's bank.

Bootstrap financing: small amounts of seed capital used in early stages of firm maturation.

Bridge financing: capital required to bridge the interim between paying and receiving funds.

Buyout: the purchase of a business, often by current management, from the current owner(s).

Cash conversion cycle: the difference between the operating cycle (inputs to cash) and the payment cycle (interval between purchasing of raw material and labour, and cash payment for them).

Cash flow: the amount and flow of funds in a firm over a designated period of time. Cash flow differs from the amounts indicated on an income statement, given that it does not include non-cash items and expenses such as depreciation.

Code of conduct: initiated by the Canadian Bankers Association, it is an agreement among the principal lending banks in Canada to communicate with their clients should they intend to change the client's credit relationship in any significant way.

Collateral: assets pledged as security for a loan. If a firm defaults on the loan, collateral is seized as a mechanism for repayment of its outstanding financial obligations.

Conditional sales contract: credit which allows the vendor of the asset to retain legal title until the purchaser has made full payment.

Commitment fee: one of the fees lenders can require on a line of credit.

Convertible debt: refers to debt or preferred stock that is convertible to a firm's common stock.

Corporate angels: larger firms that invest in spin-off, related businesses. They provide both financial and managerial support. Investments are usually complementary to existing activities.

Correspondent banking: the network of large financial institutions that engage in international business transactions and currency trading.

Covenant: contractual requirements often included in bond and term loan financing among the borrowing firm's obligation to a lender.

Credit history: a review of a firm's credit relationships. For new business owners who have not held mortgages or credit cards in their own name, the lack of credit history is particularly problematic for securing debt financing.

Credit scoring: a rating mechanism that assesses an applicant's risk based on several standardized factors such as the firm's debt to equity ratios, longevity, etc.

Creditworthiness: The generalized assessment of a firm's ability to cover (service) debt or interest expenses and maintain a reasonable level of current assets, such as accounts receivables and inventory.

Debt: a financial obligation to a lender; the amount of debt and interest payable is agreed upon over a designated period of time.

Draw: that amount of income or other capital that an owner takes from the firm to cover personal (living) expenses. This can also be thought of as an owner's salary.

Draft: a written, unconditional order to the importer to pay on presentation (sight draft) or at a specified future time (time draft).

Due diligence: a detailed examination of the firm prior to finalizing an investment arrangement. Ensures that the business is accurately described in the business plan.

Equity: a financial investment that results in a portion of firm ownership.

Equity kickers: contractual clauses or securities such as warrants that provide debt financiers with the possibility of participating in appreciation of a borrower's common shares.

Factoring: advancement of funds based on a discounted value of the firm's receivables, at interest rates competitive with those of banks. Factoring firms now provide a range of services including credit assessment, collection of payables and account administration.

Fiduciary responsibility: the obligation to act with prudence and reason in regard to the management of depositors' or investors' money.

Hybrid venture capital: funds that are government-supported but privately administered. Managed as arm's length transaction to government, these funds may include both provincial and federal investment.

Initial public offer: Also known as an IPO, or "going public": the initial sales of a firm's common shares to the public, usually in conjunction with a stock market listing.

Informal investor: an individual who invests personal capital directly in a business owned by others. Also referred to as a business angel.

Investment capital: funds required to operate a business. Can be in the form of debt or equity.

Institutional vendors: managers of large (pooled) investment funds, insurance companies, etc.

Interest rate risk: the risk taken by an investor that interests rates will rise and the market price of competitive securities such as bonds will fall.

Lease: rental agreements which can take the form of capital and operating leases. Capital leases usually provide for financing of equipment where the rights and benefits of ownership are retained by the lessee. Operating leases most often fall short of the working life of equipment.

Lessee: the individual or firm that acquires use of an asset by leasing it from the owner, the lessor.

Lessor: the individual or firm which owns an asset leased by another firm or individual.

Letter of credit: a means of facilitating international trade. Specifies the details of the transactions and documents the importer's readiness to pay for the goods or services on performance by the exporter. Letters of credit are usually documentary, meaning the seller must accompany the draft with invoices, bills of lading, and other documents. They may be revocable or irrevocable. Revocable letters of credit may be revoked, without prior notice, any time before a draft is presented to the issuing bank. An irrevocable letter of credit cannot be revoked without the consent of all parties.

Leverage: the use of financing or operating methods with fixed costs, including financial (for example, debt financing) and operating (for example, capital-intensive manufacturing processes) leverage. Both give rise to risk in the sense that net income and earnings per share are more volatile with increased leverage.

Line of credit: a type of loan in which a bank or supplier makes available a maximum amount of funding. The borrower (or client) will usually rely on only a portion of the amount made available.

Love money: financing extended by close friends and family. Lending is usually based on the relationship between individuals rather than on a formalized risk assessment.

Management capacity: the general knowledge, skills, and abilities resident in the management team of a firm. Skills include commercial, financial, domestic, network, human resource, and technological management, among others.

Micro business: a business with annual sales of less than $200,000 and fewer than three employees.

Mini business: a firm with annual sales of $200,000 to $500,000 and three or more employees.

Matchmaking services: strategic alliances between capitalists and informal investors. These function to screen investees on behalf of investors and act as a conduit to a deal.

Merchant bank: a specialized financial institution that invests in the transactions it undertakes. Provides advisory and financing services across a spectrum of applications.

Merger: the joining of two firms through share exchanges or share purchases.

Micro loans: this concept originated through very small loans provided by developing nations' banks. In the Canadian context, micro loans refer to small loans (most range from $500 to $5,000) made available through charitable institutions and the Business Development Bank of Canada. Risk assessment is often based on character and reference group support rather than collateral. Loans may be made as independent transactions or made through informal lending circles.

Mezzanine financing: a type of venture capital that can take several forms. Subordinated debt financing is usually to bridge working capital and for expansion prior to a public offering of stock or buyout. Can include equity investment along with the debt. Most often involves long-term debt, which is subordinated to the claims of existing debt.

Mortgage: a loan for the purchase of land, buildings, or equipment.

Non-residential mortgages: mortgages on land or buildings that are used for business (commercial) purposes.

Ombudsperson: a liaison officer of a bank who works at arm's length to service the concerns of small business owners.

Operating cycle: refers to the process and time required to convert the inputs of raw material to cash from sales.

Operating loan: a line of credit that allows borrowers to borrow at will up to a negotiated limit, called the operating loan ceiling.

Options: contracts that give their owners the right to buy or sell a particular stock for a fixed price on or before a given date.

Patient capital: a loan in which the terms of repayment are delayed in order that the borrower can earn revenue to pay back the capital and interest outstanding.

Payment cycle: the interval between the time at which the firm purchases raw materials and labour and the time at which it makes the cash payment for them.

Primary issue: an offering to the public of common stock on one of Canada's four stock exchanges.

Prime rate: the rate of interest set by the banks as their loan rate to their best corporate customers.

Quasi business: single ventures formed for the exploitation of temporary opportunity. They often have no employees, are short-lived, lack conventional business organization, and/or may be incubating (pre-start up) operations.

Recapitalize: to refinance the capital structure of the firm; often involves retirement of debt through issuance of equity or vice versa.

Receivables: accounts receivable, or payments due from clients.

Risk premium: that part of interest rate or yield that represents a premium over the rate on a risk-free investment.

Sale-and-leaseback: an arrangement in which a firm that owns property, buildings, or equipment sells the asset at market value, usually to a financial institution. Simultaneously, the firm executes a lease contract with the purchaser of the asset, calling for periodic lease payments.

Securitization: the sale of packages of receivables on financial markets.

Small Business Lending Act (SBLA): federal regulation which makes guaranteed or secured provision for loans to small business owners. The act specifies that even if the borrower defaults on a loan, the lender (an approved financial institution) will be able to recover a high proportion of the loan.

Subordinated debt: debt that is placed in a secondary position with respect to other specific classes of debt; it usually bears a high yield.

Sweat equity: the time and energy exerted by the business owner during the incubation, gestation, and early start-up phases of operation. While not a monetary form of equity, owners should document their time and others' in-kind contributions to demonstrate to potential investors the type and level of management activity.

Syndicate: an informal group of independent investors who each contribute a portion of investment capital to a small business. Syndication allows for a larger pool of capital and shared risk.

Term loan: a long-term loan offered by a financial institution to a business where the borrower agrees to repay interest and capital over a designated period of time.

Terms of purchase: the agreed-upon cost and repayment provisions between a buyer and seller.

Trade credit: most often unsecured credit extended by suppliers to buyers.

Venture capital: capital invested in growing enterprises by individuals or venture capital firms where risk is a significant element in the investment.

Vulture capital: discounted receivables purchased by a financial institution where the buyer is demonstrating financial distress, i.e., under bankruptcy protection.

Warrant: a contract that gives a purchaser the option of buying a specified number of shares of the company's common stock at a stated price on or before a given date.

Working capital: the difference between a firm's current assets and current liabilities.

FINANCIAL RATIO ANALYSIS
Some Key Terms

Financial statements are not just administrative paperwork or necessary evils. They are valuable tools that you should review and monitor on a regular basis. The financial ratios that emerge from the numbers in your financial statements are key indicators of how well your company is doing, and how well it is being managed.

There are certain financial ratios that are very useful. It is essential that you keep a watchful eye on them. And you won't be the only one paying close attention to these indicators. Investors of all stripes will use these key ratios to take the financial temperature of your company, to assess its financial health, and to evaluate loans and make investment decisions.

Usually, financial ratio analysis is based on the information contained in the company's historical financial statements or the *pro-forma* financial statements included with business plans. It is important to note that financial ratios are not so much *absolute* measures of performance as they are *relative* measures. Suppose, for example, that your firm has a current ratio of 1.7. By itself, this number doesn't tell you very much. However, if current ratios for firms in your industry are normally around 3.0, there might be reasons to be concerned about your company's liquidity. Therefore, ratios provide most information when compared with a benchmark. Ratios can vary from industry to industry. Firms such as Dun and Bradstreet, as well as Statistics Canada, publish industry-specific financial ratio data that you can use as benchmarks. In addition, it can be useful to monitor how the financial ratios of your business change over time. If, for example, your firm has exhibited current ratios of 1.2 to 1.4 in previous years, a value of 1.7 might signify improved liquidity.

Financial ratios can measure the performance of the firm along several dimensions. For example, the gross profit margin (ratio of sales less cost-of-goods-sold to sales) for an industry measures the ability of firms to mark up their costs. Therefore, it not only measures profitability, it also says something about the level of competition in the industry. Within each dimension, it may be useful to look at several financial ratios, to give a fuller picture of performance in that area. For example, return on equity, ROE, is defined as:

$$ROE = \frac{\text{net income}}{\text{equity}}$$

But we can extract more meaning by breaking this ratio down as follows:

$$ROE = \frac{\text{net income}}{\text{assets}} \times \frac{\text{assets}}{\text{equity}}$$

that is, ROE = return on assets x assets/equity
$$= \frac{\text{net income}}{\text{sales}} \times \frac{\text{sales}}{\text{assets}} \times \frac{\text{assets}}{\text{equity}}$$

By means of this breakdown, we can see if changes in return on equity arise from profitability (net income/sales), efficiency (sales/assets), or leverage (assets/equity).

A full treatment of financial statements, their ratios, and analysis is beyond the scope of this book. However, we want to alert you to some key terms and ratios, and to their importance.

The table that follows presents the most common dimensions of analysis, identifies the relevant ratios, and comments on how the ratios may be interpreted. For details about how the ratios themselves are computed, readers are referred to almost any introductory textbook in accounting or finance.

DIMENSION	RELEVANT RATIOS	COMMENTS
Liquidity Current Ratio Quick Ratio		Both ratios relate the firm's holdings of short-term assets (such as cash, accounts receivable, etc.) to the firm's short-term obligations. These ratios, therefore, measure the firm's solvency, or ability to pay its short-term bills
Profitability Gross Profit Margin Operating Profit Margin Net Profit Margin Return on Assets Return on Equity		The gross profit margin is the ratio of sales less the cost of goods sold to sales. It therefore measures the firm's ability to obtain a high markup and indirectly measures the firm's competitive environment. The other profit margins measure the efficiency of the firm's operations and its net income on sales. The returns on assets and equity, respectively, measure the firm's earnings expressed per dollar of total assets and per dollar of equity financing.
Debt **Management** Debt to equity ratio Times interest earned Fixed charge coverage		The debt-equity ratio measures the extent to which the firm uses debt as a source of capital. The times interest earned and fixed charge ratios measure the firm's ability to cover the obligations that arise out of interest payments, lease obligations, or from other debt-related requirements.
Asset **Management** Inventory turnover Fixed asset turnover Total asset turnover Days sales outstanding		Turnover ratios provide a measure of the efficiency with which the firm uses particular categories of assets (inventory, fixed assets, and all assets, respectively). They are sometimes called activity ratios because they measure the level of activity within the firm. Days sales outstanding measures the speed with which management is collecting on accounts receivable.

RESOURCE GUIDE FOR ENTERPRISING CANADIANS

Authors' Note: The listings that follow provide some additional resources that might be of assistance for business owners who are seeking financing or financial information. We do not presume that this list is comprehensive. Undoubtedly, we have missed other resources and we apologize for any such omissions. In addition, telephone numbers, addresses, etc. periodically change; therefore, the list below will become dated. We invite readers to help keep us up to date!

T
I
P

TIPS FOR ACCESSING SELF-HELP CENTRES

Use this list as a starting point.
This is just a sampling of the types of organizations that can assist your financing and start-up business needs. Use the list as a starting point in your research process.

Contact provincial ministries of employment and trade.
Only a sample of federal and provincial agencies is listed. Most labour and trade ministries provide a variety of small business training and targeted

support schemes for new businesses. Some provincial agencies also provide generic employee training programs.

When speaking to federal and provincial agencies inquire about equity support programs.

Several federal and provincial agencies support targeted equity group services for aboriginal, female and disabled Canadians. For example, the federal government, Atlantic Canada Opportunities Agency and Newfoundland government fund the Women's Enerprise Bureau which provides workshops, training programs, video materials, speakers, and networking opportunities for women entrepreneurs.

Crown Corporations can provide regional support.

A number of provinces also fund crown development corporations, agencies established to support industry by providing financial assistance to provincial businesses. Programs can include: term loans, loan guarantees, demand loans, equity and quasi-equity investments, and tourism incentives.

Incubation centres can also help.

These centres allow new and small businesses to take advantage of shared services. Space, business management assistance, advisory services, consulting services, administrative support, on-site day-care, seminars, and networking are often provided. Contact your provincial governments for a listing of these centres and other services.

Loan associations provide both start-up financing and consultation.

In conjunction with the federal Small Business Loans, certain provinces also provide small business loans and consultative assistance.

Universities and community colleges provide inexpensive consultation.

Contact your local universities or colleges as many provide contracted small business consulting. These small business support centres are usually run by senior undergraduate or graduate commerce students and can be a reasonably priced way to have a market analysis undertaken.

Most Canadian chartered banks produce excellent resource materials.

Most of the chartered banks produce "how to" brochures, financial management tools and business plan outlines, often free of charge. Contact your local branch managers of all the chartered banks for complimentary copies of available small business support materials.

> **Use caution before joining private small business associations.**
> Caution is suggested before paying membership fees or providing busi-
> ness information. Inquire about their consultants' small business experi-
> ence, the tenure of the organization, and attempt to obtain either a listing
> of members or written statement of services prior to payment. Our survey
> of associations resulted in many returned letters for organizations no
> longer in business!
>
> T I P

NATIONAL AGENCIES

Business Development Bank of Canada (BDC)

5 Place Ville-Marie, Suite 400
Montreal, QC, H3B 5E7
Telephone: (888) 463-6232
Fax: (514) 283-7838
E-Mail / Web Site: http://www.bdc.ca

Offers a variety of services, including term loans for expansion
projects, working capital replenishment, micro-business loans, etc.

Programs:

BDC Micro-Business Program
Provides personalized management training and term financing
to support the growth of innovative businesses.

BDC Patient Capital
A type of financing which provides firms with long-term capital
under flexible repayment terms. This program has a great deal in
common with venture capital without ownership dilution.

BDC Venture Loan Program
Businesses with strong growth potential and high-quality management may be eligible for cash flow and quasi-equity financing from $100,000 to $1 million for expansion and market
development projects.

Working Capital for Exporters
This program is designed to help small businesses finance export-related activities.

Canadian Banker's Association

Box 348, Suite 600, 2 First Canadian Place
Toronto, ON, M5X 1E1
Phone: (416) 564-7753 or toll-free 1-800-263-0231
Web site: http://www.cba.ca

This organization provides research, advocacy, information, and support to the chartered banks of Canada. They also provide a variety of information booklets on running and managing a business with emphasis on financing your business. Many booklets are free of charge.

Canada Community Investment Plan (CCIP)

235 Queen Street, 5th Floor East
Ottawa, ON, K1A 0H5
Telephone: (613) 954-5481
Fax: (613) 954-5492
E-Mail/Web Site: woods.george@ic.gc.ca

The goal of the CCIP is to help communities bring risk capital to growing small firms in non-financial centres. The federal government will cover two-thirds of the costs needed to carry out demonstration projects that help link informal investors and business owners in particular geographic regions. During 1996, the first demonstration sites were selected, with more to follow in 1997.

Canadian Finance and Leasing Association (CFLA)

151 Yonge Street, Suite 1210
Toronto, ON, M5C 2W7
Telephone: (416) 860-1133
Fax: (416) 860-1140
E-Mail / Web Site:info@cfla-acfl.ca—http://www.cfla-acfl.ca/

Organization maintains listings of firms engaged in asset-based financing. Members provide assistance directly to Canadian businesses by financing the acquisition of a wide range of equipment and vehicles by business customers and consumers.

Canadian Venture Capital Association (CVCA)

1881 Yonge Street, Suite 706
Toronto, ON, M4S 3C4
Telephone: (416) 487-0519
Fax: (416) 487-5899
E-Mail / Web Site: kryan@cvca.ca—http://www.cvca.ca/

Organization maintains listings of firms engaged in venture capital financing and provides statistical review, member directory and detailed industry preferences of Canadian venture capital companies.

Community Futures Development Corporations

Telephone: Contact your local economic development associations.

CFDCs provide financial support to communities outside metropolitan areas to develop and implement a long-term community strategic plan for the development of their local economy.

Credit Union Central of Canada/BDC Strategic Alliance

5 Place Ville-Marie, Suite 400
Montreal, QC, H3B 5E7
Telephone: (888) 463-6232
Fax: (514) 283-7838
E-Mail / Web Site: http://www.bdc.ca/

The Credit Union Central of Canada has signed an agreement with the BDC to offer clients a full range of financial products and management services specifically designed for small and mid-size business.

Human Resources and Development Canada

Phase IV, Place du Portage
Hull, QC, K1A 0J9
Telephone: (613) 990-5186
E-Mail/Web Site: info@hrdc-drhc.ca—http://www.hrdc-drhc.gc.ca/

Offers a variety of financial assistance programs designed to sub-sidize job creation activities in priority areas (areas characterized by high unemployment, job programs for groups characterized by high unemployment).

Industry Canada

235 Queen St., 5th Floor East
Ottawa, ON, K1A 0H5
Telephone: (613) 954-5481
Fax: (613) 954-5492
E-Mail / Web Site: http://strategis.ic.gc.ca/

Provides an assortment of programs to aid Canadian businesses.

The Small Business Loans Act (SBLA) is a federal government program designed to help new and existing business enterprises obtain term loans from chartered banks and other lenders toward financing the purchase and improvement of fixed assets. The maximum amount of the business improvement loan may not exceed $250,000. Further information can be obtained from lenders.

Ontario Association of Community Development Corporations

12 Barrie Blvd.
St. Thomas, ON, N5P 4B9
Telephone: (519) 633-2326
Fax: (519) 633-3563
E-Mail/WebSite: oacdcdj@snoopy.ccia.st-thomas.on.ca —
                    http://www.mwdesign.net/oacdc/main.html

Organizations whose goals are to develop business in the small communities in which they are situated; many offer financing programs. See their website for the community development corporation in your area.

Venture Capital World

E-Mail/Web Site: http://www.vcworld.com/

Worldwide marketplace for Venture Capital on the Internet.

CANADA BUSINESS SERVICES CENTRES

Newfoundland Business Service Centre

90 O'Leary Avenue, PO Box 8687
St. John's, ND, A1B 3T1
Telephone: (800) 668-1010 / (709) 772-6022
Fax: (709) 772-6090
E-Mail/Web Site: http://www.cbsc.org/

Offers a variety of information, referrals and programs to businesses in Newfoundland.

Prince Edward Island Business Service Centre

75 Fitzroy Street
Charlottetown, PEI, C1A 7K2
Telephone: (800) 668-1010 / (902) 368-0771
Fax:(902) 566-7377
E-Mail/Web Site: http://www.cbsc.org/

Business information resource centre for entrepreneurs in PEI.

Nova Scotia Business Service Centre

1575 Brunswick Street
Halifax, NS, B3J 2G1
Telephone: (800) 668-1010 / (902) 426-8604
Fax: (902) 426-6530
E-Mail/Web Site: http://www.cbsc.org/

Offers a variety of programs and information resources to Nova Scotian businesses.

New Brunswick Business Service Centre

570 Queen Street
Fredricton, NB, E3B 6Z6
Telephone: (800) 668-1010 / (506) 444-6140
Fax: (506) 444-6172
E-Mail/Web Site: http://www.cbsc.org/

Offers a variety of information, referrals and programs to businesses in New Brunswick.

Quebec Business Service Centre

5 Place Ville Marie, Plaza Level, Suite 12500
Montreal, QC, H3B 4Y2
Telephone: (800) 322-4636 / (514) 496-4636
Fax: (514) 496-5934
E-Mail/Web Site:info-entrepeneurs@bfdrg-fordq.qc.ca—
                http://www.cbsc.org/

Quebec business information resource centre.

Ontario Business Service Centre

Telephone: (800) 567-2345 / (416) 954-4636
Fax: (416) 954-8597
E-Mail/Web Site: http://www.cbsc.org/

Call-back information service for Ontario businesses. All services are conducted by telephone; no walk-in centre.

Manitoba Business Service Centre

PO Box 2609, 8th Floor, 330 Portage Avenue
Winnipeg, MB, R3C 4B3
Telephone: (800) 665-2019 / (204) 984-2272
Fax: (204) 983-3852
E-Mail/Web Site: http://www.cbsc.org/

Offers a variety of information, referrals and programs to businesses in Manitoba.

Saskatchewan Business Service Centre

122–3rd Avenue, North
Saskatoon, SA, S7K 2H6
Telephone: (800) 667-4374 / (306) 956-2323
Fax: (306) 956-2328
E-Mail/Web Site: http://www.cbsc.org/

Information, referral and assistance program; resource centre serving Saskatchewan.

Alberta Business Service Centre

100-10237 104 Street
Edmonton, AB, T5J 1B1
Telephone: (800) 272-9675
E-Mail/Web Site: http://www.cbsc.org/

Provides Canada Business Service Centre services to Albertans.

British Columbia Business Service Centre

601 West Cordova Street
Vancouver, BC, V6B 1G1
Telephone: (800) 667-2272 / (604) 775-5525
Fax: (604) 775-5520
E-Mail/Web Site: http://www.cbsc.org/

Offers a variety of information, referrals and programs to businesses in BC.

Yukon Business Service Centre

201-208 Main Street
Whitehorse, YK, Y1A 2A9
Telephone: (800) 661-0563 / (403) 633-6257
Fax: (403) 667-2001
E-Mail/Web Site: http://www.cbsc.org/

Source of information and aid to businesses serving the Yukon.

NWT Business Service Centre

3rd Floor, Northern United Place, 5004-54th Street
Yellowknife, NT, X1A 2L9
Telephone: (800) 661-0599 / (403) 873-7958
Fax: (403) 873-0101
E-Mail/Web Site: http://www.cbsc.org/

Business resource centre of NWT.

REGIONAL AGENCIES

Newfoundland

ACOA Newfoundland

215 Water St., PO Box 1060, Station C
St. John's, NF, A1C 5M5
Telephone: (800) 668-1010 / (709) 772-2751
Fax: (709) 772-2712
E-Mail/Web Site: http://www.acoa.ca/

ACOA offers a variety of loan programs to assist businesses operating or planning to start up in Newfoundland.

Prince Edward Island

ACOA Prince Edward Island

3rd Floor, 100 Sydney St., PO Box 40
Charlottetown, PEI, C1A 7K2
Telephone: (800) 871-2596 / (902) 566-7492
Fax: (902) 566-7098
E-Mail/Web Site: http://www.acoa.ca/

Helps P.E.I. small and medium enterprises with many different programs. Some financial aid programs are available.

Nova Scotia

ACOA Nova Scotia

1801 Hollis St., Suite 600, PO Box 2284, Station M
Halifax, NS, B3J 3C8
Telephone: (800) 565-1228 / (902) 426-6743
Fax: (902) 426-2054
E-Mail/Web Site: http://www.acoa.ca/

Federal government agency whose goal is to improve the economy of Nova Scotia; offers a variety of loan programs to businesses operating in that province.

Enterprise Cape Breton Corporation

4th Floor, Commerce Tower
Sydney, NS, B1P 6T7
Telephone: (800) 705-3926 / (902) 564-3600
Fax: (902) 564-3825
E-Mail/Web Site: http://www.ecbc.ca/

Development agency that aims to develop business operations on Cape Breton Island. Many loan programs are available.

Nova Scotia Economic Development and Tourism

1575 Brunswick Street
Halifax, NS, B3J 2G1
Telephone: (800) 565-2009 / (902) 424-2720
Fax: (902) 424-0508
E-Mail/Web Site:econ.ced@gov.ns.ca—
                  http://www.gov.ns.ca/ecor/

Sponsoring Organization: Canada/Nova Scotia Business Centre Offers Nova Scotia businesses information on, and provides some, financial assistance.

New Brunswick

ACOA New Brunswick

570 Queen St., 3rd Floor, PO Box 578
Fredricton, NB, E3B 5A6
Telephone: (800) 561-4030 / (506) 452-3184
Fax: (506) 452-3285
E-Mail/Web Site: http://www.acoa.ca/

Federal government agency whose goal is to improve the economy of Atlantic Canada, offers a variety of loan programs to business operating in New Brunswick.

Employment Division, Advanced Education and Labour, New Brunswick

470 York St., Room 206, PO Box 6000
Fredricton, NB, E3B 5H1
Telephone: (800) 561-4129 / (506) 453-3818
Fax: (506) 453-7967

Offers many loan assistance programs for business start-ups in New Brunswick.

Entrepreneur Program
The Employment Division of New Brunswick offers up to $10,000 to any unemployed   New Brunswicker over the age of 19 who wishes to start a business and whose start-up
costs do not exceed $50,000.

Quebec

Federal Office of Regional Development—Quebec (FORDQ)

800 Place Victoria Tower, Suite 3800, PO Box 247
Montreal, QC, H4Z 1E8
Telephone: (800) 561-0633 / (514) 283-6412
Fax: (514) 283-3302
E-Mail/Web Site: http://www.bsdrq/fordq.gc.ca/

Provides services and funding for priority areas such as innovation, R&D, design, development of markets, export trade, and entrepreneurship in Quebec.

Société de développement industriel du Québec (SDI)

Telephone: (800) 461-2433 / (514) 873-4375
Fax: (514) 873-4383
E-Mail/Web Site: http://www.sdi.gouv.qc.ca/

Allows financial assistance for fixed assets, working capital, patents, technology, etc. for business start-ups in Quebec.

Ontario

Federal Economic Development Initiative for Northern Ontario (FEDNOR)

Suite 407, 30 Cedar St.
Sudbury, ON P3E 1A4
Telephone: (800) 461-4079 / (705) 671-0711
Fax: (705) 671-0717
E-Mail / Web Site: http://fednor@ic.gc.ca/

Addresses the inadequate availability of capital through a number of financing initiatives aimed at businesses operating in Northern Ontario.

Ontario Prospectors Assistance Program (OPAP)

533 Ramsey Lake Road
Sudbury, ON, P3E 6B5
Telephone: (705) 670-5787
Fax: (705) 670-5803

Sponsoring Organization: Ontario Ministry of Northern Development and Mines

Offers financial assistance to help carry out prospecting and early grassroots exploration activities on their own properties or Crown land in Ontario.

Manitoba

Western Economic Diversification Canada / Manitoba

Suite 712, The Cargill Bldg., 240 Graham Ave.
Winnipeg, MN, R3C 2L4
Telephone: (888) 338-9378 / (204) 983-0697
Fax: (204) 983-4694
E-Mail/Web Site: http://www.wd.gc.ca/ (English) or
　　　　　　　　http://www.deo.gc.ca/ (French)

Government agency committed to helping Western Canadian SMEs grow; a variety of loan programs are available.

Saskatchewan

Western Economic Diversification Canada / Saskatchewan

Suite 601, S.J. Cohen Bldg., 119 - 4th Avenue South
Saskatoon, SA, S7K 3S7
Telephone: (888) 338-9378 / (306) 975-4373
Fax: (306) 975-5484
E-Mail/Web Site: http://www.wd.gc.ca/ (English) or
                 http://www.deo.gc.ca/ (French)

Government agency whose aim is to foster growth among
Saskatchewan SMEs. Many programs, including those that aid
small and medium business with financial matters, are available.

Alberta

Western Economic Diversification Canada / Alberta

Suite 1500, Canada Place, 9700 Jasper Ave.
Edmonton, AB, T5J 4H7
Telephone: (403) 495-4164
Fax: (403) 495-4557
E-Mail/Web Site: http://www.wd.gc.ca/

Government agency committed to helping Western Canadian
SMEs grow; a variety of loan programs are available.

Alberta Opportunity Company

(locations across Alberta)
Telephone: call your local office (their website lists the office
nearest you)
E-Mail/Web Site: aocloans@gov.ab.ca —
                 http:/www.gov.ab.ca/ ~ aoc/index.html

Helps Albertans start new enterprises or develop existing businesses.

British Columbia

Western Economic Diversification Canada / B.C.

Suite 1200, Bentall Tower 4, 1055 Dunsmuir Street
Vancouver, BC, V7X 1L3
Telephone: (888) 338-9378 / (604) 666-6256
Fax: (604) 666-2353
E-Mail/Web Site: http://www.wd.gc.ca/ (English) or
                 http://www.deo.gc.ca/ (French)

Government agency committed to helping Western Canadian
SMEs grow; a variety of loan programs are available.

BANK OMBUDS OFFICES AND WEBSITE ADDRESSES

Canadian Banking Ombudsman, Inc.

4950 Yonge Street, Suite 1602
North York, ON, M2N 6K1
Telephone: 1-888-451-4519
Fax: (416) 225-4722

Bank of Montreal

55 Bloor Street West, 15th Floor
Toronto, ON, M4W 3N5
Telephone: 1-800-371-2541
Fax: (416) 927-3006
E-Mail/Web Site: www.bmo.com

Scotiabank

9th Floor, 44 King Street West
Toronto, ON, M5H 1H1
Telephone: 1-800-785-8722
Fax: (416) 933-3276
E-Mail/Web Site: www.scotiabank.ca

TD Bank

26th Floor, TD Tower, 55 King Street West
Toronto, ON, M5K 1A2
Telephone: 1-888-361-0319
Fax: (416) 983-3460
E-Mail/Web Site: www.tdbank.ca

National Bank of Canada

7th Floor—Office 4260-1, 600 rue de la Gauchetiere ouest
Montreal, QC, H3B 4L2
Telephone: (514) 394-6440
Fax: (514) 394-8434
E-Mail/Web Site: www.bnc.ca

CIBC

Commerce Court West, 13th Floor
Toronto, ON, M5L 1A2
Telephone: 1-800-308-6859
Fax: 1-800-308-6861
E-Mail/Web Site: www.cibc.com

Royal Bank of Canada

18th Floor, North Tower, Royal Bank Plaza
Toronto, ON, M5J 2J5
Telephone: 1-800-769-2452
Fax: (416) 974-6922
E-Mail/Web Site: www.royalbank.com

Citibank

123 Front Street West
Toronto, ON, M5J 2M3
Telephone: 1-888-245-1112
Fax: (416) 947-4123
E-Mail/Web Site: www.citicorp.com

Hongkong Bank of Canada

Suite 400, 885 West Georgia Street
Vancouver, BC, V6C 3E9
Telephone: 1-800-343-1180
Fax: (604) 641-1925

Laurentian Bank

1981 McGill College Avenue
Montreal, QC, H3A 3K3
Telephone: (514) 282-4004
Fax: (514) 284-4009
E-Mail/Web Site: www.mortgagestore.com/laurent/laurent/html

MICRO-CREDIT PROGRAMS

Calmeadow Foundation

Suite 300, 4 King Street West
Toronto, ON, M5H 1B6
Telephone: (416) 362-9670
Fax: (416) 362-0769

Provides business loans to individuals investing in their own small-scale business through peer lending. Calmeadow offers several different loan funds across Canada.

Comox Valley Credit Circle Program

Box 3292 Courteney
Comox Valley, BC, V9N 5N4
Telephone: (250) 338-1133
Fax: (250) 334-9251

Micro-loan fund available to women in Comox Valley.

Edmonton Community Loan Fund

Telephone: (403) 944-1558

Micro-loan fund serving Edmonton. Call for the loan fund's orientation meeting time and places.

STARTUP—Calgary

#16 - 2936 Radcliffe Dr. SE
Calgary, AL, T2A 6N8
Telephone: (403) 272-9323
Fax: (403) 235-4646

Micro-loan fund open to anyone in Calgary

The Loan Circle—Red Deer

Suite 502, Parkland Square, 4901-48th St.
Red Deer, AL, T4N 6M4
Telephone: (403) 342-2055
Fax: (403) 347-6980

Micro-loan fund serving Red Deer, Alberta (Office will be moving soon).

Community New Ventures Program Micro-Loan Fund

10010-107A Avenue
Edmonton, AL, T5H 4H8
Telephone: (403) 424-7709
Fax: (403) 424-7736

Micro-loan fund open to Canadian immigrants who have resided in Canada for less than three years.

Credit Circle Program—Winnipeg

Telephone: (204) 944-9936
Micro-Loan program.

Women's Community Loan Fund of Thunder Bay

Telephone: (807) 625-0329
Micro-Loan fund.

Lake of the Woods Community Loan Fund

136 Matheson Ave.
Kenora, ON, P9N 1T8
Telephone: (807) 467-4640
Fax: (807) 467-4645

Micro-loan fund.

Rural Enterprise Loan Fund

379 Huron St.
Stratford, ON, N5A 5T6
Telephone: (519) 273-5017
Fax: (519) 273-4826

Micro-loan fund running in Stratford; more funds planned for Durham, Ottawa and Peterborough area.

Fond's d'emprunt économique communautaire

210 Boulevard Charest, Suite 600
Quebec, QC, J1K 3H1
Telephone: (418) 525-55260

Micro-loan program.

Cercles d'emprunt CDEST

4435 Rue Rouen
Montreal, QC, H1V 1H1
Telephone: (514) 256-6825
Fax: (514) 256-0669

Micro-loan program.

Newfoundland-Labrador Federation of Co-operatives (NLFC)

PO Box 13369, Postal Station A
St. John's, NF, A1B 4B7
Telephone: (709) 726-9435

Micro-loan fund.

EXPORT ASSISTANCE

Canadian Commercial Corporation (CCC)

50 O'Connor Street, 11th Floor
Ottawa, ON, K1A 0S6
Telephone: (613) 996-2655
Fax: (613) 992-2134
E-Mail/Web Site: http://www.ccc.ca

Aids Canadian exporters in signing contracts with foreign buyers.
The program may avert requirements for bid or performance
bonds (which would otherwise force an SME to forego bidding),
and offers some forms of financial aid to potential exporters.

Department of Foreign Affairs and International Trade

125 Sussex Drive
Ottawa, ON, K1A 0G2
Telephone: (613) 992-5726
Fax: (613) 992-5965
E-Mail/Web Site: http://www.dfait-maeci.gc.ca/

Offers a variety of financing and funding to Canadian companies
who need assistance in developing exporting capabilities or foreign markets.

Export Assistance

5 Place Ville-Marie, Suite 400
Montreal, QC, H3B 5E7
Telephone: (888) 463-6232
Fax: (514) 283-7838
E-Mail/Web Site: http://www.bdc.ca/

Sponsoring Organization: Business Development Bank of Canada—BDC

Helps companies develop export markets and take advantage of
export opportunities.

Export Development Corporation

151 O'Connor Street
Ottawa, ON, K1A 1K3
Telephone: (800) 850-9626 / (613) 598-2500
Fax: (613) 237-2690
E-Mail/Web Site:export@edc4.edc.ca — http://www.edc.ca/

Offers help with export financing and insurance, foreign investment insurance, and many other programs.

Grow Export Program

Contact your local CIBC branch, or call
Telephone: (800) 551-0606
Sponsoring Organization: CIBC and Export Development Corporation

Program provides working capital loans to knowledge-based companies to finance the costs of delivering goods and services to foreign buyers.

International Cultural Relations Program

125 Sussex Drive
Ottawa, ON, K1A 0G2
Telephone: (613) 992-5726
Fax: (613) 992-5965
E-Mail/Web Site: http://www.dfait-maeci.gc.ca/

Sponsoring Organization: Department of Foreign Affairs and International Trade

Program offers grants to people or programs that promote Canadian culture abroad.

Northstar, Inc.

Suite 205-5811 Cooney Road
Richmond, BC, V6X 3M1
Telephone: (604) 664-5828
Fax: (604) 664-5838
E-Mail/Web Site: s.shepherd@northstar.ca—
                 http://www.northstar.ca/

Supports Canadian exporters by offering fixed rate, medium-term financing to creditworthy foreign buyers of eligible Canadian goods and services.

Program for Export Market Development—PEMD

125 Sussex Drive
Ottawa, ON, K1A 0G2
Telephone: (613) 992-5726
Fax: (613) 992-5965
E-Mail/Web Site: http://www.dfait-maeci.gc.ca/

Sponsoring Organization: Department of Foreign Affairs and International Trade

Offers financing and grants to Canadian companies to help them develop foreign markets.

Working Capital for Exporters

5 Place Ville-Marie, Suite 400
Montreal, QC, H3B 5E7
Telephone: (888) 463-6232
Fax: (514) 283-7838
E-Mail/Web Site: http://www.bdc.ca/

Sponsoring Organization: Business Development Bank of Canada—BDC

This program is designed to help small businesses finance export and export-related activities.

TARGETED ASSISTANCE PROGRAMS

Agricultural

Advance Payments for Crops Act—APCA

2200 Walkley Road
Ottawa, ON, K1A 0C5
Telephone: (613) 957-4028 ext. 2701
Fax: (613) 996-2430

Sponsoring Organization: Agriculture and Agri-Food Canada—AAFC

Provides financial incentive to producers to store eligible crops immediately after harvest until later in the crop year when market conditions may result in better prices.

Agri-Food Credit Facility—ACF

Sir John Carling building, Room 1011, 930 Carling Avenue
Ottawa, ON, K1A 0C5
Telephone: (613) 759-7697
Fax: (613) 759-7499
E-Mail/Web Site:fossl@em.agr.ca — http://atn-riae.agr.ca

Sponsoring Organization: Agriculture and Agri-Food Canada— AAFC

Its purpose is to enable Canadian exporters to better meet competition from other exporting countries' export credit programs. The ACF is intended as a last resort and to match credit terms provided by foreign competition.

Business Planning for Agri-Ventures

Exchange Tower, Suite 1550, 10250—101 St.
Edmonton, AL, T5J 3P4
Telephone: (403) 495-4679
Fax: (403) 495-5665

Sponsoring Organization: Farm Credit Corporation

Provides a variety of assistance (including financial assistance) to farmers and their business associates.

CanAdapt Program

c/o 90 Woodlawn Road West
Guelph, ON, N1H 1B2
Telephone: (519) 822-7554
Fax: (519) 766-9775
E-Mail/Web Site:canadapt@adaptcouncil.org

Sponsoring Organization: Agricultural Adaptation Council

Provides funding for innovative projects designed to foster increased long-term growth, self-reliance, employment and competitiveness for Ontario's agriculture, food, and rural communities.

Farm Credit Corporation—FCC

1800 Hamilton Street
Regina, SA, S4P 4L3
Telephone: (306) 780-8100
Fax: (306) 780-6383
E-Mail/Web Site: http://www.fcc-sca.com/

Offers a variety of financial services to Canadian farmers and agri-businesses.

Aboriginal Businesses

Aboriginal Business Canada

235 Queen Street
Ottawa, ON, KA 0H5
Telephone: (613) 954-4064
Fax: (613) 957-7010
E-Mail/Web Site: abcott@ic.gc.ca — http://abc.gc.ca/

Sponsoring Organization: Industry Canada

Provides support to aboriginal entrepreneurs seeking to start or expand their own business or to improve existing ones by giving them access to financing and information.

Indian and Northern Affairs Canada

Terrasses de la Chaudire, 10 Wellington, North Tower
Hull, QC, K1A 0H4
Telephone: (819) 997-0380
Fax: (819) 953-3017
E-Mail / Web Site:InfoPubs@inac.gc.ca — http://www.inac.gc.ca/

Sponsors many programs encouraging business among Canada's Aboriginal people.

Technology-Based Firms

Industrial Research Assistance Program

National Research Council of Canada
Montreal Road
Building M-55
Ottawa, ON, K1A 0R6
Telephone: (613) 993-7082
Fax: (613) 952-2524
E-Mail/Web Site: http://www.nrc.ca/

Sponsoring Organization: National Research Council of Canada

Provides advice, technical support, contacts, and funds for R&D projects undertaken by Canadian firms with fewer than 500 employees.

Seed Capital for Technology Companies

5 Place Ville-Marie, Suite 400
Montreal, QC, H3B 5E7
Telephone: (888) 463-6232
Fax: (514) 283-7838
E-Mail/Web Site: http://www.bdc.ca/

Sponsoring Organization: Business Development Bank of Canada—BDC

Offers seed capital to Canadian entrepreneurs who wish to start up a technology-oriented company.

Young Entrepreneurs

Wage Subsidy Program

Phase IV, Place du Portage
Hull, QC, K1A 0J9
Telephone: (613) 990-5186

Sponsoring Organization: Human Resources and Development
Canada

This program provides a subsidy of wages and other costs to
non-government organizations that hire young people.

Young Entrepreneur Financing Program

5 Place Ville-Marie, Suite 400
Montreal, QC, H3B 5E7
Telephone: (888) 463-6232
Fax: (514) 283-7838
E-Mail/Web Site: http://www.bdc.ca/

Sponsoring Organization: Business Development Bank of Canada—
BDC

Program aimed at giving start-up entrepreneurs between the
ages of 18 and 34 a term loan of up to $25,000 and 50 hours of
tailor-made business management support.

Canadian Youth Business Foundation

40 Dundas Street West, Suite 221, PO Box 44
Toronto, ON, M5G 2C2
Telephone: (416) 408-2923
Fax: (416) 408-3234
E-Mail /Web Site:info@cybf.ca — http://www.cybf.ca/

Organization that offers a variety of programs geared towards
young entrepreneurs (under 29 years old).

Student Venture Capital Program

470 York St, Room 206, PO Box 6000
Fredricton, NB, E3B 5H1

Telephone: (506) 453-3818
Fax: (506) 453-7967

Sponsoring Organization: Employment Division, Advanced Education and Labour

Offers interest-free loans of up to $3000 to any small student venture.

Young Entrepreneurs ConneXion

Telephone: (800) 833-1829

Provides up to $15,000 capital and $2000 worth of free counselling for young entrepreneurs.

Enterprise Loans / Young Entrepreneur Service

5 Job Street
St. John's, NF, A1E 1H1
Telephone: (709) 739-9933
Fax: (709) 726-5231

Sponsoring Organization: Y Enterprise Centre
Offers loans up to $20,000 to young entrepreneurs (ages 19 to 30).

Société d'Investissement Jeunesse

Case Postale 385, Tour de la Place Victoria
22e etage, bureau 2226
Montreal, QC, H4Z 1J2
Telephone: (800) 875-8674 / (514) 875-8674
Fax: (514) 875-9200

Guarantees loans of up to $150,000 to young people in Quebec (ages 18 to 35).

Women-Owned Businesses

Women's Enterprise Initiative of Alberta

800-6th Avenue S.W.
Calgary, AB, T2P 3G3
Telephone: (800) 713-3558 / (403) 777-4250

Fax: (403) 777-4258

E-Mail/Web Site:awewia@compusmart.ab.ca

Offers access to a loan fund, advisory services, pathfinding to existing services and other programs to meet the needs of women entrepreneurs in the province.

Women's Enterprise Initiative of BC

#7-2070 Harvey Ave
Kelowna, BC, V1Y 8P8
Telephone: (800) 643-7014 / (604) 868-3454
Fax: (604) 868-2709
E-Mail/Web Site:wesbc@silk.net

Many services are available through this organization to female entrepreneurs in BC. A loan fund, advisory services and pathfinding services are offered.

Women's Enterprise Initiative of Manitoba

Main Floor, 240 Graham Avenue
Winnipeg, MB, R3C 0J7
Telephone: (800) 203-2343 / (204) 988-1860
Fax: (204) 988-1871

Manitoba branch of the WEI. Offers financial and consulting services to female entrepreneurs in Manitoba.

Women's Enterprise Initiative of Saskatchewan

2124B Robinson Street
Regina, SA, S4T 2P7
Telephone: (800) 879-6331 / (306) 359-9732
Fax: (306) 359-9739
E-Mail/Web Site:women@the.link.ca

Offers access to a loan fund, advisory services, pathfinding to existing services and other programs to meet the needs of women entrepreneurs in the province.

Other Targeted Programs

Action 21—Community Funding Program
Vincent Massey Place, 351 St. Joseph Boulevard
Hull, QC, K1A 0H3
Telephone: (819) 953-4950
Fax: (819) 994-1412
E-Mail/Web Site: enviroinfo@ec.gc.ca —
 http://www.ns.doe.ca/action21/menu.html

Sponsoring Organization: Environment Canada

Non-profit, non-government groups can apply for funding. Action 21 encourages projects that protect, rehabilitate or enhance the natural environment.

Transitional Job Fund
Phase IV, Place du Portage
Hull, QC, K1A 0J9
Telephone: (613) 990-5186
E-Mail/Web Site: http://www.hrdc-drhc.gc.ca/

Sponsoring Organization: Human Resources and Development Canada

Human Resources will help support job creation activities in areas with high unemployment.

TYPES
AND CONDITIONS
OF FINANCING
AVAILABLE
TO SMEs

Types and Conditions of Financing Available to SMEs

Type of Financing	Instrument and Purpose of Financing	Size and Term of Financing	Charge on Assets	Type of Return	Study and Account Management Fee	Principal Repayment
Small Business Loan (SBLA)	Debt term fiancing for fixed assets, up to 90% of value with 85% government guarantee	Up to $250,000—up to 10 years	Chattel mortgage on equipment financed or mortgage on real estate financing	Fixed or floating rates, prime +2%. Fixed residential mortgage +2.75%. Government fee also charged	2% up front fee paid to SBLA, also annual fee. Bank fees prohibited	Allowed on Floating rate at no penalty. Fixed prohibited except upon payment of penalty
Term Loan	Debt financing for all types of capital assets except tangible assets	Unlimited: i.e., 1-5 years for machinery and equipment - up to 7 years for machinery and 20 years amortization based on useful life of asset	Fixed and floating charged on assets as negotiated and considered necessary	Prime or fixed asset base rate + risk premium	Depends on complexity	Negotiated
Commercial Mortgages	Debt financing to purchase, refinance or renovate owned real estate	1 to 5 years with amortization up to 25 years depending on useful life of building	Mortgage on property. Assignment of rents and attendant security	Fixed rates—commercial rates based on money market and government bond rates	Negotiation Fee	
Leasing	Lease financing to purchase qualifying captial assets		Leasing arrangement covering assets financed	Monthly or flexible payments based on fixed or floating rates or payment needs	None	Negotiable with buyout based on providing proper return

Type of Financing	Instrument and Purpose of Financing	Size and Term of Financing	Charge on Assets	Type of Return	Study and Account Management Fee	Principal Repayment
Operating Lines of Credit	Debt financing for working capital purposes	Varies depending on need	Charge on receivables and inventories	Flexible — prime + risk premium (usually 1.5 to 3%)	Varies often minimum applies	
LSVC (Equity)	Equity financing for expansion or later stage companies	Ranges—minimum $500,000, preferred $1 to $3 million	Common shares, convertibles debentures, etc.	Expected rate of return +20% to 30%		
Equity (Angels)	Early stage financing or "seed capital" necessary to move a company from start-up to next stage of development	$5,000 to $5,000,000 (typically $50,000 to $500,000 range)	Often debt instruments with warrants or equity kicker providing a minority share position and an exit strategy			
Senior Debt	Debt financing for acquisition, expansion and restructuring	$5 to $50 million		Fixed or floating— based on performance	1% of face value	
Subordinated Debt	Debt financing for acquisition, expansion and restructuring	$5 to $50 million		Fixed or floating— based on performance	2% of face value	
Cash-Flow Venture (Business Development Bank of Canada)	Debt financing based on cash flow	$100,000 to $1,000,000 - 6 to 8 years	Mortgage, subordinated to existing charge	Fixed or floating rates—BDC base + 2-4%	Interest monthly throughout the loan	Predetermined formula

INDEX